War and Virtual War:
The Challenges to Communities

War and Virtual War:
The Challenges to Communities

Edited by

Jones Irwin

Amsterdam - New York, NY 2004

The paper on which this book is printed meets the requirements of "ISO 9706: 1994, Information and documentation - Paper for documents - Requirements for permanence".

ISBN: 90-420-1933-6
©Editions Rodopi B.V., Amsterdam - New York, NY 2004
Printed in The Netherlands

Contents

Acknowledgements   vii

Introduction   1

Part I: Understanding War and Terrorism

Roles and Identities in Old and New Wars   7
Paul Gilbert

The Impact of Ideational Interests on State Behaviour   21
and the Outcome of Militarised Disputes
Susan G. Sample

Globalisation and the Just War Tradition: The   51
Vexing Problem of Legitimate Authority
Paul Rexton Kan

System Perturbation: Conflict in the Age of Globalization   61
Bradd C. Hayes and Thomas P.M. Barnett

Cyberterrorism: Media Myth or Clear and Present   79
Danger?
Maura Conway

Part II. War and Morality

Assassination: Killing in the Shadow of Self-Defence   99
Michael L. Gross

Civil Disobedience and Military Ethics   117
Asa Kasher

Part III. Representations of War

The Exclusion of American Nurses from the Imagery   129
of Liberation
Deborah A. Gómez

Playing War in Computer Games: Images, Myths and   149
Reality
Martin Bayer

Contemporary British Cinema and the Re-imagining of   171
World War Two: A Virtual/Humane Sensibility to War
and a 'New' Grammar of Heroism
Christopher Macallister

The 'Problem' (Not the 'Theorem') of War: On Pasolini's   189
Salò
Jones Irwin

Part IV. Whither Peace?

Peace and Virtual Peace: Challenges to War   203
Edward Horgan

Cross-Track Approach: A Remedy to Post-Conflict Peace   217
Building?
Agata Dziewulska

Notes on Contributors   241

Acknowledgements

Many thanks to Rob Fisher, without whose innovative educational vision this project would never have got off the ground. Special thanks also to Peter Day and Salwa Ghaly for their additional support. My foremost thanks to Melissa Campbell for all her administrative help but, most importantly, her indispensable tender, loving care.

Welcome to a *Probing the Boundaries* Project

The *War and Virtual War: Challenges to Communities* project aims to provide an innovative, cutting-edge inter-disciplinary and multi-disciplinary research forum which will enable multiple insights and perspectives to be brought to bear on the many and various issues which relate to war and virtual war.

In particular, the project will focus on the nature, purpose and experience of war, and its impacts on all aspects of communities across the world. Viewing war as a multi-layered phenomenon, the project seeks to explore the historical, legal, social, religious, economic, and political contexts of conflicts, and assess the place of art, journalism, literature, music, the media and the internet in representation and interpretation of the experience of warfare.

Key themes will include:

- the sources, origins, and causes of war
- the 'control', conduct and limit of warfare
- the nature of warfare
- strategy, strategic thinking and the influence and effect of technologies
- types of warfare
- war crimes and crimes against humanity
- the extent of war; blockades, sanctions, defence expenditure and the impact on social and public policy
- the 'ethics' of war; just war, deterrence, defence and self-defence, collateral damage
- the experience of war; art, literature, music, poetry, and the theatre
- the role of the media - journalism, radio, television, the internet
- the prevention of war; the role of conflict resolution, peace-keeping and the role and importance of law and international legal order
- the rise and impact of non-violent movements

Dr Robert Fisher
Inter-Disciplinary.Net
http://www.inter-disciplinary.net

Introduction

If the practice of war is as old as human history, so too is the need to reflect upon war, to understand its meaning and implications. The Pre-Socratic philosopher Heraclitus asserted in 600BC that "War (*polemos*) is justice", thus inaugurating a long philosophical tradition of consideration of the morality of war. In recent times, the increased specialisation of academic disciplines has led to a fragmentation of the thematic of war within the academy – the topic of war is as likely to be addressed by sociologists, cultural theorists, psychologists and even computer scientists as it is by historians, philosophers or political scientists. This diversity of disciplinary approaches to war is undoubtedly fruitful in itself but can lead to an isolation of respective disciplinary analyses of war from each other. In July 2002, at Mansfield College, Oxford, an inter-disciplinary conference on war (entitled 'War and Virtual War') was held so as to redress some of this disciplinary isolationism and to forge an integrative dialogue on war, in all its facets. The papers below were nominated by delegates as the most paradigmatic of the ethos of the original project and the most successful in achieving its aims of inter-disciplinarity and critical dialogue.

In the opening essay to Part I, 'Understanding War and Terrorism', Paul Gilbert systematises the contrast between what have been termed 'old' and 'new' wars. While old wars are typically wars between states, seeking to promote the interests that states have *qua* states, new wars in contrast are wars between or on behalf of "peoples", whose identities may be forged in ways other than through membership of states or potential states. Such identities are formed through membership of groups whose representatives advance political claims in virtue of the kinds of people of which these groups consist. For Gilbert, the price of such new wars (of which the so-called War on Terror is paradigmatic) is that both sides are measuring rights and wrongs by reference to their own values, not by any transcultural standards.

Susan Sample's essay reflects on recent attempts to problematise traditional assumptions about the causes of war between states. Here, a certain 'constructivist turn' has set itself in opposition to an empirical and positivist approach, the latter emphasising the material interests of states whilst the former highlights the more ideological (or 'ideational') aspects of a state's identity and culture. Sample seeks an 'integrative' approach which looks at the interrelationship between the material interests *and* the ideational interests of states, as they affect the escalation of disputes to war.

Paul Rexton Kan's essay (like that of Gilbert's) puts forward its analysis in the shadow of the so-called War on Terror. Kan reflects on the problems caused by the contemporary proliferation of human social organisations (most especially transnational terrorist networks) operating in the new globalised world. For Kan, globalisation has revealed a diffusion of authorities claiming legitimacy and this implies a particularly vexing problem for the traditional Just War tenet of 'legitimate authority'. This tradition, on his view, can best be reinvigorated through the philosophy of 'cosmopolitanism' as applied to the international political environment.

In their essay "System Perturbation: Conflict in the Age of Globalisation", Bradd Hayes and Thomas Barnett address the implications of what they consider a recent re-ordering of the international system. Citing such recent events as the Asian Economic Flu, the Mexican peso crisis and, in particular, the 9:11 attacks, Hayes and Barnett argue that such a re-ordering is usually accompanied by the implementation of new sets of rules, so as to protect states from the causes of conflict. On their interpretation, what they term 'system perturbation' is the most appropriate new ordering principle. Their paper examines the underlying precepts of this principle and potential triggers that could lead to further world conflict.

Finally, in this section, Maura Conway develops the concern with the development of terrorist organisation in a specific analysis of what has come to be called 'cyberterrorism'. Conway, however, is keen to question the precipitation with which contemporary commentators rush to label this supposed new threat. While acknowledging the existence of 'hacktivism', she problematises the conceptual basis of the term 'cyberterrorism'. While terrorist groups are using the internet, they are merely using it as means of propaganda rather than as a weapon of terror in itself. To this extent, Conway argues, and contrary to popular opinion, 'cyberterrorism' has not even happened yet.

Part II, 'War and Morality', includes two essays which both begin from the specifics of the Israeli-Palestinian conflict, while also claiming wider relevance. Michael Gross' essay considers the anomalous treatment of the tactic of 'assassination' within war. Although assassination, Gross argues, in eliminating 'collateral damage' and harm to non-combatants, might appear to be an attractive tactic of war, it rather evokes particular revulsion. Gross explicates the good reasons for such revulsion, most notably its undermining of the conventions of war, while defending the specific cases of 'ticking bombs' and punitive assassination.

Asa Kasher's essay turns its attention to a refusal by Israeli soldiers to participate in military activities and the relation of such a refusal to the concept of 'civil disobedience'. Kasher's analysis compares the soldiers' refusal under two different circumstances of 'war', the Lebanon War and the current Israeli-Palestinian conflict. Kasher argues that while a philosophical conception of 'civil disobedience' was "naturally applicable" to the Lebanon War, it cannot be justified under the present circumstances of Israel.

Part III, 'Representations of War', begins with Deborah Gómez's reflection on the exclusion of American (and British) nurses from the imagery of liberation after World War II. Gómez highlights how liberation imagery in many ways determined the perception of what had occurred in the German concentration camps. In this measure, the exclusion of the female nurses from such imagery allows us a 'unique perspective' through which we can examine and reconsider the 'gendered' history of war. In her retrieval of the nurses' own photography of their experiences, Gómez sheds new light on these previously excluded images of war and liberation from war.

While war photography maintains an unquestioned cultural authority, the world of computer war games is approached by many with a certain cultural disdain. Martin Bayer's essay, 'Playing War in Computer Games: Images, Myth and Reality', seeks to debunk some of this suspicion while arguing for a serious import to these new technologies. Bayer provides an exhaustive (and informative) genealogy of computer war gaming from its basic origins in the early 1980s to its contemporary diversity and sophistication. His essay also reflects on the relationship between the development of computer war imagery and the wider question of perception as such and the increasingly problematic distinction between image and reality.

The final two essays of this section address perhaps the most prominent media representation of war, that of cinema. Christopher Macallister foregrounds an important transition in the representation of World War II by British cinema. Recent British films such as *The English Patient, Enigma and Charlotte Gray*, reflect society's changed understanding of war. These reveal, Macallister argues, a World War II of counter-myths that challenge the gender roles and boundaries established by earlier recreations of the war. The British public are no longer comfortable with 'heroism' in war, either on screen or in reality. As the individual is placed at the centre of politics, there is no room for the notion of sacrifice and the 'ethic' of heroism is critically weakened.

In my own essay, 'The 'Problem' (Not the 'Theorem') of War – On Pasolini's *Salò*', I look to the enigmatic work of the great Italian film director to question a certain moralistic simplification of war. In *Salò*, Pasolini seeks to ridicule those anti-Fascists who would consider themselves completely detached from their apparent Fascist opponents. This complex film suggests an irreducible complementarity between the Fascists and the anti-Fascists in 1940s Italy. Moreover, drawing on the work of the Marquis de Sade, and his more recent heirs such as Lautréamont and Blanchot, Pasolini, through cinema, presents the viewer with a philosophical problem – what is one's own complicity with war and violence?

The final part of the book, 'Whither Peace?', seeks to conclude on a more optimistic note. Edward Horgan's essay, 'Peace and Virtual Peace': Challenges to War' calls into question the very concept of international relations by asking whether the 'nation-state' provides the most appropriate framework to ensure an acceptable level of peace and security for humanity. Rather, Horgan argues, it is in the context of the sovereignty of the individual that progress towards a more 'perpetual peace' may be found. Against Clausewitz, Horgan argues that war is no longer acceptable as 'politics by other means'. It is rather inherently 'unnatural' and 'inhuman', and 'virtual peace' is the only alternative.

Finally, Agata Dziewulska's essay addresses the problem of post-conflict peace building in Bosnia. Dziewulska develops her analysis through a narrative which invokes the stories recounted to her by various Bosnians during a personal journey through Sarejevo. This hermeneutic approach provides a humanistic foundation for her more systematic analysis to follow. Through a reflection on the three tracks of diplomacy in Bosnia, Dziewulska argues against the 'top-down' centralised model. Instead, she calls for a decentralised 'bottom-up' model which seeks the greatest amount of cross-tracking and inclusion of all levels. This model, she argues, has been vindicated by history as the source of real democracy and societal peace.

Jones Irwin, Dublin, June 2003.

Part I

Understanding War and Terrorism

Roles and Identities in Old and New Wars

Paul Gilbert

1. Old and New Wars

The current wave of armed conflicts sweeping the world are very different from the traditional inter-state wars of modern times, so much so that they have been characterised as 'new wars', by contrast with those old ones.[1] New wars comprise a wide range of secessionist struggles and state responses, as witnessed in the former Soviet Union and Yugoslavia, and elsewhere, as well as other conflicts displaying family resemblances to these, either in their causes or in their typically low-intensity methods. They include also, I shall controversially suggest, the current so-called War on Terror and the Islamist campaign to which it is a response.

The aim of this paper is to systematise the contrast between old and new wars and to suggest an explanation of why the change has occurred. In order to accomplish the first task I shall group the features of old and new wars into those that characterise what I call the *conditions* of war, on the one hand, and what I call its *conduct*, on the other. If we follow Clausewitz's famous dictum that war is the continuation of policy by other means[2] then the conditions represent, broadly speaking, the way the war is seen as pursuing policy. The conduct of war is the way the war is fought, and this will, evidently, depend to a great extent upon its conditions.

1. Contrasting Conditions

Old wars are typically wars between states, seeking to promote the interests that states have *qua* states - secure borders and other conditions for a peaceful, prosperous and orderly life. When one side or more is not a state, as in civil wars, this is because a portion of the citizenry does not feel that it enjoys such conditions and seeks to establish these, either by effecting a change in the existing political order within the states' current borders or by changing these borders, as in secessionist struggles pursued solely because of the circumstances in which one side finds itself. New wars, by contrast, may be regarded as wars between or on behalf of *peoples*, in the sense that the sides in the war are identified in terms of identities that are given, not just through membership of states or potential states, but through membership of groups whose representatives advance political claims - including claims to separate statehood - in virtue of the kinds of people of which these groups consist.

There are a multitude of cases here. The simplest is one where two groups identify themselves as separate and where their conflicts are an expression of discord between them, as, at least at some times, between Muslims and Hindus in the Indian sub-   continent,   for   example. Partition was intended to address a conflict conceptualised in these terms, though it left a continuing legacy of bitterness with respect to Kashmir and otherwise. Many secessionist struggles have this character, but not all, even when   they are identity conflicts. For in some cases, a state will oppose secession precisely because it cannot grant that the secessionists *are* a separate people, so that now the conflict concerns not what should be accorded to peoples acknowledged to be separate, but what acknowledgement of separate identities should be made. And such acknowledgement, or its refusal, is sought from the people themselves as well as from their states and other political organisations; for self identification is needed if people are to be mobilised behind a military campaign, though the existence of such a campaign can itself influence self-identification.

The so-called War on Terror is of this sort. Whereas the Islamists regard their offensive as a war between peoples identified as Muslims on the one hand and non-Muslims generally on the other, the Americans and their allies deny they are fighting against Muslims. They view Muslims as identified in   terms not of their religion but of their nationality as given by language, territorial affiliation or whatever, just as Westerners are viewed. But such identities are quite compatible with overarching attachments to values of freedom, democracy and so on, which Islamist hard-liners are taken to reject. There is thus an ideological struggle between the Islamists and US allies to win over ordinary Muslims to the one kind of identity or the other. On the Islamist side, the war is viewed as a conflict *between* peoples, on the American, as fought by them *on behalf of* those peoples who are taken to espouse the prescribed values, but whose identities as such are threatened by those who reject them. In either case, I suggest, the war concerns the manner in which collective identities should be politically recognised, and this is a feature I take to be necessary to anything that is to count as a new war.

That new wars concern the manner in which collective identities should be politically recognised reflects, I want to say, *discord* rather than disagreement - in the simplest cases, as just mentioned, discord between peoples viewing themselves as separate, in the more complex ones, discord prior and contributory to any possible demarcation of separateness. Discord is categorically different from disagreement, since it characterises the state of a relationship rather than an event within it, even though, of course, discord can easily generate disagreements and vice versa. Discord between peoples can exist, however, without being the obvious result of any disagreement and can issue in violence or even war. Between states the case is otherwise. Their old wars are typically and explicitly the upshot of disagreements   not peaceably resolved, of which disagreements about territory or spheres of influence are, perhaps, the commonest.

Discord is characteristically either a consequence of the possession of different values or gives rise to a highlighting of real or imagined differences in values, so that the actions of one group are seen as affronts to the values of the other, as failures to show the respect that is due and, hence, as injustices. There is, therefore, a direct connection between the fact that new wars are expressions of discord, as I have put it, and that they take the form of campaigns for justice, rather than merely the securing of peaceful and orderly lives for bodies of citizens. While old wars are, of course, fought for ends represented as just, these ends are limited, to those to which citizen bodies are generally taken to be entitled, so that the disagreements which occasion old wars are typically disagreements over the precise character of these entitlements and whether they have been fulfilled, all taking place within a framework of agreement as to their general nature. In new wars the case is quite different. For without any such framework of agreement, indeed, precisely in a situation of discord in respect of values, a campaign for justice is not merely a manifestation of self-help in the absence of an authority to arbitrate on competing claims, it is itself an expression of the possession of superior authority to administer justice against those who transgress its demands.

2.   Contrasting Conduct

If the conditions of new wars, then, are that they are fought against or on behalf of peoples, over the manner in which their collective identities should be politically recognised, as expressions of discord and as campaigns for justice, then we may expect the characteristic features of their conduct to reflect this, as in the particular example we started with. Thus, whereas old wars are directed against states or other citizen bodies through attacks on their armed forces, new ones are aimed at identity groups or those who seek to constitute such groups: they are, therefore, fought in ways that either directly target members of these groups, *qua* members rather than *qua* combatants, or neglect their welfare, while often evincing disproportionate concern for that of members of one's own group. Attacks of this kind are often direct and violent means towards or against the political recognition that is sought. The most obvious case is that of "ethnic cleansing" in which ordinary people are attacked to force them from an area, either to reserve it to another identity group or to make it unavailable to one that espouses a separate or proscribed identity with political claims.

Attacks on or affecting ordinary people are easily accomplished in the atmosphere of discord surrounding new wars, which has two further related consequences for their conduct. Just as attacks upon civilians, or those that disproportionately affect them, are contrary to the rules of war, so too is the mistreatment of enemy combatants, whether through killings on a scale that has no military purpose or through the killing, torture or cruel incarceration of prisoners. Yet this is exactly what we witness in new wars, where discord obliterates respect for an enemy. One reason for the breaking of rules is that on one side, at least, troops are commonly irregulars, untrained, undisciplined and often without a clear chain of command terminating in political control. Recruitment to such irregular units is facilitated by discord and by mobilisation behind the cause of an identity group. By their nature such units are unlikely to be equipped for conventional warfare, and are forced to resort to guerrilla or terrorist tactics with all their dangers. Asymmetric struggles thus characterise new wars. But it should not be thought that the regular forces of states thereby escape the evils I have mentioned. Discord affects them too, and the massive counterforce they can employ is as much an expression of it as are terrorist attacks.

Lastly, however, the presentation of the causes of identity groups as the delivery of justice can be used to excuse many of the excesses of new wars and disguise discord and hatred behind a veil of righteous indignation. Whereas in old wars non-combatants and combatants *hors de combat* are not to be targeted because they do not, by their intentional actions, obstruct military operations to secure territory, in new wars they may be just as implicated in the supposed injustice the war is intended to rectify, as are their soldiers in action. They may, for example, in an obvious case, be occupying territory claimed by another identity group. In a less obvious case, they may be willing beneficiaries of policies that threaten the way of life of an identity group, as Islamists evidently take the American people to be. In such cases, a new war, construed as a campaign for justice, may evidently take such people as targets or, at least, as not deserving of the sorts of protection offered in old wars.

Campaigns for justice also involve different tactics from those of old wars, in which it is accepted, at least in interstate conflicts, that the armed forces of each side have a right to resist attack, however justified, since they are simply carrying out their leaders' orders as soldiers. It is otherwise in new wars, where   resisting attack is obstructing justice, in the same way that resisting the forces of law and order compounds the felony which those forces are seeking to rectify. Thus, while in old wars retaliation must have a military purpose to be justified, in new wars it serves simply to rectify yet a further perceived injustice.   Since each side will take the same view of its own superior authority to deliver justice, there ensues the apparently endless tit-for-tat attacks without any clear purpose which we witness in new wars. And, of course, these are as often aimed at other members of the group as at those who have launched the original attack. For it is the identity group as a whole, or at least its active supporters, who are taken to be "engaged in an objectively unjust proceeding",[3] not just particular attackers, as would be the case with ordinary felons.

3.   Roles and Identities

New wars, I claim, are, essentially, manifestations of the politics of identity. Their participants are groups which possess, or for which are claimed, distinctive collective identities; and they concern, in one way or another, the manner in which such identities should be recognised. What the politics of identity presupposes is that one enters political life as a person with a particular collective identity. This, it has been held, is a view deriving from German Romantic nationalism - "I am essentially a German, and I am a man through my being a German"[4] - though arguably it has an older, and ultimately religious, pedigree. That one enters politics as the possessor of a particular identity supposedly makes it appropriate that a political organisation, like a state, or, perhaps, a combination of states, should associate one with others who share that identity. It is this identity, furthermore, that equips one with the values one must employ in political action, and maybe outside of it as well. And what goes for politics generally goes for that continuation of politics which is war. New wars are fought by agents qua possessors of identities, real or imagined,[5] acting on behalf of their identity groups and in accordance with their values.

What I want to contrast with the politics of identity is an earlier - at least in recent times - politics of *role*, as I shall call it.[6] The politics of role presupposes that I enter politics without any essential collective identity but as someone set to perform a specific role, most usually, in the modern political world, the role of a citizen. One does not, that is to say, enter politics with prior attributes which the character of one's political relationships should reflect, but rather one's relationships are shaped by the way one performs one's role. How one ought to act in the political arena is not determined by values anterior to its activities, but by the duties required by the role, which, therefore, carry no implications for how one ought to act outside of it. It is, in a useful slogan, *what* one is which determines how one should act in the politics of role, *who* one is, in the politics of identity.

Typical old wars are, to paint the picture in broad brushstrokes, contests between states in which the various actors behave in ways regulated by the requirements of their roles. The leaders of states act to secure their states' vital interests while respecting the norms of international relations which make possible a range of exchanges between states, including, when peaceful dialogue breaks down, warlike ones. Leaders are, in so acting, representing people *qua* citizens - persons performing a role for which the security of the state is a precondition. Members of the state's armed forces, usually citizens themselves, have their roles too. Their task is to fight opposing forces through methods calculated to achieve military victory, which are limited to those proportionate to such goals and discriminating in their targets, so that civilians and surrendered troops are not made the object of attack. The conduct of war is, then, in the hands of soldiers, sailors and airmen and its rules are those that constrain the holders of these roles. The conditions of war, by contrast, are also governed by rules in old wars - rules about when it is permissible to resort to war and not be engaging in impermissible aggression. These international norms are what constrain the behaviour of those who occupy the role of statesmen or other relevant political leaders. It is rules in respect of both the conditions and conduct of war that get set aside when the politics of role gives way to the politics of identity.

To illustrate this process, consider what happened in Azerbaijan as the Soviet Union fell apart in the late 1980s. In the earlier part of the decade, the citizens of Azerbaijan were supporting their compatriot, Gary Kasparov, in his chess contests with the Russian, Anatoly Karpov, "regardless of the fact that Kasparov was half Armenian and half Jewish, without a drop of Azerbaijani blood".[7] By the end of the decade, however, Armenians and Azerbaijanis were locked in a civil war in which ethnic cleansing claimed thousands of lives and displaced hundreds of thousands as each side claimed Nagorno-Karabakh as part of its own historic homeland. It was to be the pattern of things to come as the Cold War balance of power broke down and nationalist movements across the world backed their claims with armed force. Identity politics had come to dominate conflict.

In the early 80s, however, the people of Azerbaijan were acting as citizens in supporting the ethnically non-Azeri, Kasparov. One of the expectations from those who perform the role of citizen is support for fellow citizens, even in sporting contests. But when ethnic Armenians and Azeris began to clash within the state they shared as citizens they were no longer performing these roles. It is not that civil war itself makes this impossible. When one body of citizens within a state is being oppressed by another, it can rise up in revolt, either to overthrow a government that permits this, or to secede, and in either case those engaged in the conflict can be acting as citizens, their leaders as representative of citizens, and their forces as the armies of citizen bodies striving for military victory. But when the civil war concerns the manner in which collective identities shall be politically recognised, as in the conflict over Nagorno-Karabakh, the participants are not acting as citizens with the interests proper to citizens in mind, but simply as members of identity groups. And the way that this conflict was fought out reflects that, with all the discord and consequent excess that new wars entail.

Identity politics and role politics are, I am suggesting, distinct modes of political activity, in the sense that participants conceive of themselves and of what is expected of them differently in the two modes. They are answerable to different ethical demands and regulate their behaviour differently accordingly, whether or not they have any clear, conscious conception of their relevant identity or role. Yet in any actual political situation there may also be practical lack of clarity as to which mode of politics is in play, with participants sometimes adopting the one, sometimes the other. The Arab/Israeli conflict is a prime example of this; with what is fundamentally an old war about the rights of an oppressed group, as against an established state's demand for security, degenerating into an identity conflict between Jews and Muslims. It would, therefore, be wrong to think of old and new wars as clear historical categories, with a transition from the former to the latter representing a sea change from role to identity politics.[8] Rather it represents, I am suggesting, a shift of emphasis in recent year from one prevailing mode to another, and with it a loss of previously accepted standards of behaviour, particularly in war, however much these standards were in fact flouted.[9] Each mode is, in the right historical circumstances, a possibility at any one time, so that the transition from the one mode to another is not a purely recent phenomenon.

The politics of role is, indeed, an essentially classical conception, deriving from Greek models of citizenship and coming to fruition in Roman notions of status as available quite independently of group identity. This conception is drawn upon in later times, most especially after the establishment of the Westphalian system of sovereign states, which put an end to the religious wars of the seventeenth century by establishing a principle of military non-intervention and other norms of international relations, many of which are now codified in the United Nations Charter.[10]

The key point about these norms is that they are *transcultural*. They have to be if they are to regulate relations between states whose members will often come from widely diverse cultural backgrounds. Thus the role of a statesman, or comparable political leader, is constrained by international norms which allow its holders to communicate and negotiate with each other on the basis of common understandings of what they are doing and what the permissible moves are. The same holds good for the role of soldier. A soldier's role is circumscribed by norms which permit military engagements to take place against a shared background of what constitutes such an engagement and how it is to be undertaken. To deviate substantially from such norms is no longer to occupy the roles, but to adopt a quite different kind of persona, perhaps that of the charismatic leader or warrior of identity politics. But whereas the norms of international roles are the result of transcultural interactions, in which certain standards have come to be fixed, what is expected of a charismatic leader or a warrior by their particular identity groups depends solely on the values which that group possesses, providing no scope for international criticism or regulation without the danger of an affront to these values.

4.   Just War and Defence

It will come as no surprise to learn that the international norms governing the roles played out in old wars are those of what is thought of as the Just War.[11] Just War Theory distinguishes two sets of requirements for a war to be accounted just. The first are the requirements for *jus ad bello* - for having a right to go to war; the second, for *jus in bello* - for right conduct in war. Now, the *jus ad bellum* requirements are, I claim, precisely the constraints that are placed upon statesmen and comparable political leaders when they decide whether to embark upon a war; the *jus in bello* ones, those placed upon soldiers and other troops involved in one. In each case, and perhaps most clearly in the latter, what it is to perform the role is determined in part by a preparedness to adhere to these requirements. Let us, then, rehearse them in relation to what I have termed, respectively, the conditions and conduct of war. The Just War Theory which results will, for reasons that will become obvious, be a *defensive* Just War Theory, and that is how I shall term it.

Consider first, then, the requirement that a war is just only if it is decided upon by *proper authority*. This may be taken to spell out the relationship which a leader who decides upon war must have to those on whose behalf it is fought. In general, it will be a constitutional relationship between statesman and state, so that the party to the war is the state itself, rather than the forces of the state being unofficially employed on behalf of some faction. Yet, as I indicated earlier, in exceptional circumstances, a leader may represent a body of citizens who do not constitute a state, as when they find themselves oppressed by one and rise up against it. This brings us to the second requirement, that of *just cause*. This, in defensive just war theory, is provided only by the war being fought in self-defence, though what amounts to self-defence can, of course, be controversial, depending upon who has the better claim to defend a given territory. But whoever it is, the purpose must, as we have seen, be to secure the territory for the purpose of governing its citizens in a lawful manner and in their own interests.

The other requirements of *jus ad bellum* follow from this and point up the role of a statesman in relation to the citizens he represents. Thus forming a *right intention* involves aiming to restore a situation of peace in which all citizens, whoever they are, can live ordered lives. The various requirements that war should be a *proportionate response* to threat, engaged in as a *last resort* and with a fair *hope of success*, all reflect the responsibility of the statesman to his own citizens and to the statesmen of other countries with analogous responsibilities. For war is always an evil, to be avoided wherever possible, not to be resorted to beyond what is strictly necessary and only where effective in restoring peace and security to citizens. To decide on war otherwise than with these requirements in mind is to endanger one's own citizens for reasons that go beyond those that derive from what one owes them. It is also to put one's fellow statesmen in a position where they will find it harder to discharge their responsibilities to their own citizens and hence it is to act in a way that defies rules that exist in order to facilitate the performance of the role of statesman.

Similar considerations apply to the requirements that must be satisfied for *jus in bello* which defensive Just War theory imposes upon soldiers. Since, if its cause is just, a war is fought to defend a territory against loss to an enemy, it follows that the role of soldiers is to do what is needed to repel enemy forces and prevent incursions. The requirements of *proportionality*[12] and *discrimination* are consequences of this. Military action is proportionate insofar as it employs only such force as is needed to secure military objectives. Anything more cannot be directed at military victory but at some other end which it is no part of a soldier's job to achieve. Discrimination involves targeting only military objectives, and that implies not attacking civilians, or enemy soldiers *hors de combat*. Again, targeting them, or, indeed, treating them badly in any way, cannot serve ends which it is part of a soldier's role to accomplish. And those who are exempt from attack include, it needs to be added, the political leaders of the enemy.

Defensive Just War Theory is, broadly speaking, that which is enshrined in international law, whether customary or codified. Here the fact that international law follows the *practice* of states[13] - a feature often regarded as quite extraordinary - actually brings out the way in which it is shaped by actual exchanges between entities whose leaders have a common interest in peace as well as particular interests in maintaining their own states' security and power. The result is two bodies of law; that which relates to the permissible use of force, as spelt out in the UN Charter and the resolutions which interpret it, and that which covers the conduct of war, as set forth in the Hague and Geneva conventions and their various codicils. The former clearly relates to the role of statesmen or other political leaders, the latter to the role of the soldier or member of the other armed forces. It is to these bodies of law which we turn in making ethical assessments of the actions of statesmen and soldiers, and rightly so, for what we are assessing is the propriety of their role performances, and that is, in large measure, determined by their adherence to these laws.

5.   Just War and Punishment

Yet what I have termed *defensive* Just War Theory is not the only version. There is another with which it is often confused, especially when Christian thinkers, and those influenced by them, debate the justice of a war. There is insufficient space here to do more than sketch out the relationship between them, but we can glimpse it in the contrast between Cicero and Augustine's conceptions of a just war. Cicero's is defensive: "There being two sorts of disputing in the world", he observes, "the one by reason, and the other by open force ... when we cannot obtain what is right by the one, we must of necessity have recourse to the other ... but it must always be with the design of obtaining a secure peace."[14] War is rightly waged, then, if all else fails, in defence of a political community's vital interests and must stop at that. St Augustine, by contrast, sees war as the punishment of a wrong, for "wars are defined as just when their aim is to avenge injury,"[15] so that it is an offence against a people's sense of what is right, rather than any objectively specifiable harm, that will lead them to what they conceive as a just war.

This *punitive* Just War theory, as I shall term it, passed into Christian thinking and into that of other religious groups. Thus the medieval crusades provide an example of wars supposedly just on Augustinian criteria, though not on Ciceronian ones, for the perceived injustice being punished and rectified was the injury that Muslims did to Christians by occupying lands sanctified by the presence of Christ.[16] An analogous consideration is in play in contemporary Muslim campaigns to expel the infidel from the lands of Islam.[18] It was precisely this sort of thinking that was held to justify the religious wars that followed the Reformation, whose participants identified themselves in terms of their religious applications. These wars were ended only by the Treaty of Westphalia in 1648, which marked a return to a more classical model of politics and put in place the state system which provided the framework, as I have already remarked, for modern role politics.

What, though, are the essential features of punitive Just War theory? It contrasts with the defensive version, not in the nominal requirements that are specified for *jus ad bellum* and *jus in bello,* but in the way that these requirements are interpreted. Thus *proper authority* consists in being able to adjudicate on whether serious public wrongs have been perpetrated, so that the emphasis falls on a leader's capacity to articulate and implement his people's values. Having a *just cause* consists in being a victim of wrongful acts, as judged against those values, and having a *right intention* in aiming to deliver justice. By contrast with the defensive theory, none of this has anything essentially to do with a leader's relationship to a body of people. Granted, the traditional theory reserves proper authority to a prince, unless he is a tyrant. But this is for theological reasons having to do with the prince being God's representative on earth in the administration of justice, not the people's.[19]

The other requirements of *jus ad bellum* in punitive theory follow from these. That war be a *proportionate* and *ultimate* sanction, and an *effective* one express the ideas that the punishment should fit the crime, and not be vengeful; that war should be resorted to only when other attempts to bring the perpetrators of wrongs to justice fail; and that war should succeed in rectifying the injustice, for otherwise evil triumphs. Similarly the *in bello* provisions reflect the war's retributive purposes. *Proportionality* in the conduct of the war is not judged in relation to purely military objectives but in relation to what is deemed necessary for delivering justice. Thus a so-called proportionate response need serve no military purpose in preventing or deterring further attack, so long as it constitutes retaliation not entirely out of scale with the attack to which it responds. *Discrimination* of response involves not targeting the innocent, that is to say, those who play no part in the original wrong or in obstructing its redress. Evidently, then, civilians are not immune, and, in particular, the leaders and active supporters of the policy that causes the wrong are not; nor are members of the armed forces not, for whatever reason, currently engaged in combat, since they are involved in perpetrating the wrong and preventing its rectification.

Now, it is this punitive version of Just War Theory, I want to suggest, that has come to the fore in new wars, with the rise of identity politics. Not, of course, that this will be readily acknowledged. For the defensive version is so engrained in international practice that those who can with any plausibility represent their actions as conforming to it will do so, while denying that their opponents have the benefit of *any* ethical justification for their war at all. The ethical position is, however, a good deal more symmetrical than this. For in new wars, I am claiming, *both* sides are measuring rights and wrongs by reference to their own values, not by any transcultural standards. Each then takes itself to have proper authority and just cause by the criteria of punitive theory, and each conducts the war largely on the lines that are entailed by its application. The reason why the *other* side's actions seem so wrong is that, judged by one's own values, indeed they are: it is, for example, the innocent who are targeted, in one's own eyes, in a cause that, far from being just, pursues odious objectives. Without the shared framework provided by role politics, there can be no resolution of such oppositions, nor any standards for the regulation of the wars they foment.

Notes

1. The old war/new war distinction originates, I believe, with Mary Kaldor, *New and Old Wars* (Cambridge: Polity, 1999). Kaldor sees only old wars as exemplifying the Clausewitzian characterisation which follows.

2. Carl von Clausewitz, *On War* (1832) (Harmondsworth: Penguin, 1968) Bk 1, Ch. 1, Sec. 24, 119.

3. G.E.M. Anscombe, *Collected Philosophical Papers* (Oxford: Blackwell, 1981), 53.

4. Louis Dumont, *Essays in Individualism* (Chicago: University of Chicago Press, 1986), 130-1.

5. Benedict Anderson claims that *all* national identities are, in a sense, imagined: *Imagined Communities* (London: Verso, 1991). That is not the sense in which I use the notion here.

6. "Role is not a well-defined and well-developed moral idea, and we will learn to make do with some sloppiness around the edges" Arthur Isak Applebaum, *Ethics for Adversaries: the Morality of Roles in Public and Professional Life* (Princeton: Princeton UP, 1999), 46. Applbaum is one of few recent philosophers to explore the ethics of role since Dorothy Emmett, *Rules, Roles and Relations* (London: Macmillan, 1996). The notion is widely used in sociology, particularly in the symbolic interactionism deriving from G.H. Mead and influential in the work of Erving Goffman.

7. See Arkadii Popov, "Ethnic Wars in the Transcaucasus" in M. Kaldor & B. Vashee (eds.), *New Wars* (London: Pinter, 1997),185.

8. *Pace* Kaldor, *New and Old Wars,* who employs the distinction, unlike me, in a literal, chronological sense.

9. E.g. in World War II, which, although an interstate war, had a strong strain of identity politics that accounted for many of its excesses.

10. Antonio Cassese, however, discerns a distinction between the Westphalian and UN Charter models of international relations. *Self-Determination of Peoples: A Legal Reappraisal* (Cambridge: Cambridge UP, 1995), 325.

11. See my *Terrorism, Security and Nationality* (London: Routledge, 1994), Ch. 2.

12. Notice the distinction between proportionality as a requirement of *jus ad bellum* and as a constraint on jus in bello.

13. See Geoffrey Best, *War and Law Since 1945* (Oxford: Clarendon Press, 1994), 5-10.

14. Cicero, *The Offices* (London: Dent, 1909), lxi.

15. Quoted W. L. La Croix, *War and International Ethics: Tradition and Today* (Lanham: University Press of America, 1988), 63.

16. See Jonathan Riley-Smith, *What Were the Crusades?* (Houndmills: Macmillan, 1977)

17. Note that holy war is not to be *contrasted* with just war in either case, since the former is taken to be a species of the latter

18. This observation does not, however, apply to Aquinas, for whom a prince's authority does depend upon his obligations to uphold the common good of his people. See La Croix op. cit., 71.

19. The material in this paper forms the bulk of Chapter One of my book, *New Terror, New Wars* (Edinburgh: Edinburgh UP, 2003). It is reproduced here by kind permission of the publishers.

The Impact of Ideational Interests on State Behaviour and the Outcome of Militarised Disputes

Susan G. Sample

1.   Introduction

Over the last few decades, research into the causes of war has successfully illuminated many old debates about the nature of the international system and the occurrence of war within it by seeking measurable patterns of behavior in state interaction. One of the great contributions of this has been researchers problematising old assumptions and addressing them as open questions about the causes of war. Do states, for instance, really act to balance power? If so, does it lend the system more stability? If states want to ensure peace and security, is it necessary to prepare for war?

Taking this approach has had enormous empirical and theoretical impact on what we know about the causes of war even while is clear that systematically testing old "truths" is not a simple task.[1] It requires scholars to theoretically confront the meanings of standard concepts like power, which is so critical to all our theories and analyses of the causes of war, and even that of war itself, while much traditional literature tended to treat these as "understood" or given. It requires scholars to find theoretically meaningful, and empirically useful, measurements of these things. In addition, the historical and theoretical foundations of the research are often inherently complex and even contradictory, as we see in the case of the research on military build-ups in war.

This study starts from the point of that empirical literature, but then engages a larger conversation on international relations theory. Customarily, the constructivist "turn" in international relations theory is set in contrast or opposition to the empirical and positivist approach, without appreciating the extent to which those approaches recognise the problematic nature of "truth." However, it is true that most traditional studies of the causes of war (empirical studies included) have focused on understanding and/or explicating how the material interests of states (such as the relative power capabilities generally, or military capabilities specifically) in conflict affect their likelihood of going to war. Constructivism's integration of socially and culturally constructed elements into our analyses of state behaviour has offered new and interesting challenges to the traditional approaches, particularly in how we understand the political context of the behaviour we are studying. New avenues of research are also suggested to us by the shift in the foreign

policy literature in the last several years, which has begun to look at the
ideational interests of states, including the way that national self-image or
values shape and define each state's definition of its interests.

Existing empirical work bringing together these strands of
research suggests a great utility in moving beyond analyses that depend
strictly on either the material aspects of social/political phenomenon, or
evaluations of the construction of social reality that do not really engage
those material interests. While a number of integrative studies exist which
look at different international/foreign policy phenomena such as
humanitarian intervention,[2] arms acquisition by states,[3] and norms on the
use of weapons of mass destruction,[4] there is not yet an explicit focus on
war causation. This study makes a first attempt at doing so.

The study addresses two related questions. First, do ideational
interests (including internal aspects like national self-image and culture,
and transnational elements, such as a global "strategic culture") have an
impact on the outcome of militarised disputes in the context of arms races,
or are outcomes understandable strictly through evaluation of material
capabilities and interests? Second, if ideational interests have an impact on
state behaviour in these situations, how? What is the nature of the
interrelationship between material interests of states and ideational
interests as they affect the escalation of disputes to war (or not) in the
context of military build-ups? Addressing these questions should
simultaneously contribute to what we know about the way wars come
about between states, and force a constructive dialogue between these
different literatures.

2.   Examining the Role of Military Build-ups in War

Satisfying research on the role of military build-ups in war has
been particularly difficult to achieve, even within the empirical literature.
Much of the reason for this is that any serious consideration of the
question immediately taps into two contradictory theoretical strands. One
is the basis of deterrence theory: if a state builds up its military, it
increases the costs of aggression against it, thus making it less likely. This
argument includes certain implicit assumptions about the making of
foreign policy; states are clearly unitary, rational actors whose behaviour
is motivated by an understanding of the states' material interests
(specifically, their interests derived from their relative power). The other
theoretical strand derives, as much as anything, from the lessons of World
War I. After the war, it was generally believed that the arms build-ups
prior to it had contributed significantly to its outbreak. Rather than

deterring aggression, the arms build-ups had convinced each state that war was inevitable or that the potential enemy had hostile intentions behind the military build-up. Thus it was concluded by many that military build-ups were profoundly dangerous and should be avoided if states did not intend to go to war. These two theoretical arguments lead to absolutely contradictory policy prescriptions if a state's goal is to ensure its own security. If this contradiction had not been sufficient to lead to a variety of research attempts to determine some semblance of the truth, certainly the absolute magnitude of the superpowers' nuclear arsenals during the Cold War gave the whole debate considerable intensity.

In 1979, Michael Wallace found a very strong relationship between ongoing arms races and the likelihood that a dispute between two major states would escalate to war.[5] His work was not replicated, however, and critics argued that measurement and sampling choices had driven his findings and conclusions.[6] Further studies cast substantial doubt on the conclusion that military build-ups had any significant independent impact on the likelihood of dispute escalation.[7] Sample resolved many of the conflicts in this debate by evaluating the original critiques regarding sampling and measurement, and, using updated data, established that the probability of the escalation of a dispute between two major states was increased by the presence of an ongoing military build-up.[8] While the relationship was not as strong as Wallace had found, it was robust and held up in multivariate analysis.[9]

The limited scope of this research had some interesting consequences for the way we thought about the disputes and the dynamics of their outcomes. Until recently the research has addressed the question of the role of military build-ups for major state disputes only, apparently assuming that major states would provide a good reflection of the behaviour of all states in the international system, rather than asking if this were true.[10] Much previous research also lacked a real contextualisation of the timeframe of the study. Using the whole Correlates of War timeframe from 1816 forward can have both benefits and costs. The obvious cost comes from the fact that by treating the whole time frame as essentially similar, real differences between the eras can be obscured.

Regarding these two issues, Sample has found that major states and minor states do not show identical patterns of escalation, all else being equal, and that there are clear differences between pre- and post-World War II in the ways states interact. For instance, the patterns that characterised major state dispute escalation essentially vanished after the war.[11] While one could attribute these changes to the overwhelming power of nuclear weapons, and thus a change in the material damage that the states could do to one another, that would not explain why minor states interacted differently after the war as well. All the patterns changed, even for those states not directly touched by the power of nuclear weapons. With the two world wars and the advent of nuclear weapons, and perhaps the significance of decolonisation as well, the context of international politics was altered, not just the distribution of international power. These findings indicate the importance of a more in-depth examination of the changing context, both material and ideational, of foreign policy decisions, including the decision to escalate a dispute to war.

3.   Constructivism, Foreign Policy, and the National Interest

Other tools are required if our intent is to examine the dynamics of war causation beyond material interests (represented in the first instance by power calculations). The first of these tools is a serious integration of foreign policy research into our analysis of war causation. To a great extent, the empirical studies cited began from the point of a rational actor model of foreign policy making in which the state is assumed to be a unitary actor with interests determined by external forces in the international system. There is, however, a considerable literature that empirically challenges those assumptions through careful investigation of sub-national influences on policymaking. The second "tool" is a shift in our perspective about the nature of the international system. The constructivist approach to international relations theory, rather than assuming the nature of the system and accepting that states have given national interests, problematical both. This does not mean that constructivism is incompatible with empirical analysis; rather, national interests become a variable in the analysis, and the international system is recognised as a flexible framework for state action. Any analysis using these tools is bound to be much more complex and contextualised than one without them, but it might also be more realistic.

The relationship between material and ideational interests is being addressed both directly and indirectly in foreign policy case studies and more comparative, theoretical work on policymaking.[12] In the historically dominant rational actor model of foreign policy making, states are assumed to be unitary actors, seeking to maximise (in the neo-realist version) their power (and thus their security) in the international system.[13] In this formulation, domestic politics is, whether within the bureaucracies of the government, or relating to societal groups and their access to policymakers, not particularly relevant to policy outcomes, nor are other unique national characteristics, such as national culture and identity and national regime type.

There is now ample evidence that challenges the realism of the rational actor model of foreign policy making. The research comes from several different origins, but leads to the common conclusion that the hard line that neo-realists wanted to draw between international politics on the one hand, and domestic politics on the other hand, is unrealistic. Evidence from cognitive psychology explores the ways that individuals, including policymakers, interpret and use data in ways that are not predicted by assumptions of rationality.[14] Cognitive psychology provides, for instance, a good theoretical framework for the "hostile spiral" explanation for World War I.[15] In addition, Kong's work and others examine the manner in which analogical reasoning, or psychological referral to past events as a means of understanding and determining policy in current events, has affected foreign policy making decisions.[16] Janis explores the way that "groupthink" can alter the discussion and evaluation of possible alternative policy choices in non-rational ways that have more to do with the psychological need for group unity than the foreign policy question before the group.[17] In international relations, research on the democratic peace suggests that the regime type of states probably has an impact on whether or not they are likely to engage in violent conflict with one another.[18] And finally, "middle power theory" looks at the foreign policy of countries like Australia and Canada who have attempted (with relative success) to forge an international identity for themselves that includes a leadership role in international institutions in ways unanticipated by the power-delineated world of neo-realism.[19]

Studies focusing on the construction of national identity and its impact on foreign policy of states obviously have a theoretical grounding in constructivism.[20] Constructivism is more an approach to international relations than a theory in itself. The key distinction, as we have seen, between the constructivist approach and more traditional theories of international relations like neo-realism is that constructivists hold that ideas both matter and have a constructing impact on the material world, including states' perception of their interests.[21]

In neo-realism, ideas are largely epiphenomenal.[22] The anarchy of the international system being what it is, states have certain fairly specific material national interests: they must constantly be prepared to defend themselves in the event of aggression from others, aggression which is always possible given the nature of the system. Given their need for preparation and defence, they must be concerned with their power relative to other states at all times. States that do not attend to these concerns will fail to survive in the end. The material world is concrete, and it generates clear interests and prescriptions for necessary behaviour.[23] The role of ideas in this neo-realist context is minimal. Ideologies, nationalism, and national identities reflect the material interests of the actors in the system. They may serve a useful role in helping the state to act on its interests—nationalism serves to make young men willing to die for the preservation of the state, for instance—but these things are shaped by the interests that are pre-existing, they do not shape them.

In contrast, constructivism begins with the understanding that humans are social creatures who through interaction create social and cultural narratives that are meaningful psychologically and materially.[24] Middle power "theory" is worth looking at because of its conscious inclusion of both material and ideational elements in its explanation of the changing foreign policy role taken on by certain states.[25] It argues, significantly, that a country's *perception* of itself and its role in the international system strongly contributes to the country's definition of its national interest. In other words, national interest is not a given, but a variable, a function of both the material context of a state and its perception and everything that contributes to that (ideology, history, culture, etc.)

The literature on the foreign policy of states like Canada, Australia, and some of the Scandinavian countries suggests that these states perceive their role in the international system as keepers of international order and peace.[26] This role has both material justification and ideational explanation. Cooper, et al, do not take the line that Canada and Australia have pursued international co-operation simply because they are "good international citizens," but rather that co-operation in international politics has been vital to their material interests as well.[27] While international co-operation suits their material interests, history provides evidence of conscious identity as good citizens as well. At the founding of the United Nations, Canada attempted to get a special role for itself based on that good citizenship—its willingness to co-operate and provide leadership for a peaceful order in international relations beyond its material power.[28] Canada's view of itself has had a clear impact on its choices in foreign policy, and the same can be said of the Scandinavian states, like Norway, which has disproportionate representation in United Nations peacekeeping missions and other cooperative international enterprises. Self-image matters.

The way a country's image impacts its foreign policy choices is not limited to middle powers by any means. The notion of American "exceptionalism" is certainly about American culture and its impact on American policy.[29] Part of the American cultural identity is the belief that democracy is obviously the best form of government. The Wilsonian strand of this (which has historically competed with opposing beliefs) argues that it is the moral responsibility of enlightened Americans to spread democracy to the rest of the world, one way or another.[30] While American foreign policy has exhibited inconsistency over the years, there can be little doubt that the self-image of the United States has led to an adoption of "spreading democracy" as a "national interest" of the country independent of any material gain. Even an avowed realist like Samuel Huntington may unconsciously indicate the importance of ideational elements in the creation of national interest; there is a fundamental distinction to be made, he argues, between American leadership in the international system and even that of another democratic, relatively free-trading state such as Japan. The Americans have an "interest" in actively encouraging democracy abroad that Japan simply does not have because it is not part of the Japanese national culture or identity.[31]

Beyond questions of foreign policy, the implications of constructivism in international relations are substantial. Constructivists problematise each element of the neo-realist narrative in its description of an anarchical world. Constructivists question both the meaning of anarchy and its implications for state behaviour.[32] They also, fundamentally, challenge the notion that any social reality, including the nature of the international system, is actually "natural" in the sense that it exists independent of human behaviour constructing and/or reconstructing it.

Wendt argues that anarchy "is what states make of it." States do in fact exist in a world without an overarching political authority; however, Wendt argues, the implications drawn from this state of affairs, including that states must constantly seek power and engage in power politics, are socially constructed, not inherent to the system. Rather, a self-help system, where each state identifies its interests individualistically, is one way that states can interact in an anarchical international system. If they interact this way, the system is created and reinforced, and eventually believed to be "natural".[33] This does not mean, however, that the system that emerges is the only one that was or is possible. States could interact (or could have interacted) in more co-operative patterns, thus leading to the belief that co-operation was the "nature" of anarchy.

None of this is intended to imply that constructivism as an approach to understanding international political phenomenon is entirely uniform. Variations in constructivist approaches lead some scholars to essentially reject the idea that the material world exists at all apart from socially constructed understandings of it (moving toward post-modernism). Others are likely to examine the interactions between the existing material world and the social and cultural meanings that we construct in that world.[34] The latter assumes relevant and meaningful interaction between the ideational and the material—the causal arrow does not go only one direction.

4.   (Re)Examining the Patterns of Dispute Escalation

In the literature on the role military build-ups play in dispute escalation, there are several empirical findings, alluded to earlier, that are of particular theoretical interest because they seem to pose real explanatory challenges to traditional international relations theory. By challenging the explanatory ability of traditional international relations theory, they may serve as a proving ground for a study that examines interaction between the material and the ideational. The first of these findings is that military build-ups do play a role in patterns of dispute escalation, both for major states and for minor states. The finding itself is fairly straightforward (though the subject of much controversy), but it sits at the nexus of a serious theoretical battle that has implications for both international relations theory and decision-making theory. The second finding worthy of more in-depth discussion is that major states, all else being equal (including relative power balance between opposing parties) have been more war-prone than minor states historically. Overall, their disputes have been more likely to escalate than those between small states have. Finally, there is a post-war change in all the patterns of dispute escalation, whether involving major states or minor ones. Major states exhibit no pattern of escalation, and while minor states do, it seems that military build-ups no longer have any statistical impact on the likelihood of escalation after World War II.

Each of these findings could be explained individually by appeal to one theory or another.   However, the argument here is that constructivism can offer a way of explaining all of these findings that both recognises the empirical patterns and their material aspects, and shows how the behaviour of states has been influenced by socially constructed, shared meanings about state interaction on the part of policymakers. Taken together, it becomes evident that an understanding of the interaction of states in militarised disputes requires the approach that constructivism offers by standing at the crossroads between material and ideational explanations for human behaviour.[35]

Throughout the 20th century, most of the theoretical and empirical work on arms races conceptualised an arms race as an action–reaction cycle: one country built up its military and its rival followed suit.[36] More in-depth analysis has indicated, however, that military build-ups are sometimes far less interactive than that. Countries may build up their militaries for domestic reasons due to party politics, bureaucratic politics, etc..[37]   In fact, Eyre & Suchman argue that the conventional military build-ups of minor states throughout the Cold War could be explained better by their quest for international social status than material threats to their national interests.[38] This does not mean, however, that the outcomes of military build-ups have to be related necessarily to their cause.[39]   It is possible for a military build-up to have unanticipated consequences.

It is evident that perception of military build-ups and the way they are interpreted within a state's interests are not defined solely in material terms. All else being equal, the United States will not judge a military build-up on the part of the United Kingdom and China as equivalents in the way they impact American national interests. Certain realist scholars have tacitly acknowledged this as well, as we see in Walt's move beyond the basic realist formulation of balancing power by injecting the notion that states balance threats.[40] What is missing from his analysis, however, is a thorough analysis of the extent to which "threats" are defined by both the material (power) and the ideational (social constructed identities, particularly those of "enemies").[41]

The behaviour of states can be explained both by their individualised perceptions of the international system and their place in it, and by socially shared norms in the international system. There is a growing literature on the role of norms in international relations, including analyses of possible norms against the use of nuclear weapons and for humanitarian intervention.[42] This literature fits within the larger constructivist framework in its explication of the way states have developed new, shared meanings and means of interacting over time. There has been, in the literature on norms, something of a tendency to focus on those norms or institutions that encourage or reinforce co-operative behaviour,[43] but there is no theoretical reason to suggest that conflictive norms and institutions may not be constructed and reinforced just as easily as co-operative ones.[44]

When it comes to militarised interaction between states, and issues of national security, there is a system of shared meanings and an existing full international strategic culture. Realism, *realpolitik*, itself can be interpreted within the constructivist approach as a set of institutions that help shape states' perceptions and behaviour. Realism defines and helps construct the shared meanings of sovereign states, and certainly of the inherently conflictual nature of the anarchical international system.[45] Having defined the system in this way, states also share common prescriptions of appropriate behaviour in international relations, particularly regarding issues of "national security." These appropriate behaviours include typically choosing to balance power through alliances or military build-ups, the purpose of which policies is to deter aggression.[46]

Why then would there be an increased chance of war for states involved in militarised disputes when they are building up their militaries for the purpose of increasing stability and security? A full understanding of how the dynamic works includes delving deeper into the constructed realist narrative, recognising its interaction with the real material threat involved in a militarised dispute, and acknowledging the importance of human psychology.[47] States build up their military in the first instance because international anarchy in the realist narrative is an inherently dangerous place, and they must ensure their survival.[48] Those military build-ups should deter aggression. When a militarised dispute occurs, then, the first question a state must ask itself is "we were building up our military: why weren't they deterred?" Evidence from cognitive psychology tells us that human beings tend to assume that they are at the centre of others' attention and plans,[49] so the realist narrative offers a clear answer to the question: if the other state was not deterred by the visible military build-up, and the military build-up of the other was directed at them all along (whether that is actually true or not), then it must be that the opposing state actually has hostile intentions (which may, or may not, be true). Within the realist narrative, the appropriate response to that situation is to indicate your willingness to take a conflict "to the next level," either to convince the other state to back down, or to prepare to defend yourself and prosecute your cause in event of war.

Thus, the states move closer to war through an interaction between potential material threat and shared and socially constructed perceptions about the "nature" of the international system. The constructed narrative of realism shapes the perceptions of both states to judge the situation as deliberately threatening to their national security. This is independent of whether the military build-ups actually impact the power balance between the two states or not: the dynamic of the build-up and the way it affects perceptions have an impact on dispute escalation beyond the material aspect. Of course, there is a material aspect to this in that both sides *are* armed and *can* threaten each other. Then the socially shared culture of international security suggests that in the face of aggression (the occurrence of the dispute despite its own military build-up) it is a gamble to not assume hostility on the part of the other. While most militarised disputes still end peacefully, this dynamic certainly increases the chance of dispute escalation to war.[50]

In the empirical findings regarding dispute escalation, we also know that major states were more war prone in general than were minor states, at least in the pre-war era.[51] A strictly material explanation for this finding is not particularly easy to construct. Minor states facing each other should judge their power relative to their opponent and make a rational decision on that basis. There is no obvious reason why major state disputes and minor state disputes would come out differently given the individualistic definition of anarchy offered by neo-realism.

A treatment of national identity and image as a variable in the analysis creates a richer and more complete explanation for this finding (one that simultaneously provides a challenge to traditional international relations theory and sounds like common sense). In sum, major states have an identity as major states, which leads them to perceive their interests in conflictive situations differently. The identity of a major state includes the perception of having global interests, and interest in having an impact on the global system, that goes beyond any strict material need of the state. Indeed, our definition of major power status includes these identity issues as much as it includes measures of power.

There is ample evidence that such an "identity" for major states exists, and that this identity is socially constructed by the state itself and interactively with other states in the international system. A state's perceptions, however, may not be in accord with the way other states see it, and in the end, whether a state is a "major power" or not depends on international recognition as such, not solely on its own perception. One simple example goes back a hundred years: if their power is measured in strictly material terms,[52] it is clear that both the United States and Japan met the material "standard" of being a major power years before they attained that political status at the end of the nineteenth century. However, their peripheral position in the dominant European state system of the time meant that they were not recognised until they politically began to "play the game" of being major states. In both cases, the states were victorious in an imperial war, drawing European respect and thus status as "major" players in that system.

A more recent example of the importance of socially constructed international status and its impact on state behaviour can be seen in India's quest for major power status. While India perceives itself as ready to have major power status, it has been unable to attain that political goal. By strictly material measures, India has more "power" than the United Kingdom, but that has not translated into political meaning in the international system, particularly among other major states. India has shown itself to be well aware of the importance of the complex construction of international status; the acquisition of nuclear weapons was about more than the threat of Pakistan or China, it was an attempt to join the "club" and gain international recognition and respect which was not, in fact, forthcoming. Instead, India's more or less declared nuclear status in 1998 just got it sanctioned by the United States—essentially treated as a "small" country that got out of line—because the major states, while understanding that India has potential, do not yet perceive it as one of their own.[53]

It seems that there are two avenues to recognition as a major state. First, there is the traditional path of fighting a major state (well) or fighting a recognised major war. This path can explain the enhanced international political status of the United States after the Spanish-American War in 1898, the Japanese after the Sino-Japanese War of 1894-95, and (to some extent) China in the Korean War in 1950-53. The other path, which has arguably been forged more recently and is therefore somewhat less certain still, is to be a large and extraordinarily rich country: both Japan and Germany are perceived as major states now, despite not seeking military dominance in their regions or the global system.[54]

The complex social construction of "major power status" is strongly supported by the evidence of real international politics over time. There is no "natural" reason for major states to treat each other differently in the anarchy of the international system from the way minor states treat each other, but they do so because of the socially constructed nature of the international system itself. The major states have shared a set of meanings about their role and their interaction in the political world that goes beyond material power. This is not meant to imply that both the shared meanings and the implied role of those meanings have been consistent or stable across time. Rather, that the "culture" of being a major state exists, and it evolves like any other culture in which we see both continuity and change over time.

Generally speaking, despite some small change in the way they are defined, major states have a constructed role that has granted them the perceived right and/or obligation to project their power across the globe whether it seems strictly in their materially defined national interest or not. The United States has ideational national interests (competing always with material ones) that lead it to humanitarian interventions on some occasions, and ill advised (materially) crusades on others. It is not only the United States, however; France sees itself as having interests in small, poor African countries which can really contribute little to French well being or material power. The Europeans certainly wanted American involvement in the Bosnian war, which had no clear relevance to anyone living in Peoria. And, because of a constructed definition of appropriate roles, we find that major states, as distinguished by recognised status as much as by actual power holdings, also behave differently than minor states do when they are involved in militarised disputes.

Militarised disputes between major states (before World War II) were more likely to escalate than those between minor states were. Having global status and global interests meant that major states were competing for global influence, not just immediate material interests. While there were clear statistical patterns in the escalation of minor state disputes, the overall likelihood of their escalation was smaller than for major states. Major state disputes are more likely to be multi-layered: immediate local interests, regional interests, and global interests creating a network of overlapping issues. If inter-linking issues can contribute to co-operation on several of them, there is ample evidence before World War II that they could contribute to complex conflicts as well. For minor states, perception of interests is far narrower, and more "local," thus making for a less complex situation, and more diplomatic solutions.

After World War II, however, the defined patterns of interaction profoundly changed for both the major states and the minor states. There are no more statistical patterns in the escalation of disputes involving major states, either with each other, or with minor states. The military build-ups of the major states in this period have no statistically recognisable impact on the likelihood of a dispute's escalation. Similarly, mutual military build-ups do not increase the chance that minor states will escalate a dispute to war. Minor states do, however, retain a clear empirical pattern of dispute escalation, just a different one: both recent power transitions (where one state passes the other in power) and conflicts over territory make disputes more likely to escalate between small states.[55]

The question then is whether power-based explanations are sufficient to explain these changes, or whether constructivism can offer real input here. Obviously, the power-based explanations of choice for the change in major state behaviour are the nature of the bipolar international system on the one hand, and deterrence theory on the other. Neo-realists argued that the material nature of the bipolar system, dominated by two overwhelming superpowers, so constrained the behaviour of the other major states that they were unable to act, and the bipolarity itself made the interaction between the superpowers generally stable.[56] They also argued, however, that once the bipolar system collapsed, that we could expect a resurrection of instability and conflict among the major states (Mearsheimer 1990) which has not been forthcoming. The other element of the post-war behavioural change that must be assessed is deterrence theory, which argued that due to the overwhelming destructive nature of nuclear weapons, states that had them were essentially immune from aggressive behaviour and had to be entirely more cautious in disputes with each other.

Deterrence theory is appealing on its face because we know, after all, that the great rivals of the Cold War did refrain from war. The historical record, however, does not really offer deterrence theory the support that is usually taken for granted. There are many examples during the Cold War of non-nuclear states challenging nuclear states, and sometimes getting what they wanted.[57] Britain's nuclear capability (independent or not) certainly did nothing to deter the Argentines in 1982, and neither China in 1950, nor North Vietnam twenty years later, were particularly concerned with US nuclear dominance (when at least China probably should have been).

A host of other explanations for the long post-war peace among the major states has been offered, in addition to bipolarity and deterrence; these include war-weariness, learning, displacement of conflict to the periphery, liberal economic exchange, etc.[58] Critically, virtually all of these involve, in one way or another, a restructuring of the way the major states perceived the nature of the system, a change in perceptions that went beyond the material dangers of war to them.

The dynamic of US-Soviet relations during the Cold War illustrates well the interaction between material national interests and social construction of relationships. In this period, the two countries had an unprecedented number of militarised disputes in a relatively short time, but unlike earlier major state rivalries (like France and Germany), these disputes never escalated to the point of war. An evaluation of pre- and post-Cuban Missile Crisis superpower relations shows a clear process of social learning over the course of the Cold War, with the CMC being a critical juncture in it. The Cuban Missile Crisis illustrates both the fact that war was entirely possible between the superpowers at that time (in spite of the proposed deterrent effect of nuclear weapons), and that they did hesitate because of the fear of nuclear war. There are patterns of change across the Cold War that cannot be attributed to changing threat (once both countries could destroy each other, nothing else was really of material importance) but must be attributed to learned social interaction between the enemies.

The most dangerous disputes of the Cold War all took place before the Cuban Missile Crisis. After that, their conflict rapidly took on routinised, and learned patterns of behaviour that involved continued disputes, but gave little indication that either party intended to escalate, and every indication that both parties knew that. The risk of nuclear war created an environment that allowed the United States and Soviet Union to construct new social patterns for these rivals to deal with each other, even though the material threat and the unquestionable animosity remained.[59] However, the causal arrow did not just run one direction: once the new patterns of interaction, even in rivalry, were created, they contributed to the reshaping of social interaction among the major states more generally.

The major states have redefined the nature of the their interaction profoundly since World War II. Their behaviour indicates that they now assume that their relationship is "naturally" co-operative, and even real disagreements and material conflicts must be dealt with in this larger social context of co-operation. These are the same states that have exhibited some of the most dangerous international rivalries in history, and still retain the power (even without nuclear capability) to present enormous material threat to one another. Wendt offers a constructivist argument that suggests that the material world and the ideational world interact, and that international anarchy can take on different characteristics based largely on the variation of socially constructed norms.[60] The now co-operative "nature" of major state relations would seem to provide an example supporting this thesis.

The creation of nuclear weapons toward the end of a devastating world war created both a material and an ideational critical juncture in history that is evidenced by many things. The rivalry between the superpowers ended differently than essentially every other major state rivalry in recent history. Perhaps more importantly, for distinguishing between material and ideational explanations for the peace, the major states did not abandon co-operation at the end of the Cold War despite the material changes in the international system. Rather, co-operation continued because the social context of major state relationships had changed: war between them, as Mueller has argued, is virtually unthinkable because their behaviour and perceptions have created a different interactive environment for them.[61]

While there is some evidence of growing "zones of peace" among minor states, there are still statistically verifiable patterns of escalation among them, which suggest that these "critical junctures" were quite different for them. The changes in the patterns of minor state escalation before and after the war indicate that the context of the international system changed for them, too, but not in the same way. This could be the result of their lack of nuclear capability (giving no direct material spur to self-reinforcing ideational change), or perhaps decolonisation (itself the *product* of ideational change in the international system). It is evident, though, that the shared culture of co-operation that we see now among the major states does not yet translate itself to the whole of the international system (despite the best efforts of the United Nations to construct that system). As a whole, the culture of the international political system is still largely grounded in the socially-constructed European (then global) state system, with states acting on their concerns for sovereignty and security defined in relatively traditional ways.

6.   Conclusion

An examination of the empirical findings relating to dispute escalation, and the role military build-ups have played in them, indicates that it is indeed valuable to take a constructivist approach in analysing state behaviour. This study obviously does not abandon the material, but rather seeks to uncover ways that material and ideational aspects of international politics interact, while recognising that ideational elements have causative effects on behaviour, and are not merely consequences of behaviour. Constructivism offers an understanding of each of the observable, but theoretically difficult, patterns that we find in the empirical literature on the role of military build-ups in war.

While traditional international relations theories, such as neo-realism, and traditional rational actor models of foreign policymaking purport to explain international politics, the many unexplained empirical patterns must force us to re-examine their value in the absence of ideational variables. If we accept that ideas matter, we can create more complex, but also more realistic explanations for international events that incorporate global (strategic) cultural elements, as well as particular national identities, and their influence on the way states define their national interests.

Including these elements offers us a more robust understanding and explanation for both why military build-ups increased the likelihood of disputes escalating to war before World War II, and why they no longer seem to have the same impact. Because of their self-reinforcing socially shaped identity, recognised major states have made different policy choices than minor states have. There is a group of major states, defined both by independent ideational factors and material ones, that constructs separate rules for interacting with each other, and the rest of the world. While once that meant an ongoing competition for dominance in an inherently conflictive international system, it now appears to be an understanding that conflicts between them go on in the context of a general assumption of international co-operation among major states.

There is little doubt that ideas do matter and have an independent impact on human behaviour. This can be the source of comfort in the sense that it means that the world may, in fact, get "better" if, for instance, the assumptions of major state co-operation spread to the larger international system either through evolution or the diligent effort of international organisations committed to the notion. We might also remember that ideas do not have to be benevolent, as both Stalin and Hitler provide ample historical evidence to the contrary. It does mean that the world is far more complex than neo-realism or neo-liberalism, the two apparent contestants for theoretical dominance for many years, have led us to believe. We cannot *expect* either co-operation or conflict in the system because of its "nature." Both are entirely possible. In the end, however, we must recognise in our studies of war that human agency and decision, both through the unconscious continuity of accepted cultural frameworks and through conscious efforts to alter ideology and identity, do matter to the outcome, whether that is war or peace. And we can make of that what we will.

Notes

1. John A., Vasquez, ed. *What do We Know about War?* (Lanham MD: Rowman & Littlefield Publishers, 2000). and Manus I. Midlarsky, ed. *Handbook of War Studies II.* (Ann Arbor MI: University of Michigan Press, 2000.) See also John A. Vasquez, *The War Puzzle.* (Cambridge: Cambridge University Press, 1993).

2. Martha. Finnemore, "Constructing Norms of Humanitarian Intervention," In *The Culture of National Security: Norms and Identity in World Politics,* ed. Peter J. Katzenstein. (New York: Columbia University Press, 1996).

3. Dana P. Eyre and Mark C. Suchman, "Status, Norms, and the Proliferation of Conventional Weapons: An Institutional Theory Approach," In *The Culture of National Security: Norms and Identity in World Politics*, ed. Peter J. Katzenstein. (New York: Columbia UP, 1996), 79-113

4. Richard Price and Nina Tannenwald, "Norms and Deterrence: The Nuclear and Chemical Weapons Taboos," In *The Culture of National Security: Norms and Identity in World Politics*, ed. Peter J. Katzenstein (New York: Columbia UP 1996), 114-152.

5. Michael D Wallace, "Arms Races and Escalation: Some New Evidence," *Journal of Conflict Resolution* 23.1 (1979): 3-16.

6. Erich Weede, "Arms Races and Escalation: Some Persisting Doubts," *Journal of Conflict Resolution* 24.2 (1980): 285-287; Michael F. Altfeld, "Arms Races?—And Escalation? A Comment on Wallace," *International Studies Quarterly* 27.2 (1983): 225-231.

7. Paul F. Diehl, "Arms Races and Escalation: A Closer Look," *Journal of Peace Research* 20.3 (1983): 205-212.

8. Susan G. Sample, "Arms Races and Dispute Escalation: Resolving the Debate," *Journal of Peace Research* 34.1 (1997): 7-22.

9. Susan G. Sample, "Military Buildups, War, and Realpolitik: A Multivariate Model," *Journal of Conflict Resolution* 42.2 (1998): 156-175; Susan G. Sample, "The Outcomes of Military Buildups: Minor States vs. Major Powers," *Journal of Peace Research* 39.6 (2002): 669-692.

10. Sample, 2002.

11. Ibid.

12. Examples include Laura Neack, "Linking State Type with Foreign Policy Behavior," In *Foreign Policy Analysis: Continuity and Change in its Second Generation*, eds Laura Neack, Jeanne A. Hey, and Patrick J. Haney (Englewood Cliffs, NJ: Prentice Hall, 1995), 215-228; Walter Russell Mead, *Special Providence: American Foreign Policy and How it Changed the World* (New York: Alfred A. Knopf, 2001); Shona Dodds, "The Role of Multilateralism and the UN in Post-Cold War US Foreign Policy," (Dissertation draft Australian National University, 2002).

13. Neo-liberals assume states are maximising their material well-being rather than power. This distinction has some very interesting implications for the likelihood of co-operation and conflict in the international system, but in terms of determining how policy is actually made, the differences between neo-liberalism and neo-realism are negligible. For a discussion of the dominance of the rational actor model in studies of foreign policy, as well as popular discourse, see Allison & Zelikow (1999).

14. Robert Jervis, "Hypotheses on Misperception," *World Politics* 20.3 (1968): 454-479. Robert Jervis, *Perception and Misperception in International Politics* (Princeton, NJ: Princeton UP, 1976); Jerel A. Rosati, "A Cognitive Approach to the Study of Foreign Policy." In *Foreign Policy Analysis: Continuity and Change in its Second Generation,* eds. Laura Neack, Jeanne A. Hey, and Patrick J. Haney (Englewood Cliffs, NJ: Prentice Hall, 1995), 49-70.

15. Ole R. Holsti, Robert C. North, and Richard A. Brody, "Perception and Action in the 1914 Crisis." In *Quantitative International Politics*, ed J. David Singer (New York: The Free Press, 1968), 123-158.

16. Yuen Foong Khong, *Analogies at War: Korean, Munich, Dien Bien Phu, and the Vietnam Decisions of 1965.* (Princeton, NJ: Princeton UP, 1992); Keith L. Shimko, "Foreign Policy Metaphors: Falling 'Dominoes' and Drug 'Wars.'" In *Foreign Policy Analysis: Continuity and Change in its Second Generation,* eds Laura Neack, Jeanne A. Hey, and Patrick J. Haney (Englewood Cliffs, NJ: Prentice Hall, 1995), 71-84.

17. Irving L. Janis, *Groupthink: Psychological Studies of Policy Decisions and Fiascos*, 2nd ed. (New York: Houghton Mifflin, 1986).

18. See as one example of a large and continuing literature, Bruce M. Russett, *Grasping the Democratic Peace: Principles for a Post-Cold War World.* (Princeton, NJ: Princeton UP, 1993).

19. Andrew F. Cooper, et al. *Relocating Middle Powers: Australian and Canada in a Changing World Order.* (Melbourne: Melbourne University Press, 1993). Neack, 1995.

20. See Thomas Risse-Kappen, "Ideas do not Float Freely: Transnational Coalition, Domestic Structures, and the End of the Cold War," *International Organization* 48.2 (1994): 185-214.

21. Alexander Wendt, "Anarchy is what States Make of it: The Social Construction of Power Politics," *International Organization* 46.2 (1992): 391-425; Risse-Kappen, 1994; Ronald L Jepperson, et al. "Norms, Identity, and Culture in National Security." In *The Culture of National Security: Norms and Identity in World Politics,* ed. Peter J. Katzenstein (New York: Columbia UP, 1996), 33-78; John Gerard Ruggie, "What Makes the World Hang Together? Neo-utilitarianism and the Social Constructivist Challenge," *International Organization* 52.4 (1998): 855-

885; Jeffrey T. Checkel, "The Constructivist Turn in International Relations Theory," *World Politics* 50.2 (1998): 324-348.
22. Checkel, 1998.

23. Kenneth N. Waltz, *Theory of International Politics*. (New York: Random House, 1979).

24. Ruggie, 1998.

25. Cooper, et al., 1993; Neack, 1995.

26. For one example, see Neack 1995.

27. Cooper, et al, 1993.

28. Neack 1995.

29. Dodds, 2002.

30. Walter Russell Mead, *Special Providence: American Foreign Policy and How it Changed the World* (New York: Alfred A. Knopf, 2001).

31. Samuel P. Huntington, "Why International Primacy Matters," *International Security* 17.4 (1993): 68-84.

32. Wendt, 1992.

33. Wendt, p. 408, suggests that the existence of a predator state in the system, one that does seek to dominate and maximise power, can have the effect of creating a self-help anarchical system. Once other states learn the behaviour, it becomes difficult for the system to change its "nature."

34. Emanuel Adler, "Seizing the Middle Ground: Constructivism in World Politics," *European Journal of International Relations* 3.3 (1997): 319-363.

35. Ibid.

36. Samuel P. Huntington, "Arms Races: Prerequisites and Results," *Public Policy* 8 (1958): 41-86. Lewis F. Richardson, *Arms and Insecurity*. (Pacific Grove, CA: The Boxwood Press, 1960); Wallace, 1979.

37. Charles W. Ostrom, "Evaluating Alternative Foreign Policy Decision-Making Models," *Journal of Conflict Resolution* 21 (1977): 235-266; Charles W. Ostrom, "A Reactive Linkage Model of the US Defence Expenditure Policymaking Process," *American Political Science Review* 72 (1978): 941-957; A.F.K. Organski and Jacek Kugler, *The War Ledger* (Chicago: Chicago UP, 1980); Michael D. Ward, "Differential Paths to Parity: A Study of the Contemporary Arms Race," *American Political Science Review* 78 (1984): 297-317.

38. Eyre &. Suchman,1996.

39. Suzanne Werner and Jacek Kugler, "Power Transitions and Military Buildups: Resolving the Relationship between Arms Buildups and War," In *Parity and War: Evaluations and Extensions of 'The War Ledger*, eds. Jacek Kugler and Douglas Lemke (Ann Arbor, MI: University of Michigan Press, 1996): 187-210

40. Stephen M. Walt, *The Origins of Alliances*. (Ithaca, NY: Cornell UP, 1987.)

41. Wendt, 1992.

42. Price & Tannenwald, 1996; Finnemore, 1996.

43. Jervis (1998) criticised constructivism on the grounds that it appears to be driven by a normative agenda. In other words, to the extent that the political world is socially constructed, it can be made "better." From his point of view, there are at least two problems with this: first, even if we take the position that socially constructed norms influence the material world, the reality is that influential ideas in the system may be "evil" as well as "good," and in that case, traditional realpolitik may be valued as providing a moderating influence on foreign policy otherwise driven by frightening radical plans for change (just think about the Nazis) (Jervis p. 974). Moreover, he fears that that the normative desire to believe that the world can be made better will overshadow the scientific enterprise of understanding and explaining real politics. His first point is absolutely valid, and made by many constructivists as well; his second point, while a valuable critique and an important point to keep in mind, may have been based on an underestimation of the systematic nature of much of the work done in the constructivist vein. Many of the empirical studies in

Katzenstein's *The Culture of National Security* wed the material and the ideational in systematic and analytical fashion.

44. Wendt, 1992.

45. Jim George, *Discourses of Global Politics: A Critical (Re)Introduction to International Relations*. (Boulder CO: Lynne Rienner Publishers, Inc., 1994).

46. Sample, 1998; Sample 2000.

47. Sample, 1998.

48. It is important to note that mutual military build-ups are not all that common. The definition used for a military build-up (trying to tap into the idea of an arms race) ensures that only unusually high rates of military spending are included. States embark on rapid build-ups rarely, so the likelihood of a dispute taking place in the context of two states building up their militaries rapidly is relatively small. For a full explanation of the measures and data used, see Sample, 1998; Sample, 2002.

49. Jervis, 1968; Jervis, 1976.

50. Empirical research tells us that in a dispute between major states, the chance of escalation is six and a half times higher when both states are engaged in a military build-up. Disputes between two minor states are more than twice as likely to escalate if a military build-up is ongoing, Sample, 2002. It is important to note, as subsequent discussion will illuminate, that these are the figures for disputes occurring before World War II.

51. A pattern noted by Quincy Wright (1962) is his classic *A Study of War*. In Sample (2002), the statistics are as follows: of 268 total dyadic disputes between major states between 1816-1993, 14.9% (40) escalated to war. Of 1433 dyadic disputes between two minor states, 9.5% (136) escalated. Disputes involving one major state and one minor state escalated 13.7% of the time.

52. For instance, if one uses the Correlates of War capabilities data, a fairly standard and useful measure for power in the empirical literature. Gross National Product is also a good measure, but the data does not go back as far—the two are highly correlated (Organski & Kugler 1980). As

with any case of an operationalised measure of a concept as complex as power, both of these measures can be debated in their outcomes for specific cases, but both have proven valid and reliable in research.

53. Amil Gupta, "India's Third-Tier Nuclear State Dilemma: N plus 20?" *Asian Survey* 41.6 (2001),1044-1063.

54. The definition of Japan and Germany as "major" states here is taken from the Correlates of War project designations as such as of 1990. Also, there are other differences between "major" states and "minor" ones. India consciously linked the two characteristics of having permanent membership and veto status in the United Nations Security Council, and possessing nuclear weapons. However, while nuclear weapons possession might have been meaningful in terms of political status in the 1950s, the non-proliferation movement and the recognition by the recognised major states that proliferation among middle powers was entirely possible and even likely removed much of the political cachet from possession (Gupta 2001).

55. Whether or not a conflict is over an issue of territory is the single most robust variable in these analyses, across classes of disputes, independent of whether the states are contiguous or not (Sample, 2002).

56. Kenneth N. Waltz, *Theory of International Politics*. (New York: Random House, 1979.)

57. Jacek Kugler, "Terror Without Deterrence: Reassessing the Role of Nuclear Weapons," *Journal of Conflict Resolution* 28 (1984): 470-506.

58. John Mueller,"The Essential Irrelevance of Nuclear Weapons." In *The Cold War and After: Prospects for Peace*. Eds. Sean M. Lynn-Jones and Steven E. Miller, revised edition (Cambridge, MA: MIT Press, 1993): 45-69; David Singer, J., "Peace in the Global System: Displacement, Interregnum, or Transformation?" In *The Long Postwar Peace: Contending Explanations and Projections*, ed. Charles W. Kegley Jr., (New York: HarperCollins, 1991): 56-84

59. Victor Kremenyuk, "The Cold War as Cooperation," In *From Rivalry to Cooperation: Russian and Americans Perspectives on the Post Cold War Era*, ed. Manus I. Midlarsky, John A. Vasquez, and Peter V. Gladkov, (New York: HarperCollins, 1994): 3-25. More recently, we see this quote by a senior US administration official: " ' In dealing with the

old Soviet Union, we all knew the rules. We worry that the Indians and the Pakistanis don't have any rules' " David E. Sanger, "On Visit to Paris, Bush Tries to Ease Concern in Europe." *New York Times* 27 May 2002: sec. A, p. 1. The quote clearly indicates a recognition that it was not just a matter of mutual material threat that defined US-Soviet interaction during the Cold War, but their shared (social) understanding of the way the interaction was supposed to go. One implication of the argument that deterrence created a learning environment for the United States and Soviet Union is that we cannot assume that all nuclear rivals will exhibit the same pattern of behaviour. Perhaps India and Pakistan will also learn routinised ways of interacting that do not actually involve violence because they fear the implications of war in the nuclear age, perhaps they will not. It also leaves me somewhat uneasy about the empirical existence of a blanket "norm" against the use of nuclear weapons. However, it could be possible that deterrence would work to the extent that states believe that it works— deterrence itself could be perceived as a social construct that impacts the behaviour of states in rivalry situations.

60. Wendt, 1992.

61. Mueller, 1993.

Bibliography

Adler, Emanuel. "Seizing the Middle Ground: Constructivism in World Politics." *European Journal of International Relations* 3.3 (1997): 319-363.

Allison, Graham, and Philip Zelikow. *Essence of Decision.* 2nd Edition. New York: Long man, 1999.

Altfeld, Michael F. "Arms Races?—And Escalation? A Comment on Wallace." *International Studies Quarterly* 27.2 (1983): 225-231.
Checkel, Jeffrey T. "The Constructivist Turn in International Relations Theory." *World Politics* 50.2 (1998): 324-348.

Cooper, Andrew F., Richard A. Higgott, and Kim R. Nossal. *Relocating Middle Powers: Australian and Canada in a Changing World Order.* Melbourne: Melbourne University Press, 1993.

Diehl, Paul F. "Arms Races and Escalation: A Closer Look." *Journal of Peace Research* 20.3 (1983): 205-212.

Dodds, Shona. "The Role of Multilateralism and the UN in Post-Cold War US Foreign Policy." Dissertation draft Australian National University, 2002.

Eyre, Dana P. and Mark C. Suchman. "Status, Norms, and the Proliferation of Conventional Weapons: An Institutional Theory Approach." In *The Culture of National Security: Norms and Identity in World Politics,* edited by Peter J. Katzenstein, 79-113. New York: Columbia UP, 1996.

Finnemore, Martha. "Constructing Norms of Humanitarian Intervention." In *The Culture of National Security: Norms and Identity in World Politics,* edited by Peter J. Katzenstein. New York: Columbia University Press, 1996.

George, Jim. *Discourses of Global Politics: A Critical (Re)Introduction to International Relations.* Boulder CO: Lynne Rienner Publishers, Inc., 1994.

Gupta, Amil. "India's Third-Tier Nuclear State Dilemma: N plus 20?" *Asian Survey* 41.6 (2001). 1044-1063.

Holsti, Ole R., Robert C. North, and Richard A. Brody. "Perception and Action in the 1914 Crisis." In *Quantitative International Politics,* edited by J. David Singer, 123-158. New York: The Free Press, 1968.

Huntington, Samuel P. "Arms Races: Prerequisites and Results." *Public Policy* 8 (1958): 41-86.

Huntington, Samuel P. "Why International Primacy Matters." *International Security* 17.4 (1993): 68-84.

Janis, Irving L. *Groupthink: Psychological Studies of Policy Decisions and Fiascos,* 2nd Edition. New York: Houghton Mifflin, 1986.

Jepperson, Ronald L., Alexander Wendt, and Peter J. Katzenstein. "Norms, Identity, and Culture in National Security." In *The Culture of National Security: Norms and Identity in World Politics,* edited by Peter J. Katzenstein, 33-78. New York: Columbia UP, 1996.

Jervis, Robert. "Hypotheses on Misperception." *World Politics* 20.3 (1968): 454-479.

Jervis, Robert. *Perception and Misperception in International Politics.* Princeton, NJ: Princeton UP, 1976.

Jervis, Robert. "Realism in the Study of World Politics." *International Organization* 52.4 (1998): 971-992.

Khong, Yuen Foong. *Analogies at War: Korean, Munich, Dien Bien Phu, and the Vietnam Decisions of 1965.* Princeton, NJ: Princeton UP, 1992.

Kremenyuk, Victor. "The Cold War as Cooperation." In *From Rivalry to Cooperation: Russian and Americans Perspectives on the Post Cold War Era,* edited by Manus I. Midlarsky, John A. Vasquez, and Peter V. Gladkov, 3-25. New York: HarperCollins, 1994.

Kugler, Jacek. "Terror Without Deterrence: Reassessing the Role of Nuclear Weapons." *Journal of Conflict Resolution* 28 (1984): 470-506.

Mead, Walter Russell. *Special Providence: American Foreign Policy and How it Changed the World.* New York: Alfred A. Knopf, 2001.

Mearsheimer, John J. "Back to the Future." *International Security* 15.1 (1990): 5-56.

Midlarsky, Manus I. *Handbook of War Studies II.* Ann Arbor MI: University of Michigan Press, 2000.

Mueller, John. "The Essential Irrelevance of Nuclear Weapons." In *The Cold War and After: Prospects for Peace,* edited by Sean M. Lynn-Jones and Steven E. Miller, revised edition, 45-69. Cambridge, MA: MIT Press, 1993.

Neack, Laura. "Linking State Type with Foreign Policy Behaviour." In *Foreign Policy Analysis: Continuity and Change in its Second*

Generation, edited by Laura Neack, Jeanne A. Hey, and Patrick J. Haney, 215-228. Englewood Cliffs, NJ: Prentice Hall, 1995.

Organski, A.F.K. and Jacek Kugler. *The War Ledger*. Chicago: Chicago UP, 1980.

Ostrom, Charles W. "Evaluating Alternative Foreign Policy Decision-Making Models" *Journal of Conflict Resolution* 21 (1977): 235-266.

Ostrom, Charles W. "A Reactive Linkage Model of the US Defence Expenditure Policymaking Process" *American Political Science Review* 72 (1978): 941-957.

Price, Richard and Nina Tannenwald. "Norms and Deterrence: The Nuclear and Chemical Weapons Taboos." In *The Culture of National Security: Norms and Identity in World Politics*, edited by Peter J. Katzenstein, 114-152. New York: Columbia UP, 1996.

Risse-Kappen, Thomas. "Ideas do not Float Freely: Transnational Coalition, Domestic Structures, and the End of the Cold War." *International Organization* 48.2 (1994): 185-214.

Richardson, Lewis F. *Arms and Insecurity*. Pacific Grove, CA: The Boxwood Press, 1960.

Rosati, Jerel A. "A Cognitive Approach to the Study of Foreign Policy." In *Foreign Policy Analysis: Continuity and Change in its Second Generation,* edited by Laura Neack, Jeanne A. Hey, and Patrick J. Haney, 49-70. Englewood Cliffs, NJ: Prentice Hall, 1995.

Ruggie, John Gerard. "What Makes the World Hang Together? Neo-utilitarianism and the Social Constructivist Challenge." *International Organization* 52.4 (1998): 855-885.

Russett, Bruce M. *Grasping the Democratic Peace: Principles for a Post-Cold War World*. Princeton, NJ: Princeton UP, 1993.

Sample, Susan G. "Arms Races and Dispute Escalation: Resolving the Debate." *Journal of Peace Research* 34.1 (1997): 7-22.

Sample, Susan G. "Military Buildups, War, and Realpolitik: A Multivariate Model." *Journal of Conflict Resolution* 42.2 (1998): 156-175.

Sample, Susan G. "Military Buildups: Arming and War." In *What do We Know about War?* edited by John A. Vasquez, 165-196. Lanham MD: Rowman & Littlefield Publishers, 2000.

Sample, Susan G. "The Outcomes of Military Buildups: Minor States vs. Major Powers" *Journal of Peace Research* 39.6 (2002): 669-692.

Shimko, Keith L. "Foreign Policy Metaphors: Falling 'Dominoes' and Drug 'Wars.'" In *Foreign Policy Analysis: Continuity and Change in its Second Generation*, edited by Laura Neack, Jeanne A. Hey, and Patrick J. Haney, 71-84. Englewood Cliffs, NJ: Prentice Hall, 1995.

Singer, J. David. "Peace in the Global System: Displacement, Interregnum, or Transformation?" In *The Long Postwar Peace: Contending Explanations and Projections*, edited Charles W. Kegley Jr., 56-84. New York: HarperCollins, 1991.

Vasquez, John A. *The War Puzzle*. Cambridge: Cambridge UP, 1993.

Vasquez, John A., ed. *What do We Know about War?* Lanham MD: Rowman & Littlefield Publishers, 2000.

Vasquez, John A. "Re-examining the Steps to War: New Evidence and Theoretical Insights." In *Handbook of War Studies II,* edited by Manus I. Midlarsky. Ann Arbor MI: University of Michigan Press, 2000.

Wallace, Michael D. "Arms Races and Escalation: Some New Evidence." *Journal of Conflict Resolution* 23.1 (1979): 3-16.

Walt, Stephen M. *The Origins of Alliances*. Ithaca, NY: Cornell UP, 1987.

Waltz, Kenneth N. *Theory of International Politics*. New York: Random House, 1979.

Ward, Michael D. "Differential Paths to Parity: A Study of the Contemporary Arms Race." *American Political Science Review* 78 (1984): 297-317.

Weede, Erich. "Arms Races and Escalation: Some Persisting Doubts." *Journal of Conflict Resolution* 24.2 (1980): 285-287.

Werner, Suzanne and Jacek Kugler. "Power Transitions and Military Buildups: Resolving the Relationship between Arms Buildups and War." In *Parity and War: Evaluations and Extensions of 'The War Ledger*, edited by Jacek Kugler and Douglas Lemke, 187-210. Ann Arbor, MI: University of Michigan Press, 1996.

Wendt, Alexander. "Anarchy is what States Make of it: The Social Construction of Power Politics." *International Organization* 46.2 (1992): 391-425.

Wright, Quincy. *A Study of War*, revised edition. Chicago: University of Chicago Press, 1962.

Notes

1. ... the old and new wars ... (Mary Kaldor, *New and Old Wars* (Cambridge: Polity, 1999) ... the Clausewitzian characterisation which ...

2. Carl von Clausewitz, *On War* (1832) (Harmondsworth: Penguin, 1968) Bk. 1, Ch. 1, Sec. 24, 119.

3. G.E.M. Anscombe, *Collected Philosophical Papers* (Oxford: Blackwell 1981), 52.

4. Louis Dumont, *Essays in Individualism* (Chicago: University of Chicago Press, 1986), 130-1.

Globalisation and the Just War Tradition:
The Vexing Problem of Legitimate Authority

Paul Rexton Kan

"This is a guy [Osama bin Laden] who, three months ago, was in control of a country. Now he's maybe in control of a cave."
-President George W. Bush
28 December 2001

Before President Bush uttered these words, Osama bin Laden was in control of more than just a cave or a country. Operating from the mountains of Afghanistan, bin Laden was the "CEO" of a vast terrorist network that spanned over fifty countries. The international reach of the criminal conspiracy that planned the September 11th attacks highlights the truly transnational quality of violence in a globalising world.

The hijackers included Egyptian, Saudi and Lebanese citizens. The apparent leaders came from a cell headquartered at a technical university in Hamburg, Germany. Arrests in other countries such as Spain, Britain, Germany and France targeted Kuwaiti, French, Algerian, Yemeni, Moroccan, Libyan, Syrian and Tunisian activists among others. One group was apparently organizing a parallel plot to attack the American embassy in Paris. The organisers were mostly Al Qaeda second-generation Algerians in France[1].

Like all human endeavours, violence is subject to ethical comment and moral reflection. When a political community purposefully uses violence against another political community, it becomes war and special comment is deserved. War is not just simply murderous violence—killing for the sake of killing. War has a political goal and appeals to morality are made to justify the violence employed to meet a particular goal. Even bin Laden, however repugnant his actions, makes a moral argument to justify his violence. For those of us in the West, it will become increasingly important to understand the moral boundaries that will shape the justifications for our responses to terrorist acts.

Throughout Western history, the just war tradition has provided the framework to begin a moral inquiry of those boundaries, when the purposeful application of violence is used by one political community against another. This essay does not use just war tenets to assess bin Laden's moral claims or to examine America's response to September 11th. Instead, this essay seeks to examine how the proliferation of human social organisations (such as transnational terrorist networks) operating in a new international context (a globalising world) and using asymmetric techniques (low-tech methods and commercially available technology) illustrates a particularly vexing challenge to the just war tradition. Specifically, this challenge is to the just war tradition's key tenet of legitimate authority. This challenge can no longer be overlooked as we head into a century that seems to hold new and more vicious security threats to the current international order.

1.   The Saliency of Legitimate Authority

The legitimate authority tenet states that only a competent public authority has the right to declare and wage war. Only public authority can lawfully take life. The ultimate sanction of taking life could alone make the legitimate authority tenet the lynchpin of the just war theory. However, legitimate authority is the lynchpin of the just war because of the cohesiveness it provides to the entire doctrine. Deciding who or what is the legitimate authority outlines the parameters of the other just war tenets. For example, answering the questions of whether a war has a just cause, is fought with the right intention and in the right manner, depends on the conduct of the entity imbued with the legitimacy to use violence. Whoever or whatever is vested with legitimate authority utilises rhetoric, designs the strategy and carries out tactics that are to be judged. In essence, the legitimate authority becomes the accountable entity, subject to moral approbation or disdain.

Another crucial function of the legitimate authority tenet is delineating public and private violence. As such, the just war seeks to limit violence by permitting only certain groups to wage war while proscribing others. In many respects, this delineation separates war from crime and can determine the type of violence that will be employed— armed intervention or police action. Globalisation and the war on terrorism demonstrate that this delineation is less than clear in today's international political environment.

The decision to focus on legitimate authority may seem like a mundane choice when examining the war against terrorism. There does not seem to be any basis for debating who or what is the legitimate authority. It would seem that, in the war against terrorism, the only legitimate authority in such a war would be the aggrieved party—the United States. After all, September 11th was a series of deliberate attacks on the United States and, under international law, the US is recognised as having the legitimate authority for declaring war. Some may suggest that the United Nations is the appropriate organisation to mount a response to a series of attacks that killed not just Americans, but citizens from nearly two dozen countries. However, since the US sits on the Security Council, any independent UN action would be unlikely and the magnitude of the viciousness inflicted on the US makes UN action unwelcomed by the American public. At first glance, an argument that the war on terrorism poses a problem, for the legitimate authority tenet of the just war theory, is seriously flawed.

The argument, however, is not that the United States has no authority to declare war. Rather, the war on terrorism shows that, in a globalising world, too many entities believe they have the authority to declare war. Moreover, they have the means and the willingness to follow through and wage war. In short, globalisation has revealed a diffusion of authorities claiming legitimacy. Such authorities include the United Nations, NATO, sovereign states, ethnic communities, clan-based warlords, terrorist organisations and even criminal syndicates. Many would argue that the Cold War was rife with a large number of entities claiming that they had legitimate authority to wage war. There were national liberation movements, guerrilla insurgents, communal groups, and terrorist organisations. It appears, at first glance, that the post Cold War era, marked by increased globalisation, is no different and therefore does not present any greater challenge to the just war doctrine. However, the main difference in today's world is that the present international system contains groups that can carry out acts that have more acute international effects, while commanding greater and wider allegiance.

This diffusion of authority, and its potentially lethal effects, runs counter to the universalistic vision of globalisation that portrays an increasingly integrated world based on free trade, democracy and respect for fundamental human rights. Globalisation is occurring in a world rife with particularisms, a world that Hedley Bull called a "neo-medieval" order. In such a world, states would "share their authority over their citisens, and their ability to command their loyalties, on the one hand with regional and world authorities, and on the other hand with sub-state or sub-national authorities".[2] From merely "sharing authority", it is a short step to *empowering* that authority with violent means. There should be no wondering why the post Cold War era has seen a massive proliferation in small arms--merely declaring one's organisation legitimate does not render *de facto* recognition or even assure acknowledgement. However, as September 11th demonstrates, this empowering of authority can rise to a devastating level of danger. And, in a globalised world filled with easily attainable weapons and dual-use technology, more entities are likely to seek to empower themselves with the authority to wage war.

Although deeply disturbing, this is not the first time the just war tradition has found multiple authorities vexing its coherence as a moral doctrine. In response, many key just war theorists through history have sought to consolidate or spread a certain political order at the expense of challengers to that order, by designating who or what constitutes legitimate authority. Whether it was to uphold the Roman emperor, who embraced Christianity, to sustain the power of the Papacy or to imbue the newly empowered monarchs and their kingdoms with legitimacy, the just war doctrine was a political project as much as it was an attempt at moral theorising. It is worth examining the political projects that the just war tradition sought to maintain or build in the past, in order to know what political order those of us who oppose transnational terrorism wish to maintain or design in the future. Identifying this political order will more clearly delineate the moral boundaries within which the war against terrorism will be operating.

There is a critical lack of vision in today's war. Many commentators and decision makers have said that we will not know when we have won the war against terrorism; there will not be anything akin to a surrender on the deck of a battleship. However, understanding the political order we wish to maintain or design will give us something to strive for, a way to know how we have won this war. So far, no national leader at the forefront of the war effort has outlined what this order would resemble. Vague declarations of this war being about "freedom" and a "return to normalcy" hearken back to the continuation of the pre-September 11th status quo, which was in essence globalisation without a goal. Moreover, as argued, the status quo has proven to be extremely dangerous. An examination of past international environments and the debates over legitimate authority may contribute to charting the way ahead for not only the current war, but for globalisation as well.

3. Three Pivotal Eras of the Just War

The three historical periods when the just war doctrine was reinvigorated each epitomise a world order that may be useful to designing a goal for the war on terrorism and for globalisation itself. The first period is that of the Christian Roman emperor Constantine, whose authority was challenged from within the empire by Christians resisting Rome's influence, and from without by the Vandals. During a time when the early Christian church was largely pacifist, Ambrose and St. Augustine argued that legitimate authority was vested in the emperor and public authority, allowing Christians to serve in Rome's legions and to protect the empire that had once persecuted them. In today's world, *Pax America* is not only due to its economic and military strength, but many nations have come to share its values of tolerance, democracy and respect for human rights. These values have a transnational, co-opting force. Should the war on terrorism be a US centered process, in the same way that globalisation appears to many as "Americanisation"? Will the war on terrorism come to resemble the Cold War with shifting alliances and proxy wars?

The second historical period is the Middle Ages and the decentralised political order of Europe. Legitimate authority was divided among many types of human social organizations, that held overlapping jurisdiction over the inhabitants of the continent. The Church, kingdoms, fiefs and guilds all competed for people's allegiance. Yet Aquinas did attempt to limit the violence of such a decentralised order by allowing only public authorities to declare and wage war. The Papacy also tried to limit war by using its moral authority to intervene in disputes. In this sense, the UN of today can be said to be similar to the Catholic Church of the Middle Ages. Much like the Church, the UN promotes a universal vision of the unity of humankind and issues resolutions to limit and manage global violence and its effects, while authorising its members to use force in its name. Should the end goal of war on terrorism be the granting of greater authority to the UN? How can the UN gain more legitimacy as an institution in a globalising world?

The third historical period is a time after the religious wars of the Reformation and the Thirty Years War, when the monarchs had wrested power away from the Catholic Church and began subduing restless nobles. Francisco Vitoria and Alberico Gentili tried to consolidate this order by arguing that wars should not be waged for religious reasons or sanctioned by religious authorities. Hugo Grotius argued that only the monarchs who controlled their states were legitimate authorities. Should the war on terrorism be prosecuted only by nation-states? Are legitimate governments only those that have a functioning government that can eliminate terror groups? Does this mean that the triumph of globalisation can only be guaranteed when a certain type of state sovereignty exists?

Each age serves as a metaphor and raises questions for today's war on terrorism in an era of globalisation. However, the questions that are posed by each age cannot be answered through the application of metaphor alone; after all, each historic period is unique. The sum of the questions from each period provide the context for managing the diffusion of legitimacy in the current international political system. This diffusion contributes to the deficit of consensus on key norms that define international peace and security, and on the justified use of violence to protect global order. Filling this deficit, as the war on terrorism plays itself out, should be one of the key features of any victory.

4.   Rethinking Cosmopolitanism in a Globalising World

Each of the political orders explored in the three historical periods contains similarities to today's international environment. Although each provides approaches for the conduct of the war on terrorism and ideas for constructing a goal for globalisation, the political orders examined are unique and do not completely match the complex reality of current international relations. Metaphors and analogies can only go so far. A combination of approaches, however, is more beneficial as a way to formulate a basis of legitimate authority that can reinvigorate the just war tradition.

A starting point for a reinvigoration is to revisit the idea of cosmopolitanism for the international political environment. Many aspects of cosmopolitanism can already be found in today's globalising world. Cosmopolitanism has the advantage of incorporating multiple authorities, overlapping allegiances and diverse beliefs, but under an umbrella of unifying principles that members of the cosmopolitan community accept and share. It is a framework of moral cohesion across boundaries and between peoples. Cosmopolitanism would include "both a positive political vision, embracing tolerance, multiculturalism, civility and democracy, [and] a more legalistic respect for certain overriding universal principles which should guide political communities at various levels."[3] Since the level of analysis used in this essay is the international political environment and the interaction of agents of political violence within it, a global perspective is best suited for cosmopolitanism. This means a cosmopolitan outlook would conceptualise the world as a nearly unified entity. However, a note of caution is warranted. Adopting such a global perspective does not mean that a single global, or supranational institution, is the *only* logical manifestation of legitimate authority in a cosmopolitan world order. Cosmopolitanism means *inter*national governance, not world government.

Central to cosmopolitanism is the acceptance of diverse sources of legitimacy and distinguishing them from illegitimate entities and the violence that they use. Illegitimate entities would be those which threaten the values and order of cosmopolitanism. Petty tyrants, ethno-nationalist zealots, terrorist organisations and criminal syndicates and their violence would be illegitimate since they do not accept the commonly agreed upon norms of "tolerance, multiculturalism, civility and democracy". Their violence is akin to the disruption that the vandals, feudal nobility, robber-barons and pirates posed to the Emperor, Church and monarchy of the past. The violent activities of these disruptive groups came to be likened to criminal acts, giving authorities more legitimacy to use force against them in the name of a public good. The current international public good is an emerging social order based on cosmopolitan ideas, but it is threatened by certain violent acts that were once tolerable but which are now exceptionally damaging.

Such a transition in perception reflects the blurring of the distinction between war and crime in today's world. "Once the legal monopoly of armed force, long claimed by the state, is wrested out of its hands, existing distinctions between war and crime will break down. Often, crime will be disguised as war, whereas in other cases war itself will be treated as if waging it were a crime".[4] Nurturing a cosmopolitan world order means looking at the current war on terrorism through new lenses. Taking a global perspective, rather than a narrow national perspective, raises an interesting question: Is transnational terrorism a kind of crime in the global village?

If war is indeed coming to resemble something more akin to criminal activity, then it might be worthwhile to borrow from the vocabulary of police work to meet the transnational terrorist threat and other challenges to global order. Much like the British government considered IRA terrorism an "emergency" and not necessarily a civil war, there should be the option to declare a "global emergency". Unlike the current UN Charter that recognises only the resisting of interstate aggression as a justification for war, a global emergency would move beyond the Charter and recognise other forms of violence as threats to global order. The British used an emergency to suspend specific individual liberties until the emergency had abated. In a global emergency, the right of sovereignty that is accorded to states could be suspended if certain states do not conform to specific norms of decent governance. Those sub national and transnational groups that use violence against the cosmopolitan order would also fall under a global emergency. In short, certain states would be considered illegitimate and certain groups would be international outlaws, allowing the application of force to proceed.

The British also offer an example of how to proceed with a declared emergency. British police and intelligence services were given exceptional powers which were linked with military force when warranted, but "all continued to operate within a peacetime framework of civil authority".[5] A global emergency would be similar, but the larger question of this paper is what type of institution could call a global emergency or, more simply, what represents a "global civil authority"? For the cosmopolitan order to be viable and sustainable, the blurring between war and crime requires some sort of institution to clearly delineate what violent actions permit the use of force and in what degree. The answer lies in those institutions that currently uphold a version of cosmopolitanism. Nowadays, they are those states existing in what Cooper has described as the "modern" and "post modern" worlds that are well-ordered, respectful of human rights and uphold democratic principles.

The nation-state is an impressive institution; it has evolved and shown remarkable adaptability throughout its existence. Whether it will be an enduring form of human social organisation is an open question, but it does have advantages that can be brought to bear in the war on terrorism and manage the negative aspects of globalisation. Nation-states are flexible enough to react to new forms of illegitimate violence, in a new international political environment.

The traditional paradigm of security and insistence upon its traditional requirements naturalises a sharp boundary between external and internal security, as well as military and police matters, and in the process obscures the fact that such a demarcation was produced as part of the development of the modern war fighting state. Recognising that the functional distinction between military and police was an artifact of the emergence of a particular kind of state, at a particular period, leaves us better placed to consider the kinds of contemporary developments that may be the harbingers of another kind of state, in another historical epoch, with other forms of organised violence.[6]

Those nation-states that exhibit cosmopolitan qualities would have to adopt some features of Cooper's post-modern state, in order to give greater governance to globalisation. For Cooper, post-modern states practice a type of "mutual transparency"—the rejection of war as a means of settling disputes among members of the community, mutual interference in domestic affairs and the breaking of the monopoly of force.[7] This means the creation of new institutions and *fora* that cut across political boundaries and use distributed decision making to reach consensus on the use of force.[8] The threats of the future are organised as transnational networks; countering them with another type of network may be part of the solution. Distributed decision-making would be a type of democratic internationalism which, in the process, leads to a democratisation of the just war doctrine.[9]

Just war in a cosmopolitan world would not mean universal intervention, but something more like the Medieval Church's conception of the just war: the restoration of justice and solidarity with the aggrieved across boundaries. This is not a carte blanche for the developed world or for the United States to act unilaterally-in fact, greater cooperation and accountability will have to accompany any application of military force. But it is this moment of transition when the US, and its hegemony, can be most useful in helping the world move further down the road to cosmopolitanism. After all, the values that under gird cosmopolitanism are the values that the US hegemony has sought to promote. If the US commits itself more fully to a vision of cosmopolitanism, the war on terrorism and the process of globalisation will be, in turn, vested with more legitimacy across the globe.

The just war is much more than a type of checklist; check each box appropriately and the bombs fall and the killing begins. It does not only have an instrumental function. The just war has a deeply speculative nature that imagines a just world order and creates the tenets of moral cohesion that will protect the order from the most devastating of all human activity—war. As James Turner Johnson writes, "the nature of war changes continually, and the moral questions posed by one form of war often turn out to be less pressing in another, which in turn produces its own particular quandries."[10] The world is now in such a moment, where it needs to revisit the speculative nature of the just war tradition to address the particular quandaries of today. Such a commitment will require not just boldness of action, but a bold imagination to envision a more just tomorrow.

Notes

*The views expressed in this chapter do not necessarily represent those of the United States Department of Defence or the United States Air Force.

1. Martha Crenshaw, "Why America? The Globalization of Civil War", *Current History* 100, (2001): 432.

2 Hedley Bull, *The Anarchical Society: A Study of Order in Politics*, (New York, NewYork: Columbia University Press, 1977), 254.

3 Mary Kaldor, *New and Old Wars: Organized Violence in a Global Era*, (Stanford, California: Stanford University Press, 1999), 115.

4 Martin Van Creveld, *The Transformation of War*, (New York, New York: The Free Press, 1991), 204.

5 Michael Howard, *Evening Standard*, 1 November 2001.

6 Peter Andreas and Richard Price, "From War Fighting to Crime Fighting: Transforming the American National Security State", *International Studies Review* 3, (2001): 34.

7 Robert Cooper, *The Post-Modern State and World Order*, (London: Demos, 2000), 17-19.

8. The idea of distributed decision making comes from the discussion of managing the information revolution in "Transcendental Destination: Where Will the Information Revolution Lead?" www.rand.org/publications/randreview/issues/rr.12.00/transcendental.htm

9. For a more thorough discussion on democratic internationalism, see Alan Gilbert, *Must Global Politics Constrain Democracy*, (Princeton, New Jersey: Princeton University Press, 2000).

10. James Turner Johnson, *Morality and Contemporary Warfare*, (New Haven, Connecticut: Yale University Press, 1999), 1.

System Perturbation: Conflict in the Age of Globalisation

Professor Bradd C. Hayes
Dr. Thomas P. M. Barnett

1.   Background

Aperiodically, the international system reorders itself — normally in the aftermath of a major conflict. This reordering is accompanied by the implementation of new rule sets in an attempt to firewall states from the causes of the conflict. Policymakers have openly enquired whether the end of the Cold War and the birth of the information age requires a new firebreak and the implementation of a new set of rules. Because "great power war" has been the proximate cause of past restructuring, great power war has been the ordering principle for international (and national) rules and institutions. Recent events (from so-called the Asian Economic Flu, to the Mexican peso crisis, to the Love Bug computer virus, to the heinous events of 11 September 2001) indicate that a new ordering principle is required (one in which great power war is but one possible outcome).

In helping America's Defence Department think through the future of international security, we have proposed that "system perturbation" be examined as the new ordering principle. The best way to describe this ordering principle is to examine what happened on and after 11 September. The attacks of 9/11 were not acts perpetrated by a nation-state using traditional methods of warfare. Yet their effect was momentous, like a giant stone dropped in a calm pond. The initial vertical shock was spectacular, but the resulting horizontal ripples had longer-lasting effects that went well beyond the security field. This paper examines the underlying precepts of system perturbation and potential triggers that could lead to great power conflict. It argues that these triggers will likely foment in places where globalisation is actively resisted and by individuals who will use information age tools to oppose globalisation's spread and content. We argue that great powers are less likely to confront one another than they are to cooperate to eliminate super-empowered individuals (or groups) trying to disrupt the global economy.

2.   Firewalling the Past

The military is constantly accused of planning and training for the last war instead of the next one. Military leaders deny it, of course, but the truth is that planning for the unknown — and getting it right — is extremely difficult. The military is an easy target for critics, yet, if it has had a chequered past when it comes to planning for the next great upheaval, others in the national security community (including politicians, diplomats, and economists) have done even worse. The best they have been able to do is firewall the future from the past. Political scientists trace the roots of the nation-state to the 1648 Treaty of Westphalia. That treaty, in effect, was one of the first modern firewalls as it attempted to isolate religion from secular politics. Leaders believed that religious competition had fostered needless unrest and suffering. The treaty came after 30-years of bloodshed, during which one-third of Europe's population died either in battle or from plague, malnutrition, or similar war-related causes. Who wouldn't want to firewall themselves from such a catastrophe? As noted above, that kind of firewalling has accompanied almost all major conflicts.

Some 150 years later, at the beginning of the 19th century, the Congress of Vienna and the Concert of Europe were established following the Napoleonic Wars. The Hague Conventions were drafted after the unification of Germany. Something else was happening as well. Although the term was yet to be invented, globalisation was cracking its shell. This first period of globalisation began with European colonisation, but really hit its stride during the industrial revolution with its huge appetite for raw material. It was marked by the massive movement of resources from colonies to the motherland and distribution of finished goods from the motherland to the world. It was accompanied by the free movement of labour, otherwise known as emigration. It was possible to travel the length of Europe without a passport. Huge corporations dominated the landscape and helped form foreign policy. The period was also marked by economic nationalism, as domestic manufacturers and growers were confronted, for the first time, with competitive goods from distant lands. As the 19th century ended, Europe faced an arms race and an ambitious German state. To counter Germany's rise, states entered into secret combinations of alliances in order to maintain a balance of power which led, inevitably, to the First World War.

The consequences of that war are well known. It cost nearly $350 billion in 1918 dollars, resulted in nearly 12 million war dead and over 20 million people were wounded[1]. The aftermath of war was even worse when more people died from epidemics than were killed during the war. The Bolshevik revolution gained a purchase it would never have achieved without these horrendous conditions. The call for new rules and a break with the past was clarion. Unfortunately, policymakers were too myopic in their vision when they established those rules. They failed to look much beyond the security dimensions of the problem and their shortsightedness, especially to economic issues, meant that the instruments and institutions of peace (such as Treaty of Versailles and League of Nations) either exacerbated the problem or couldn't deal with them. The international monetary system in the mid-war years rested precariously on loans (principally from the United States) instead of on a system of extensive gold reserves and securities. The result was repression, depression, and the Second World War — the conclusion of which also marked the end of Globalisation I. Once again the call for new rules and a break with the past sounded forth.

This time policymakers (especially from the United States and the United Kingdom) took a much broader view of the international system and they tried to firewall the present from the past by replacing the League with the United Nations (UN) and establishing an economic system, devised at Bretton Woods, that would help achieve economic stability and social well-being in the pursuit of international peace and security. One of the negative experiences that spurred economic action was the instability of exchange rates prior to the war. The International Monetary Fund (IMF) was created as the centrepiece of a new international monetary system that was designed to guarantee an orderly and reliable exchange of currencies in order to promote the international flow of goods and capital[2]. Its sister institution, the International (World) Bank for Reconstruction and Development, was established to provide financing and guarantees for reconstruction following the war.[3] Unfortunately, a large part of the global economy (the communist bloc) isolated itself from the economic system and stalemated the United Nations. Those nations that were positively influenced by the new rule sets, underwent an enormous transformation and they flourished. Those who fared worst under this system lived in the seams between the east and west. They literally fell between the cracks. Nevertheless, the firewall, with its new rule sets, basically worked and marked the beginning of Globalisation II.

3.   A Taste of the Future

Our first exposure to the possibility that the world was again on the verge of changing its rule sets came when we were asked to think about the security consequences of Y2K, if things went badly. Since we were not computer experts, nor air traffic control experts, nor electrical grid experts, nor electronic financial transaction experts, we realised we would have to take a systemic approach to the question. We did this by examining several alternative ways that the scenario could play out and then populated a scenario dynamics grid that looked at lingering effects through four lenses (business, government, networks, and society) over six periods: 1) the initial mania created by the possibility of a serious problem, 2) the countdown to the actual event, 3) the onset of the event, 4) the unfolding of the event's aftermath, 4) the event's peak, and, finally, 5) the event's exit. We asked experts to help fill in the types of events we would expect to see in each of the boxes created in this grid. Some of the eventualities we contemplated were:

•   Catastrophic terrorism targeting Americans in highly symbolic venues (e.g., New York City, Washington, DC, Rome, and/or Jerusalem).
•   Opportunists taking advantage of chaos to sow additional fear through acts of mischief (likely millenarian).
•   A major stock market disabled for days, then market quakes around world, followed by global recession.
•   A significant rise in people buying guns and private security.
•   "Islanding" — wherein firms refused customers certain basic services—especially insurance.
•   Firms stockpiling industrial inputs due to anticipated delays at critical network nodes — e.g., borders and ports.
•   Leaders telling the public to stay calm (no scapegoating) but accepting security measures to keep peace just in case domestic tranquillity deteriorates (many feared loss of liberties).
•   Preventable wars, as leaders employed desperate measures to show people they were in control.
•   US law enforcement and national security agencies being called into action simultaneously all over the country/world to deal with fantastic scenarios (lots of covert/special operations) with most interventions targeted for backward states.

In the darkest scenarios, people started acting differently and living by new rules in order to protect themselves from the more vicious effects of global turmoil. It didn't happen, of course, but we were struck by the enormity of the possibilities and never once did the spectre of great power warfare rear its head. The possibilities were so intriguing that we teamed with the powerful, but then little known, brokerage firm of Canter-Fitzgerald, and began a series of workshops under the collective title of NewRuleSets.Project. We had conducted three extremely interesting meetings (out of a proposed series of five) before the World Trade Centre and Canter-Fitzgerald's headquarters were lost. We were convinced new rule sets were emerging, but saw them evolving naturally over time as opposed to being drafted at a Dumbarton Oaks type of international forum. Enough of the series was completed before 11 September that we, along with Hank Gaffney, a colleague at the Centre for Naval Analyses in Alexandria, Virginia, had already begun thinking about a new organising principle for national and international security, that looked different from the great power war model. The signs were everywhere. More and more individuals were calling for a break with the past, as a result of sea changes in the global economic and security environments. Meetings of organisations that represent the current rule sets (such as the IMF) were plagued by increasingly angry protestors, who used the tools and freedoms of globalisation to work against its spread.

These protestors remain a symptom of a deeper trend that puzzles policymakers, who, like their counterparts over the past 350 years, have used interstate war as the organising principle for their institutions and plans. The depth of this underlying reality was driven home on 11 September. The most oft-heard statement following those attacks was, "This changes everything." Donald Rumsfeld, the American Secretary of Defence, decried the fact that people didn't know how to adjust to this new reality. "Almost every day in meetings," he lamented, "I am confronted by people who come to me with approaches and recommendations and suggestions and requests that reflect a mindset that is exactly the same as before September 11th. They understand that September 11th occurred, but the power of this institution [the Department of Defence] to continue 'what is' is so great that we all need to be reminded and indeed jarred to realise the urgency that exists."[4]

4.   New Asymmetries

If the old rules are not working and everything has changed, who makes the new rules and how are they going to come into effect? To answer these questions, we like to start with a framework proposed by Kenneth Waltz in his seminal work, *Man, the State, and War*. He looked at the sources of conflict using three images. The first image was the individual. Wars start because there are evil people in the world. The second image was the state. Wars start because there are aggressive nations that desire what others have and are willing to take it by force. The final image was the international system. Wars start because there is no Hobbesian leviathan to prevent them so that man's natural aggression runs amok. What, you may ask, has changed about that? For one thing, nuclear weapons are a fact of life. Since their first use at the end of the Second World War, there have been no great power wars — a period of over 50 years. We think that is likely to remain the case. That does not mean we believe the world will be a peaceful place. The past 50 years have been some of the bloodiest in history and there is no end of the bloodshed in sight.

Looking at Waltz' three images we see western militaries "frozen" in the nation-state image, while much of the violence has migrated down to the individual image. At the same time, much of the competition and power has migrated up to the system image. As a result, militaries are fixated on rogue states and their weapons of mass destruction programs or on the wistful hope that a new near-peer will rise up to fill the void left by the demise of the Warsaw Pact. That militaries remained transfixed on the nation-state image is not surprising. After all, that is the image where money is legally aggregated to buy the weapons of war and where rules exist for its conduct. In the meantime, we see economics racing ahead of politics, technology dashing ahead of today's rules, potential threats staying one step ahead of realised enemies, and vulnerabilities remaining allusive of robustness. This leaves an enormous governance gap that tried-and-true, "stovepiped" government organisations are incapable of filling.

There has been much talk, at least in the United States, about asymmetrical warfare. Until 11 September, these discussions were more often about how a country like China might use asymmetrical strategies to counter a frontal U.S. military assault than about how America could be attacked asymmetrically at home. The Cassandras did exist, but they were largely ignored. Today Waltz' framework might be populated a bit differently. The first image would not be national leaders, but Thomas Friedman's super-empowered individuals (SEI), such as Usama bin Laden and those who carry out his wishes. Jumping to the system image, we find transnational networks, such as Al-Qaeda, that can connect directly with super-empowered individuals (bypassing nation-states) to wreak havoc and create chaos. These transnational networks wield sufficient clout to trigger systemic stress. Militaries were lucky that, at the beginning of the war on terrorism, the link between the super-empowered individual and the transnational network ran through a nation-state sponsor (Afghanistan), making a conventional response both swift and executable. Finding individuals, such a bin Laden, proved more difficult and required, at the individual level, both special operations and extraordinary human intelligence. Attacking the network at the systemic level was even more challenging, especially since there was no overarching organising principle to coordinate these disparate activities. Once Afghanistan was under control, selecting the next target was problematic. President Bush went looking for other nation-states (such as Iraq) to attack.

5.   New Battle Lines

At a conference we participated in at the US Naval War College, one presenter showed a picture montage of Earth taken at night. The striking feature about the photograph was that the places drawing the world's attention, like Afghanistan and North Korea, were mostly dark. They were also the places that, in large measure, were (or had been) fighting the onslaught of globalisation. From a western perspective, if a country, group, or individual is fighting against or resisting globalisation, that country, group, or individual is likely to be a problem for the west. The obverse of that foreign policy corollary is that if a country, group, or individual is not resisting globalisation they should join the solution set. Using that standard, if you look at a Mercator projection of the world, solution set countries lie in a ring along the edges. Potential problem countries largely rest in the middle, forming a black hole of trouble for those embracing globalisation (see figure 1).

Figure 1. Functioning Core States of Globalisation and Non-Functioning

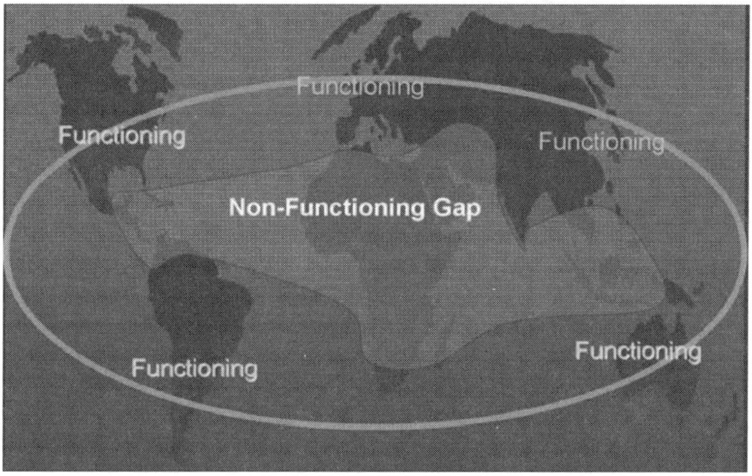

Gap States

Another way of looking at how things have changed is to examine the Cold War paradigm and compare it to today's paradigm. You'll see that it is a paradigm flipped on its head. The Cold War world was bipolar and each side saw its foreign policy as a zero sum game. It was capitalism against communism — you were one or the other. If communism gained the upper hand, Americans feared they would lose their free markets and with them their way of life. In order to prevent this, the west firewalled its market system (at the individual level) by adopting a foreign policy aimed at containing communism from spreading (at the system level). Today, America believes that globalisation (at the system level) will preserve free markets (at the individual level), and thus maintain their way of life. The threat that needs to be isolated is the super-empowered individual. In order to protect against this new threat, America is trying to place a firewall between globalisation (at the system level) and those who oppose it by containing them (at the individual level).

Since nuclear weapons made great power conflict (the current organising principle) unthinkable during the Cold War, America's military strategy was one of deterrence. It worked for many reasons. Among those reasons was the fact that Marxism taught that communism had time on its side. It was historically inevitable, Marx claimed, that the world would turn to communism. As a result, Soviet leaders were unwilling to risk regime control by engaging in a precipitous war that could send them tumbling from power. What about today's super-empowered individual? He has no regime to risk and sees time running out for him to stop the encroachments of globalisation into his world. How does deterrence work in this instance? President George W. Bush immediately reverted to the Cold War solution by trying to deter nation-states ("you harbour terrorists, we will come"). But how does one deter transnational networks or super-empowered individuals? This is one of the conundrums the globalised world now faces.

6.   Whither Globalisation?

Although we believe that globalisation is a *fait accompli* for most of the world, its end state is still unclear. We juxtapose two pairs of end states about globalisation on X-Y axes to create four possible futures. The vertical axis represents those participating in globalisation (or not) and how competition between them could lead to conflict. At the top we place "the best against the rest," meaning that supporters of globalisation join to contain those who oppose it. At the bottom, we place "the west against the rest," meaning that Asia doesn't cooperate and each region pursues globalisation differently. The horizontal axis addresses who is going to lead, as the world globalises. On the left, we place "governance gap continues," meaning that business and technology advance faster than rules controlling them. On the right, we place "new rule sets emerge," meaning that the developed world agrees about how globalisation should proceed while protecting local cultures and values (see figure 2).

Figure 2. Possible Globalisation Futures

If new rules don't emerge and the developed world doesn't get together to challenge those who oppose globalisation, the world could remain a very messy place in which to live. We call this future "Globalisation Traumatised." If the world cooperates to advance globalisation, but fails to adopt a new rule set, economic growth will proceed haltingly and governments will be reactive rather than proactive. We call this future "Globalisation Compromised." Those are the darker scenarios we posit. On the brighter side, if developed nations agree on some broad rules directing how globalisation proceeds (rules, for example, that would protect workers, the environment, and tax bases), but fail to cooperate when dealing with those opposing globalisation, they should expect to be plagued by continual, large-scale protests. We call this future "Globalisation Stabilised." The best scenario would see developed countries cooperating to ensure that the world's economy expands smoothly and justly. They agree on rules that protect workers' rights, local cultures, and the environment. They also cooperate to contain disaffected groups and work to bring opponents into the fold. We call this future "Globalisation Normalised."

7.   New Crises

Having laid out our case for a new organising principle and new rules, we examine the kinds of conflicts or crises that we can expect in the era of globalisation. The great power war paradigm assumed that conflict would be proceeded by a period of tension, during which parties would gather the 'dogs of war' and then unleash them in an intense combat to the finish. We call these vertical scenarios. The classic vertical scenario unfolds with lightning speed. Opponents, allies, strategy and battle plans are all known beforehand. Once the war begins, you come as you are. The scenario develops quickly and there is not time for evolution or change. In the great power war scenario, time is static because the world is frozen in place. This scenario fits the American psyche. Americans like things to happen quickly, believe a solution is possible, and they assume that if they toss enough resources at a problem they will triumph.

Some have argued that the Cold War represented a new type of protracted conflict "that would continue until one side or the other was transformed. Either the United States would cease to be a democracy or the Soviet Union would cease to be a Leninist dictatorship. The ideological divide was too deep and wide for any lasting peace, and while tensions might grow or diminish, these were tactical decisions dictated by geopolitical convenience, not strategic changes. Try as Western statesmen might to bridge this divide with detente or, from the Soviet side, with the ideological sleight of hand called 'peaceful coexistence,' the conflict would not end until one side or the other triumphed."[5] We argue that globalisation takes protracted conflict even further and, in fact, will be the norm in the future. It will look much different, however, than it did during the Cold War. There will be no clear beginning or end as it drags slowly on. The definition of who the enemy is will likely change over time. Allies will come and go; moreover, some former "allies" may turn on you. Strategy for fighting the conflict evolves over time to meet these changing circumstances. The conflict is characterised more by strikes than battles. As the conflict lingers, definition of the "problem" will be subject to debate. Unlike great power warfare, the world goes on while the situation seems frozen.

The dilemma with horizontal scenarios, in the era of globalisation, is that more than the security dimension is involved. The more the world becomes connected, the more that every segment of human endeavour is drawn into the fray. Globalisation's growing density of network connectivity is spawning a category of conflict or war, whose main attributes are the dynamics of disruption. As a result, a new way for thinking about how to organise defences and responses to crises needs to be adopted. We offer system perturbation as one possibility.

8.   A New Organising Principle

We noted at the beginning of this paper that a system perturbation is like a giant stone dropped into a calm pond. The initial vertical shock is spectacular, but the resulting horizontal ripples have even wider spread and longer lasting effects. Let's again examine 9/11 and its aftermath. In one morning, a series of relatively simple terrorist acts set in motion a system perturbation that has not only rearranged our sense of national security, but redirected our nation's foreign policy and recast states' relationships with one another — all over the world. Much of this change will be temporary, but some changes will be permanent, generating path-dependencies that nation-states will have to deal with for decades to come. The key point is this: the strategic environment is in flux for some indeterminate period of time. That is the essence of system perturbation — as it unfolds, all bets are off. The old rule set evaporates, the new one is not yet gelled. Both direct and sympathetic ripples spread horizontally from the perturbation. We will now look at a few of 9/11's threads from six different areas: security, environment, technology, culture, health, and economics.

A. Security.

Security at airports was immediately strengthened and screening procedures tightened, with the inevitable result that permanent additional taxes (or fees) were levied in order to pay for heightened enforcement measures. People started asking about the security of other forms of transportation, including trains, buses, trucking, and shipping. This led to discussions of immigration and border security. A crackdown on immigration had an immediate effect on some industries, including high tech industries and agriculture that rely heavily on foreign employees. Soon, security issues were affecting areas that had never been touched directly by such challenges. For example, Pakistan was critical in the operation against Afghanistan and remained critical for hunting down terrorists that fled into its territory. By cooperating fully, Pakistani leaders expected a quid pro quo, not on the security front but on the economic front, by having the United States lower its tariffs on Pakistani textile goods — a move that was vigorously opposed by textile manufacturers in America. Thus, within months, the American textile industry took the stage in the war on terrorism. Increased reliance on Pakistani cooperation also affected the calculus in the ongoing tension between India and Pakistan. Additionally, America found itself developing bases in Central Asia, an area the Iranians had hoped to bring into their sphere of influence. As a result, Iran opened its borders to fleeing Al-Qaeda terrorists and covertly supported anti-American forces in Afghanistan. President Bush then felt free to link Iran, Iraq, and North Korea into an "axis of evil."

B. Environment.

The Bush administration came to office with an energy agenda that was furthered by 9/11. As gas prices increased sharply in the months succeeding 9/11, people started to hint of a "third" oil crisis. Calls for less reliance on Arab oil re-emerged. This led to President Bush calling for more domestic oil drilling and production. Environmentalists decried this plan and mobilised into action, moving them closer to the militant anti-globalisation camp than they already were. To soften the criticism, hybrid cars were parked on the White House lawn so that President Bush could tout them as cars of the future. Thus, environmentalists joined the fray.

C. Technology.

Events of 9/11 spurred the production of several new technologies, including detection devices that could be used to find explosive, biologic, and radioactive material. It also spurred the transformation of the military and the increased use of unmanned vehicles in combat. Exactly where the technology thread will lead is unclear, but surely technologies that can be both helpful and misused will emerge. Civil libertarians are already protesting technologies that can automatically monitor, scan, and identify individuals, whether they are trying to board a plane or simply walking down the street.

D. Culture.

Analysts who had written off Samuel Huntington's "Clash of Civilisations" arguments began to re-examine them. The longer the strikes continued against Afghanistan and the more vituperative the language used against Iraq, the more uneasy the Arab world grew. Xenophobia increased. Opponents of globalisation found themselves in an uncomfortable alliance with bin Laden's supporters; agreeing with some of his aims, but stopping short of supporting all of his tactics. As Muslim frustration and disbelief increased as a result of the tension, a door was opened for some of the deadliest attacks ever carried out against Israel. Martyrdom became a cause célèbre among young, disaffected Muslims. In the West, this only reinforced a negative stereotype about the Arab world and Islam.

E. Health.

Fellow travellers used the opportunity presented by 9/11 to send anthrax in the mail and raise fears about widespread bio-terrorism. One result was an outcry for more ciprofloxacin, but Bayer, a German pharmaceutical company, held the patent on the medication and they couldn't manufacture the required amounts quickly enough. A call was raised in many quarters, both public and private, demanding that US companies ignore the patent and make the drug. Advocates for African AIDS victims had been making the same demand about drugs, including ciprofloxacin, used to fight that deadly malady. When Bayer cut a deal with the United States, it also helped reduce the cost and increase the production of AIDS drugs for use in Africa. Security was now tied directly to suffering populations in the underdeveloped world.

F. Economics.

The immediate effect of 9/11 on the stock market was stunning, but the effect on the travel and leisure industries was greater. People stopped flying and hotels emptied. Amusement parks didn't seem quite as amusing. This was not just an American phenomenon, it occurred worldwide, and it came at a time when the world was already slipping into a recession. Unemployment grew and foreign direct investment dried up. Government surpluses evaporated and deficits returned. Only the stocks of the military industrial complex saw a silver lining. To stimulate the US economy, President Bush returned the government to deficit spending, risking the downstream viability of social security and Medicare — issues close to the heart of an aging American population.

As you can see, the tendrils of 9/11 expanded outward in every direction changing lives, creating havoc, and demanding a response. Governments realised that stovepiped approaches to governance were no longer workable and they started to forge networks between previously unconnected departments and even proposed the creation of a new department. We have only begun to see the enormous changes that will be wrought as a result of the events on 11 September. So how does system perturbation theory help us get our arms around all of these problems and allow us to use it as a new organising principle?

9.   System Perturbation Theory

What do we mean when we talk about system perturbation? The following is our working definition:

• An international security order thrown into a state of confusion by a perversely shocking development somewhere in the increasingly interconnected global economy.

• This "vertical" shock generates an outflow of "horizontal" waves whose cascading effects cross sectoral boundaries (which may not dampen but amplify the waves) to the point where nearly all rule sets are disturbed, knocked out of equilibrium, questioned, or intrinsically rearranged.

• This *fluxing* of the system is temporary, but path dependent and chaotic. End states encompass the return of old rules, the rise of entirely new rule sets, and/or the merging of old and new.

• The potential for conflict is maximised when divergent rule sets are forced into collisions.

In the past, as we have noted, great power war has led to changes in the international order. Under economic globalisation, which generates an increasingly denser medium for shock wave transmission, great power war becomes less likely the cause and more likely one possible effect of a system perturbation. If true, then system perturbation, not great power war, needs to be the organising principle governments use to build their strategies and field their resources, since it covers a greater number of adverse situations. Under this new arrangement, we ask, "Who makes the rules?" For the US Department of Defence, we developed a decision tree that helped explain why this was such an important question for them (see figure 3).

The higher up the tree you go the greater the degree of transformation required. First we ask if 9/11 represented a new form of crisis (that is, was it "existence proof" for system perturbation theory)? If it was not, then the Department of Defence probably requires only slight modification. If 9/11 does represent a new kind of crisis, then simply modifying a few organisations might be an insufficient transformation. If the kind of crisis one must get involved in has changed, does it mean the rules of the game have changed? Does system perturbation become the new ordering principle for the Department of Defence? It must be willing to give up some of the old product lines in order to make room for new ones. If a new ordering principle is required, we wonder who establishes the rules for the game. Is it the new super-empowered individuals? Transnational networks? If not, and states continue to make the rules, the Department of Defence must understand what the new rules are and reposition themselves to succeed under them. This would probably require a major organisational transformation as well as a major technological change. If the newcomers do make the rules, then the Department of Defence may be in the wrong business.

The philosophy behind asymmetrical warfare has always been to do things that render major segments of your opponents' forces useless. What good did America's mighty military do to deter the terrorists who attacked the World Trade Centre? What good were the Army's heavy forces in Afghanistan, or the Air Force's bombers before there were nearby bases, or the bulk of the Navy's ships that floated hundreds of miles from a landlocked country? What good are armaments at all against cyber attacks? Or biological attacks? That doesn't make military power irrelevant in every case, but more and more people now realise that military power is not relevant in every case either. The resources required to combat the latter two eventualities are probably not resident in the military at all, nor should they be. Yet having tools that can be used effectively in every circumstance is critical. That is why a new organising principle is essential — so that the disparate parts that need to coordinate their efforts have a framework for doing so.

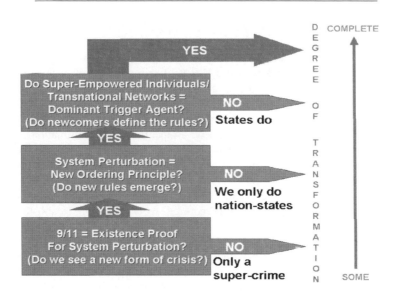

10.   What is to be Done?

As we think narrowly about US security, we see the following changes. There will be a merging of national and personal security issues. The antiseptic *posse comitas* approach of the past will find the lines between military action and law enforcement being blurred. Private security agencies will likely come under closer scrutiny and heavier regulation — but that sector of society will inevitably grow. Police forces will become paramilitary. American defence policy, which has supported a US foreign policy that prefers fighting "over there," will have to balance "home" and "away" responsibilities even as the defence dollar is squeezed by requirements of an aging population and a cry for more homeland security provided by non-defence agencies.

On the battlefield, nations cooperating to contain super-empowered individuals and transnational networks will find conflict defined increasingly by a values-based response to globalisation; hence, the rise of values-based targeting. The threats will primarily be non-state, non-nodal, asymmetric and without restrictions and both sides will wage wars of "perversity." Militaries will have to transform dramatically, in terms of equipment, concepts of operation, and strategy. The old industrial age model will not work because battlefield density no longer matters. Intelligence will become the most critical resource a military can have. Massing of weapons will yield to directed energy weapons and the military will have to answer all the ethical questions that will arise from their use. Armed reconnaissance units will be the norm as stealth helps define lethality. Shooters will be directly coupled to sensors in a new way. Some battlefields may be completely autonomous and the protection of innocents will raise difficult challenges. Games of hide and seek will replace classic battlefield engagements. Prosecution of some conflicts will be equal parts military action, economic sanction, and law enforcement. Turf battles over who is in charge will undoubtedly rage.

If system perturbation theory has any relevance beyond being an ethereal model of a complex world, then we need to identify who or what the trigger agents are that can "drop the big rocks in the pond," what media they will use, how the shockwaves will be transmitted, what connections exist between the initial shock and the horizontal scenarios, what barriers can be erected to stop the spread of adverse effects, and what the consequences are of both the threat and the cure. We need to understand what capabilities are needed for both system perturbations and great power war, and which are distinct to system perturbation. Some of the tools we may need may not yet exist. We suspect that research and development in this area will be critical. We need to continue to identify essential rule sets and understand who is making particular rules along with who is following them and who is not. Governments, especially the US Government, needs to forge new links across departments and agencies and possibly needs a reorganisation of major portions of the bureaucracy. Because system perturbation implies that the international system is affected, some functions are probably beyond the ken of national governments and transnational solutions will have to be worked out. New links with business must be established, because globalisation is primarily an economic phenomenon. The dilemma for governments is that some deterrence and consequence management resources may be beyond their political reach and rest with actors tied to no nation-state. As the theory is explored and refined, we may find new venues and new alliances that need to be established in addition to current ones such as the United Nations and Interpol.

Right now, we are good only at tracing the dynamics of a system perturbation after they happen, much like a detective recreating a crime scene during an investigation. What we need to understand better is who or what are the agents that can trigger system perturbations. What devices can they use? How fast will the effects of the perturbation spread as globalisation creates a denser medium through which such effects can flow? What forms of transmission will these effects assume? Are there naturally occurring breakers within the globalisation system? We need to understand the difference between the paths of least resistance (in effect, the usual suspects for transmission) and the paths of greatest resistance (what is most fit in this landscape to resist shockwaves). Where we find naturally occurring breaks, we need to identify, bolster, and exploit them.

This nascent theory currently raises more questions than it answers. But we believe it will help governments think more broadly about national security by forcing them to forge new connections between politics, diplomacy, economics, culture, and security. Done correctly, international relationships will be strengthened and possibilities of great power wars reduced. The venues required to counter super-empowered individuals and transnational networks will make international relations more transparent, thus enhancing trust.

Notes

1.   Garraty and Gay, 1972, 992.
2.   Simma, 1995, 810. Since 1971 and the beginning of free floating rates of exchange, the Fund "ensures that floating is orderly and that the international transfer of payments is as free as possible, and it provides the money used for balancing deficits in the balance of payments. This has caused the Fund to be one of the most important actors in the management of the international debt crisis." (ibid.)
3.   Ibid., 811. "Today it focuses on financing development projects, especially in the field of infrastructure." (ibid.) The World Bank has two affiliate organisations, The International Finance Corporation (IFC) and the International Development Association (IDA).
4.   Remarks during a 31 January 2002 press conference.
5.   Strausz-Hupe, 2002.

References

Garraty, J.A. and P.Gay (eds.)   (1972)   *The Columbia History of the World*. New York: Harper and Row.
Simma, B (ed.) (1995)   *The Charter of the United Nations: A Commentary*. Oxford:Oxford University Press.
Strausz-Hupe, R. (2002) 'The New Protracted Conflict', *Orbis*, Spring 2002
Weltz, K (1965) *Man, the State and War*. New York: Columbia Press.

Cyberterrorism: Media Myth or Clear and Present Danger?

Maura Conway

1.   Introduction

The Internet is the instrument of a political power shift. It is the first many-to-many communication system. The ability to communicate words, images, and sounds, which underlies the power to persuade, inform, witness, debate, and discuss (not to mention the power to slander, propagandise, disseminate bad or misleading information, engage in misinformation and/or disinformation, etc.) is no longer the sole province of those who own printing presses, radio stations, or television networks. Every machine connected to the Internet is potentially a printing press, a broadcasting station, a place of assembly. And in the twenty first century, terrorists are availing of the opportunity to connect.

The Internet is an ideal propaganda tool for terrorists: in the past they had to communicate through acts of violence and hope that those acts garnered sufficient attention to publicise the perpetrators cause or explain their ideological justification. With the advent of the Internet, however, the same groups can disseminate their information undiluted by the media and untouched by government sensors. In 1998 it was reported that 12 of the 30 terrorist organisations identified by the US State Department had their own websites. Today, a majority of the 33 groups on the same list of Designated Foreign Terrorist Organisations maintain an official online presence.[1] The question that then arises is this: Are terrorist groups who use the Internet in such a manner 'cyberterrorists'? The answer hinges on what constitutes cyberterrorism.

The term cyberterrorism unites two significant modern fears: fear of technology and fear of terrorism. Both of these fears are evidenced in this quote from Walter Laqueur, one of the most well known figures in terrorism studies: "The electronic age has now made cyberterrorism possible. A onetime mainstay of science fiction, the doomsday machine, looms as a real danger. The conjunction of technology and terrorism make for an uncertain and frightening future"[2]. It is not only academics that are given to sensationalism. Cyberterrorism first became the focus of sustained analysis by government in the mid-1990s. In 1996 John Deutch, former director of the Central Intelligence Agency (CIA), testified before the Permanent Subcommittee on Investigations of the United States' Senate Governmental Affairs Committee:

International terrorist groups clearly have the capability to attack the information infrastructure of the United States, even if they use relatively simple means. Since the possibilities for attacks are not difficult to imagine, I am concerned about the potential for such attacks in the future. The methods used could range from such traditional terrorist methods as a vehicle-delivered bomb -- directed in this instance against, say, a telephone switching centre or other communications node -- to electronic means of attack. The latter methods could rely on paid hackers. The ability to launch an attack, however, are likely to be within the capabilities of a number of terrorist groups, which themselves have increasingly used the Internet and other modern means for their own communications. The groups concerned include such well-known, long-established organisations as the Lebanese Hizballah, as well as nameless and less well-known cells of international terrorists such as those who attacked the World Trade Center.[3]

It was Deutch who, in the same testimony, warned that an "electronic Waterloo" was a real possibility thus coining a neologism employed with startling frequency since.

In 1998 the Center for Strategic and International Studies, located in Washington DC, published their report entitled *Cybercrime, Cyberterrorism, Cyberwarfare: Averting an Electronic Waterloo*. The document's authors view cyberterrorism as a sub-species of Information Warfare (IW). And although they fail to provide a definition of what it is they mean by 'cyberterrorism,' they are at pains to illustrate its potentially disastrous consequences:

A smoking keyboard does not convey the same drama as a smoking gun, but it has already proved just as destructive. Armed with the tools of Cyberwarfare, substate or nonstate or even individual actors are now powerful enough to destabilise and eventually destroy targeted states and societies... Information warfare specialists at the Pentagon estimate that a properly prepared and well-coordinated attack by fewer than 30 computer virtuosos strategically located around the world, with a budget of less than $10 million, could bring the United States to its knees. Such a strategic attack, mounted by a cyberterrorist group, either substate or nonstate actors, would shut down everything from electric power grids to air traffic control centers.[4]

A focus on such 'shut-down-the-power-grid' scenarios is increasingly a feature of analyses of the cyberterrorist threat. This chapter is concerned with the origins and development of the concept of cyberterrorism. It seeks to excavate the story of the concept through an analysis of both popular/media renditions of the term and scholarly attempts to define the borders of same. Let me say at the outset that, in both realms, confusion abounds. This is startling, particularly given that since the events of 9-11, the question on everybody's lips appears to be 'Is Cyberterrorism Next?'. In academic circles the answer is generally 'not yet.' The media are less circumspect, however, and policy makers appear increasingly to be seduced by the latter's version of events. It seems to me that both question and answer(s) are hampered by the lack of certainty surrounding the central term. Let me begin by putting forward some concrete illustrations of this definitional void culled from newspaper accounts.

2.   Cyberterrorists Abound

In June 2001 a headline in the *Boston Herald* read 'Cyberterrorist Must Serve Year in Jail'. The story continued: "Despite a Missouri cyberterrorist's plea for leniency, a Middlesex Superior Court judge yesterday told the wheelchair-bound man 'you must be punished for what you've done' to Massachusetts schoolchildren and ordered him to serve a year in jail." Christian Hunold, 21, pleaded guilty to "launching a campaign of terror via the Internet" from his Missouri home, including directing Middle School students to child pornography Web sites he posted, telephoning threats to the school and to the homes of some children, and posting a picture of the school's principal with bullet holes in his head and chest on the Net.

In December 2001 a headline in the *Bristol Herald Courier*, Wise County, Virginia, USA read 'Wise County Circuit Court's Webcam "Cracked" by Cyberterrorists'. The webcam, which allows surfers to log on and watch the Wise County Circuit Courts in action, was taken offline for two weeks for repairs. "(Expletive Deleted) the United States Government" was posted on a web page, but the defaced page could only be seen by the Court's IT contractors. Internet surfers who logged on could only see a blank screen. The 'attack' is thought to have originated in

Pakistan or Egypt, according to the report. "This is the first cyberterrorism on the court's Internet technology, and it clearly demonstrates the need for constant vigilance," according to Court Clerk Jack Kennedy. "The damage in this case amounted to a $400 hard drive relating to the Internet video server. The crack attack has now resulted in better software and enhanced security to avoid a [*sic*] further cyberterrorism." According to Kennedy, cracking can escalate to terrorism when a person cracks into a government- or military-maintained Web site; he said cyberterrorism has increased across the United States since the events of 9-11 and law enforcement has traced many of the attacks to Pakistan and Egypt [5].

The scare mongering is not confined to the US, however. In March 2002 British IT security specialists Digilog published what has been described as "the most comprehensive study of the insecurity of wireless networks in London"[6]. The survey discovered that over 90 per cent of those networks are open to drive-by hacking. Unfortunately, this potentially worthwhile survey is undermined by the emphasis placed on the supposed link between drive-by hackers and international terrorism: "And networks are not only at risk from attacks at close quarters. University research in Hawaii has shown that signals can be intercepted from a distance of over 25 miles, raising fears of large-scale cyber-terrorism. Computer-controlled power grids, telephone networks and water-treatment plants are at risk"[7]. Also in March linkLINE Communications, described as "a small, but determined Internet service provider" located in Mira Loma, California received telephone and e-mail threats from an unnamed individual who claimed to have accessed- or be able to access- the credit card numbers of linkLINE's customers. He said that he would sell the information and notify linkLINE's customers if $50,000 wasn't transferred to a bank account number that he supplied. The ISP refused to concede to the cracker's demands: "We're not going to let our customers, or our reputation, be the victims of cyber-terrorism," said one of the company's founders. linkLINE contacted the authorities and learned that the cracker and his accomplices may have extorted as much as $4 billion from other companies. The account was subsequently traced through Russia to Yemen.

A similar incident had taken place in November 2000. An attack, originating in Pakistan, was carried out against the American Israel Public Affairs Committee, a lobbying group. The group's site was defaced with anti-Israeli commentary[8]. The attacker also stole some 3,500 e-mail addresses and 700 credit card numbers, sent anti-Israeli diatribes to the addresses and published the credit card data on the Internet. The Pakistani hacker who took credit for the crack, the self-styled Dr. Nuker, said he was a founder of the Pakistani Hackerz Club, the aim of which was to "hack for the injustice going around the globe, especially with [*sic*] Muslims"[9].

In May 2001 'cyberterrorism' reared its head once again when supporters of the terrorist group Laskar Jihad (Holy War Warriors) hacked into the websites of the Australian embassy and the Indonesian national police in Jakarta to protest against the arrest of their leader. The hackers intercepted users logging on to the Web sites and redirected them to a site containing a warning to the Indonesian police to release Ja'far Umar Thalib, the group's leader. Thalib was arrested in connection with inciting hatred against a religious group and ordering the murder of one of his followers. According to police, the hackers, the self-styled Indonesian Muslim Hackers Movement, did not affect police operations. The Australian embassy said the hackers did not sabotage its Web site, but only directed users to the other site.

It is clear that the pejorative connotations of the terms 'terrorism' and 'terrorist' have resulted in some unlikely acts of computer abuse being labelled 'cyberterrorism'. According to the above, sending pornographic e-mails to minors, posting offensive content on the Internet, defacing Web pages, using a computer to cause $400 worth of damage, stealing credit card information, posting credit card numbers on the Internet, and clandestinely redirecting Internet traffic from one site to another all constitute instances of cyberterrorism. And yet none of it could be described as terrorism- some of it not even criminal- had it taken place without the aid of computers. Admittedly, terrorism is a notoriously difficult activity to define; however, the addition of computers to plain old criminality it is not.

3.   What is Cyberterrorism?

There are a number of stumbling blocks to constructing a clear and concise definition of cyberterrorism. Chief among these are the following:

(a.) A majority of the discussion of cyberterrorism has been conducted in the popular media, where the focus is on ratings and readership figures rather than establishing good operational definitions of new terms.

(b.) The term is subject to chronic misuse and overuse and since 9/11, in particular, has become a buzzword that can mean radically different things to different people.

(c.) It has become common when dealing with computers and the Internet to create new words by placing the handle *cyber*, *computer*, or *information* before another word. This may appear to denote a completely new phenomenon, but often it does not and confusion ensues.

(d.) Finally, a major obstacle to creating a definition of cyberterrorism is the lack of an agreed-upon definition of terrorism.

This does not mean that no acceptable definitions of cyberterrorism have been put forward. On the contrary, there are a number of well thought out definitions of the term available, and these are discussed below[10]. However, no single definition of cyberterrorism is agreed upon by all, in the same way that no single, globally accepted definition of classical political terrorism exists.

Barry Collin, a senior research fellow at the Institute for Security and Intelligence in California, coined the term 'cyberterrorism' in the 1980s. The concept is composed of two elements: cyberspace and terrorism. Cyberspace may be conceived of as "that place in which computer programs function and data moves"[11]. Terrorism is a less easily defined term. In fact, most scholarly texts devoted to the study of terrorism contain a section, chapter, or chapters devoted to a discussion of how difficult it is to define the term. This chapter employs the definition of terrorism contained in Title 22 of the United States Code, Section 2656f(d). That statute contains the following definition:

> The term 'terrorism' means premeditated, politically motivated violence perpetrated against non-combatant targets by sub-national groups or clandestine agents, usually intended to influence an audience[12].

Combining these definitions results in the construction of a narrowly drawn working definition of cyberterrorism as follows:

> Cyberterrorism refers to premeditated, politically motivated attacks by sub-national groups or clandestine agents against information, computer systems, computer programs, and data that result in violence against non-combatant targets[13].

The above definition is similar to that put forward by Professor Dorothy Denning in numerous articles and interviews, and in her testimony before the United States Congress's House Armed Services Committee. According to Denning:

Cyberterrorism is the convergence of cyberspace and terrorism. It refers to unlawful attacks and threats of attacks against computers, networks and the information stored therein when done to intimidate or coerce a government or its people in furtherance of political or social objectives. Further, to qualify as cyberterrorism, an attack should result in violence against persons or property, or at least cause enough harm to generate fear. Attacks that lead to death or bodily injury, explosions, or severe economic loss would be examples. Serious attacks against critical infrastructures could be acts of cyberterrorism, depending on their impact. Attacks that disrupt nonessential services or that are mainly a costly nuisance would not[14].

Utilising these definitions, the 'attack' on the Web-cam of the Wise County Circuit Court does not qualify as cyberterrorism, nor do any of the other 'cyberterrorist attacks' outlined. It's hardly surprising; the inflation of the concept of cyberterrorism may increase newspaper circulation, but is ultimately not in the public interest. Despite this, many have suggested adopting broader definitions of the term.

In an article, which appeared in the journal *Terrorism and Political Violence* in 1997, Devost, Houghton and Pollard defined 'information terrorism' as "the intentional abuse of a digital information system, network or component toward an end that supports or facilitates a terrorist campaign or action"[15]. They conceive of information terrorism as "the nexus between criminal information system fraud or abuse, and the physical violence of terrorism" (ibid). This allows for attacks that would not necessarily result in violence against humans- although it might incite fear- to be characterised as terrorist. This is problematic because, although there is no single accepted definition of terrorism, more than 80% of scholars agree that the latter has two integral components: the use of force or violence and a political motivation. Indeed, most domestic laws define classical or political terrorism as requiring violence or the threat to or the taking of human life for political or ideological ends. Devost, Houghton and Pollard are aware of this, but wish to allow for the inclusion of pure information system abuse (i.e. that does not employ nor result in physical violence) as a possible new facet of terrorism nonetheless. Others have followed their lead.

Israel's former science minister, Michael Eitan, has deemed "sabotage over the Internet" as cyberterrorism[16]. According to the Japanese government 'Cyberterrorism' aims at "seriously affecting information systems of private companies and government ministries and agencies by gaining illegal access to their computer networks and destroying data"[17]. A report by the Moscow-based ITAR-TASS news agency states that, in Russia, cyberterrorism is perceived as "the use of computer technologies for terrorist purposes" (ibid). In 1999, a report by the Center for the Study of Terrorism and Irregular Warfare (CSTIW) at the Naval Postgraduate School in Monterey, California, defined cyberterrorism as the "unlawful destruction or disruption of digital property to intimidate or coerce people"[18.] "We shall define cyberterrorism as any act of terrorism…that uses information systems or computer technology either as a *weapon* or a *target*," states a NATO brief [19.] Yael Shahar, Web master at the International Policy Institute for Counter-Terrorism (ICT), located in Herzliya, Israel, differentiates between a number of different types of what he prefers to call 'information terrorism': 'electronic warfare' occurs when hardware is the target, 'psychological warfare' is the goal of inflammatory content, and it is only 'hacker warfare', according to Shahar, that degenerates into cyberterrorism[20].

John Leyden, writing in *The Register*, described the way in which a group of Palestinian hackers and sympathisers established a Web site that provides one-stop access to hacking tool and viruses, and tips on how to use the tools to mount attacks on Israeli targets. They are, he said, using the techniques of cyberterrorism[21]. Leyden and others wish to conflate politically motivated hacking- so-called hacktivism- and terrorism. Such unwarranted expansion of the concept of cyberterrorism runs contrary to the definitions outlined earlier. Advancing one step further, Johan J. Ingles-le Noble, writing in *Jane's Intelligence Review*, had this to say:

> Cyberterrorism is not only about damaging systems but also about intelligence gathering. The intense focus on 'shut-down-the-power-grid' scenarios and tight analogies with physically violent techniques ignore other more potentially effective uses of IT in terrorist warfare: intelligence-gathering, counter-intelligence and disinformation[22].

Noble's comment highlights the more potentially realistic and effective uses of the Internet by terrorist groups (i.e. intelligence-gathering, counter-intelligence, disinformation, etc.). However, he mistakenly labels these alternative uses 'cyberterrorism.' Such a taxonomy is uncalled for: even had Dr. Nuker broken into the headquarters of the American Israel Public Affairs Committee and physically stolen the credit card information and e-mail addresses, this would not be considered an act of terrorism, but a criminal undertaking. It is only acting on the information obtained to perpetrate an attack in furtherance of some political aim that could be considered terrorist. Noble contends, furthermore, that "disinformation is easily spread; rumours get picked up by the media, aided by the occasional anonymous e-mail." That may be so, but spreading false information whether via word-of-mouth, the print or broadcast media, or some other medium, is oftentimes not even criminal, never mind terrorist. Why should things be any different in cyberspace?

In fact, Ingles-le Noble (1999) himself recognises that:

There is undoubtedly a lot of exaggeration in this field. If your system goes down, it is a lot more interesting to say it was the work of a foreign government rather than admit it was due to an American teenage 'script-kiddy' tinkering with a badly written CGI script. If the power goes out, people light a candle and wait for it to return, but do not feel terrified. If their mobile phones switch off, society does not instantly feel under attack. If someone cracks a web site and changes the content, terror does not stalk the streets[23].

Nonetheless, there is widespread concern that a catastrophic cyberterrorist attack is imminent particularly in the wake of the events of 9/11. However, the bulk of the evidence to date shows that while terrorist groups are making widespread use of the Internet, so far they have not resorted to cyberterrorism, or shown the inclination to move heavily in that direction. Dramatic predictions to the contrary certainly make good copy, generate high ratings and sell many books and journals, but do not contribute to an intelligent, well-informed analysis of the threat of cyberterrorism. Unfortunately, such predictions appear to have had a significant impact in policy circles. It has been observed that "there is a lot of fear around and perhaps governments are in possession of the most of it"[24]. These inchoate fears have led to the introduction of a raft of legislation that, in many instances, fails to distinguish between crime and terrorism, malicious hacking and cyberterrorism thus setting a dangerous precedent.

4.   Distinguishing Characteristics

When it comes to discussion of cyberterrorism, there are two basic areas in which clarification is needed. First, the confusion between cyberterrorism and cybercrime. Such confusion is partly caused by the lack of clear definitions of the two phenomena. A UN manual on IT-related crime recognises that, even after several years of debate among experts on just what constitutes cybercrime and what cyberterrorism, "there is no internationally recognised definition of those terms"[25]. Second, it is useful to distinguish two different facets of terrorist use of information technology: terrorist use of computers as a facilitator of their activities, and terrorism involving computer technology as a weapon or target. Utilising the definitions outlined above, it is possible to clarify both difficulties. Cybercrime and cyberterrorism are not coterminous. Cyberspace attacks must have a 'terrorist' component in order to be labelled cyberterrorism. The attacks must instil terror as commonly understood (that is, result in death and/or large-scale destruction), and they must have a political motivation. "The words cyberterrorism should refer to an act or acts of terrorism carried out through the use of a computer"[26]. As regards the distinction between terrorist use of information technology and terrorism involving computer technology as a weapon/target, only the latter may be defined as cyberterrorism. Terrorist 'use' of computers as a facilitator of their activities, whether for propaganda, communication, or other purposes, is simply that: 'use.'

Kent Anderson[27] has devised a three-tiered schema for categorising fringe activity on the Internet, utilising the terms 'Use,' 'Misuse,' and 'Offensive Use.' Anderson explains:

> Use is simply using the Internet/WWW to facilitate communications via e-mails and mailing lists, newsgroups and websites. In almost every case, this activity is simply free speech…Misuse is when the line is crossed from expression of ideas to acts that disrupt or otherwise compromise other sites. An example of misuse is Denial-of-Service (DoS) attacks against websites. In the physical world, most protests are allowed, however, [even] if the protests disrupt other functions of society such as train service or access to private property…The same should be true for online activity. Offensive use is the next level of activity where actual damage or theft occurs. The physical world analogy would be a riot where property is damaged or people are injured. An example of this type of activity online is the recent attack on systems belonging to the world

economic forum, where personal information of high profile individuals was stolen [28].

5.   Legislative Measures

In February 2001, the UK updated its Terrorism Act to classify "the use of or threat of action that is designed to seriously interfere with or seriously disrupt an electronic system" as an act of terrorism[29]. In fact, it will be up to police investigators to decide whether an action is to be regarded as terrorism. Online groups, human rights organisations, civil liberties campaigners, and others condemned this classification as absurd, pointing out that it placed hacktivism on a par with life-threatening acts of public intimidation[30]. Notwithstanding, in the wake of the events of 9-11, US legislators followed suit. Previous to 9/11, if one successfully infiltrated a federal computer network, one was considered a hacker. However, following the passage of the USA Act[31], which authorised the granting of significant powers to law enforcement agencies to investigate and prosecute potential threats to national security, there is the potential for hackers to be labelled cyberterrorists and, if convicted, to face up to 20 years in prison. Clearly, policymakers believe that actions taken in cyberspace are qualitatively different from those taken in the 'real' world.

It is not the Patriot Act, however, but the massive 500-page law establishing the US Department of Homeland Security that has the most to say about terrorism and the Internet. The law establishing the new department envisions a far greater role for the United States' government in the securing of operating systems, hardware, and the Internet in the future. In November 2002, US President Bush signed the bill creating the new department, setting in train a process which will result in the largest reshuffle of US bureaucracy since 1948. At the signing ceremony, Bush said that the "department will gather and focus all our efforts to face the challenge of cyberterrorism"[32]. The Department of Homeland Security will merge five agencies that currently share responsibility for critical infrastructure protection in the United States: the FBI's National Infrastructure Protection Center (NIPC), the Defence Department's National Communications System, the Commerce Department's Critical Infrastructure Office, the Department of Energy's analysis centre, and the Federal Computer Incident Response Center. The new law also creates a Directorate for Information Analysis and Infrastructure Protection whose task it will be to analyse vulnerabilities in systems including the Internet, telephone networks and other critical infrastructures, and orders the establishment of a "comprehensive national plan for securing the key resources and critical infrastructure of the United States" including information technology, financial networks, and satellites. Further, the law dictates a maximum sentence of life-imprisonment without parole for those who deliberately transmit a program, information, code, or command that impairs the performance of a computer or modifies its data without authorisation, "if the offender knowingly or recklessly causes or attempts to cause death." In addition, the law allocates $500 million for research into new technologies, is charged with funding the creation of tools to help state and local law enforcement agencies thwart computer crime, and classifies certain activities as new computer crimes.

6.   Conclusion

In the space of thirty years, the Internet has metamorphosed from a US Department of Defence command-and-control network consisting of less than one hundred computers to a network that criss-crosses the globe: today, the Internet is made up of tens of thousands of nodes (i.e. linkage points) with over 105 million hosts spanning more than 200 countries. With a current (December 2002) estimated population of regular users of over 600 million people, the Internet has become a near-ubiquitous presence in many world regions. That ubiquity is due in large part to the release in 1991 of the World Wide Web. In 1993 the Web consisted of a mere 130 sites, by century's end it boasted more than one billion. In the Western world, in particular, the Internet has been extensively integrated into the economy, the military, and society as a whole. As a result, many people now believe that it is possible for people to die as a direct result of a cyberterrorist attack and that such an attack is imminent.

On Wednesday morning, 12 September 2001, you could still visit a Web site that integrated three of the wonders of modern technology: the Internet, digital video, and the World Trade Center. The site allowed Internet users worldwide to appreciate what millions of tourists have delighted in since Minoru Yamasaki's architectural wonder was completed in 1973: the glorious 45-mile view from the top of the WTC towers. According to journalists, the caption on the site still read 'Real-Time Hudson River View from World Trade Center.' In the square above was deep black nothingness. The terrorists hadn't taken down the Net, they had taken down the towers. "Whereas hacktivism is real and widespread, cyberterrorism exists only in theory. Terrorist groups are using the Internet, but they still prefer bombs to bytes as a means of inciting terror," wrote Dorothy Denning just weeks before the September attacks. Terrorist 'use' of the Internet has been largely ignored, however, in favour of the more headline-grabbing 'cyberterrorism.'

Richard Clarke, White House special adviser for Cyberspace Security, has said that he prefers not to use the term 'cyberterrorism,' but instead favours use of the term 'information security' or 'cyberspace security.' This is because, Clarke has stated, most terrorist groups have not engaged in information warfare (read 'cyberterrorism'). Instead, he admits, terrorist groups have at this stage only used the Internet for propaganda, communications, and fundraising[33]. In a similar vein, Michael Vatis, former head of the US National Infrastructure Protection Center (NIPC), has stated that "Terrorists are already using technology for sophisticated communications and fund-raising activities. As yet we haven't seen computers being used by these groups as weapons to any significant degree, but this will probably happen in the future"[34]. According to a 2001 study, 75% of Internet users worldwide agree, they believe that 'cyberterrorists' will "soon inflict massive casualties on innocent lives by attacking corporate and governmental computer networks." The survey, conducted in 19 major cities around the world, found that 45% of respondents agreed completely that "computer terrorism will be a growing problem," and another 35% agreed somewhat with the same statement.[35] The problem certainly can't shrink much, hovering as it does at zero cyberterrorism incidents per year. That's not to say that cyberterrorism cannot happen or will not happen, but that, contrary to popular perception, it has not happened yet.

Notes

1. The European Union (EU) has recently updated its list of prohibited organisations (see http://ue.eu.int/pressData/en/misc/70413.pdf). Canada is the latest country to establish such a list (see http://www.sgc.gc.ca/publications/news/20020723_e.asp).

2. Laqueur, W. (1999), *The New Terrorism: Fanaticism and the Arms of Mass Destruction*. Oxford: Oxford University Press, 254.

3. Deutch, J. (1996), *Statement Before the US Senate Governmental Affairs Committee* (Permanent Subcommittee on Investigations), June 25. Available on the Internet at http://www.nswc.navy.mil/ISSEC/Docs/Ref/InTheNews/fullciatext.html.

4. Centre for Strategic and International Studies (CSIS), (1998), *Cybercrime, Cyberterrorism, Cyberwarfare: Averting an Electronic Waterloo*. Washington DC: CSIS, xiii.

5. It was predicted that an escalation in hack attacks would occur in the aftermath of 9-11 (ISTS 2001). However, the predicted escalation did not materialise. In the weeks following the attacks, Web page defacements were well publicised, but the overall number and sophistication of these remained rather low. One possible reason for the non-escalation of attacks could be that many hackers- particularly those located in the US- were wary of being associated with the events of September 11th and curbed their activities as a result.

6. Leyden, J. (2002), 'Drive-By Hacking Linked to Cyberterror', *The Register*, March 27. Available on the Internet at http://www.theregister.co.uk/content/55/24611.html.

7. ibid.

8. The defacement may be viewed online at http://www.attrition.org/mirror/attrition/2000/11/02/www.aipac.org/.

9. Schwartz, J. (2000), 'When Point and Shoot Becomes Point and Click', *The New York Times*, November 12.

10.One of the most accessible sound bites on what defines cyberterrorism is that it is 'hacking with a body count' (Collin, quoted in Ballard *et al* 2002, 992).

11. Collin, B. (1996), 'The Future of Cyberterrorism', presented at the 11th Annual International Symposium on Criminal Justice Issues, University of Illinois at Chicago. Available on the Internet at http://www.afgen.com/terrorism1.html.

12. Title 22 of the United States Code, Section 2656f(d) may be viewed online at http://www.lii.warwick.ac.uk/uscode/22/2656f.html. This is the definition employed in the US State Department's annual report entitled *Patterns of Global Terrorism*. These are available online at http://www.state.gov.

13. Pollitt, M. (n.d.), *Cyberterrorism: Fact or Fancy?* Washington DC: FBI   Laboratory. Available:http://www.cs.georgetown.edu/~denning/infosec/pollitt.html.

14. Denning, op cit
15. Devost, M., B. Houghton & N. Pollard (1996), 'Information Terrorism: Can You Trust Your Toaster?', *The Terrorism Research Centre*, 75

16. Sher, H. (2000), 'Cyberterror Should be International Crime- Israeli Minister', *Newsbytes*, November 10.

17. Foreign Broadcast Information Service (FBIS) (2002b), 'Government Sets Up Anti-Cyberterrorism Homepage', *Sankei Shimbun*, FBIS-EAS-2002-0410, April 10.

18. Daukantas, P. (2001), 'Professors Hash Out Emergency Response, Cyberterrorism Strategies', *Government Computer News*, December 14. Available on the Internet at http://www.gcn.com/vol1_no1/daily-updates/17642-1.html.

19. Mates, M. (Rapporteur) (2001), *Technology and Terrorism*. Brussels: NATO.

20. Hershman, T. (2000), 'Cyberterrorism is Real Threat, Say Experts at Conference', *Israel.internet.com*, December 11.

21. Leyden, J. (2000), 'Palestinian Crackers Give Out Tools to Attack Israelis', *The Register*, December 4. Available on the Internet at http://www.theregister.co.uk/content/6/15199.html.

22. JJ Ingles-le Noble *Jane's Intelligence Review* 1999, 6

23. ibid., 6

24. Stanton, J.J. (2002), 'Terror in Cyberspace: Terrorists Will Exploit and Widen the Gap Between Governing Structures and the Public', *American Behavioral Scientist* 45(6): 1017-1032.

25. Mates, M. (Rapporteur) (2001), *Technology and Terrorism*. Brussels: NATO.   Available   on   the   Internet   at

http://www.tbmm.gov.tr/natopa/raporlar/bilim%20ve%20teknoloji/AU%2
0121%20STC%20Terrorism.htm.

26. Embar-Seddon, A. (2002). 'Cyberterrorism: Are We Under Siege?',
American Behavioral Scientist, 45(6): 1035.

27. Anderson was formerly senior vice-president of IT Security and
Investigations for information security firm Control Risks Group.

28. Weisenberger, K. (2001), 'Hacktivists of the World, Divide',
SecurityWatch.com, April 23, 2. Available on the Internet at:
http://www.securitywatch.com/TRE/042301.html.

29. The full text of the UK Terrorism Act 2001 is available online at
http://www.legislation.hmso.gov.uk/acts/acts2000/20000011.htm.

30. Furthermore, ISPs in the UK may be legally required to monitor some
customers' surfing habits if requested to do so by the police under the
Regulation of Investigatory Powers Act 2000.

31. The Uniting and Strengthening America by Providing Appropriate
Tools Required to Intercept and Obstruct Terrorism (USA PATRIOT) Act
of 2001 was signed into law by US President George Bush in October
2001. The law gives government investigators broad powers to track
wireless phone calls, listen to voicemail, intercept e-mail messages and
monitor computer use, among others. I cannot enter into a discussion of
the Act here due to limitations of space. However, the full text of the Act
is available at http://www.ins.usdoj.gov/graphics/lawsregs/patriot.pdf
(Section 1016 pertains to critical infrastructure protection). See also
Johnson 2001; Matthews 2001.

32. McCullagh, D. (2002), 'Bush Signs Homeland Security Bill', *CNET
News*, November 25. Available on the Internet at
http://news.com.com/2102-1023-975305.html

33. Wynne, J. (2002), 'White House Advisor Richard Clarke Briefs Senate
Panel on Cybersecurity', *Washington File*, February 14.

34. Veltman, C. (2001), 'Beating Cyber Crime', *The Daily Telegraph*
(UK), March 1: 12E.

35. Poulsen, K. (2002), 'Lawyers Fear Misuse of Cyber Murder Law', *SecurityFocus Online*, November 21. Available on the Internet at http://online.securityfocus.com/news/1702

Part II

War and Morality

Assassination: Killing in the Shadow of Self-Defense

Michael L. Gross

As a tactic of war, assassination is most puzzling. Morally abhorrent to most students of war, assassination has the singular virtue of virtually eliminating collateral damage and harm to noncombatants. In an age when low intensity war is increasingly replacing conventional armed conflict, and pinpoint attacks against combatants are preferred to indiscriminate assaults on mixed populations of civilians and soldiers, assassination should be particularly attractive. Time-tested, it is the paradigmatic "smart" weapon: identify your prey, hunt him down and kill him.

But for reasons that are difficult to understand this is not the case at all. As a tactic of war, assassination evokes particular revulsion. Morally odious, it seems to violate a deep seated and inviolable moral norm. "The most imperative military necessity," wrote Spaight in 1911, "could not justify the use of poison, or the torture ("inhumane treatment") of a prisoner of war, or *assassination*.[1] Spaight offers no explanation for his conclusion, suggesting instead that the prohibition against assassination is self-evident and incontestable.

In war, where killing of combatants excites little consternation, the ban on assassination stands out as something of an anomaly. The ban is all the more perplexing in light of changing concepts of warfare that move from conventional conflagrations to low intensity conflict. For policy makers fearful of extensive civilian casualties, tactics like assassination or "targeted killings" exert a certain appeal if they can avoid the widespread devastation associated with conventional war. Why then the anathema? Is there any reason to avoid assassination in the context of war of any kind? The answer I propose to this last question is a guarded "yes." Assassination, often described as "murder by treachery" faces serious difficulties as a method of warfare. It undermines conventions of war, harms civilian communities and confounds our intuitions of self-defense that allow soldiers to kill in wartime. There are, however, some cases of defensible assassination. These include "ticking bombs" and punitive assassination.

1.   Assassination: Murder by Treachery

Assassination, often described simply as "murder by treachery" attracts particular denunciation. "What scourge," wrote Vattel in 1758, "could be more terrible in its effects on the human race than the practice of

securing the assassination of one's enemy by means of a traitor?"[2] Vattel
poses a rhetorical question and no more provides an answer than Spaight
does. But what is self evident about it? Why is murder by treachery a
scourge?

Assassination brings with it two kinds of harm: harm to the
conventions of trust that operate in wartime thereby impinging on the
ability of adversaries to wage anything less than total war, and harm to
civilians as the traitors and informers necessary to effect assassination
infiltrate and undermine the civilian community.

A.   Treachery: Undermining the Conventions of Trust During
Wartime

Although some military codes explicitly prohibit assassination, the
practice is not banned unequivocally by international law and convention.[3]
Instead it must be teased out of the general prohibition against killing by
"perfidious" means, that is, acts inviting the confidence of an adversary to
lead him to believe that he is entitled to, or is obliged to accord, protection
under the rules of international law applicable in armed conflict, with
intent to betray that confidence...[4]

At first blush, perfidy resembles other acts of devious warfare such
as ambushes, ruses and deceptions. But the difference is significant. Ruses
aim to deceive one's enemy but not by invoking legal protections. Perfidious
acts, on the other hand, are a "deliberate claim to legal protection for hostile
purposes."[5] Common examples include assaults by enemy soldiers
masquerading as civilians or neutrals, soldiers feigning surrender and
attacking their unsuspecting captors, and un-kept promises of safe passage,
particularly those extended for the purposes of peace negotiations. Each of
these acts undermines the legal protections afforded combatants during
wartime. Assassination is but a subset of perfidious killing characterised by
named victims.

While the prohibition against perfidy serves to protect civilians it
also protects important interests of belligerents. Without some modicum of
trust between adversaries, it is impossible - short of unconditional surrender
or total annihilation - to end a battle or a war. The convention of surrender
rests upon legal protections that individual soldiers or armies can invoke as
they lay down their arms and gain noncombatant status and immunity from
harm. In return, their captors expect non-belligerence from surrendering
forces. If these protections are abused, by a soldier suddenly firing from
under the protection of a white flag for example, the convention collapses.
Next time there will be no prisoners leaving armies no choice but to fight to
the death. Adversaries cannot surrender or conduct negotiations if wary that

the protection offered by a white flag or safe passage will be violated. Assassination engenders similar suspicions as victims are often lured to their death under the guise of the few conventions of trust and protection that operate during wartime. When these conventions are violated the fragile confidence needed to end war and make peace is eroded. It is for this reason that the Geneva conventions ban perfidy in the strongest language, aware that perfidious warfare and, by extension, assassination, "destroy the necessary basis for reestablishing peace."[6]

B.   Treachery: Harm to Civilians and Their Communities

While assassination may take the form of treachery described above it may also hinge upon information provided by spies, informers and traitors who betray their community. Betrayal is perhaps one of the most odious forms human behavior can take. More than a violation of a promise, betrayal takes advantage of an individual's good faith to do him or his community harm. Communities, and particularly traditional communities, are built on loyalty, friendship, fidelity and allegiance. Practices like assassination abuse these norms and risk undermining communal integrity and well-being.

The harmful consequences of assassination are perhaps best exemplified by Israel's policy of targeted killings in its current conflict with the Palestinians.[7] Responding to an increasing number of terror attacks that were an integral part of Palestinian strategy to pry additional concessions from Israel, Israel undertook a policy of "liquidating" Palestinian militants engaged in terrorist activity. Aside from the question of whether assassinations are a legitimate form of self-defense (see below) the policy can be assessed by its costs and benefits.

At one level it is difficult to assess the efficacy of assassination. Thwarted attacks remain unobserved, and counterfactuals - attacks that would have been launched had there never been a firm assassination policy - are difficult to gauge. Nevertheless, it seems clear, even to security forces, that terror groups were only temporarily disabled. New leaders emerged often more radical that their predecessors and determined to avenge their deaths.[8] Following Israel's month long invasion of Palestinian territory in April 2002, terror networks were reportedly dismantled only to mount deadly suicide attacks within weeks. Many of these came in the wake of the very assassinations designed to prevent them.[9] Equally important, an assassination policy fueled by collaboration wreaks havoc on the Palestinian community. Herein lies one scourge of assassination.

Collaborators are the mainstay of Israeli intelligence in the occupied territories. In a recent report, B'tselem, The Israeli Information Center for Human Rights in the Occupied Territories, describes how Palestinians are offered cash, goods and/or reduced prison sentences in return for collaboration. Those who refuse risk losing work permits or access to medical care. The number of collaborators is large and estimates range widely from 40,000 to 120,000 individuals (1% to 4% of the population).[10] Anecdotal evidence suggests that collaboration has far reaching effects on Palestinian society. Vigilante justice characterised by torture and summary execution of suspected collaborators is a common problem. Sometimes serving as a cover to allow rival gangs to settle political scores or eliminate those accused of moral turpitude, vigilante justice often erodes respect for law and order across the entire community. Its effects are pervasive. "The Palestinian collaborator in the Israeli strategy," notes Abdel-Jawad, "serves the purpose of creating mistrust, spreading confusion and undermining collective self-confidence within Palestinian society."[11] Once facilitated by spies, informers and compromised friends and family members, assassination subverts strongly held beliefs about integrity, trust, honor and loyalty that hold together traditional societies. And, it creates a vicious cycle of violence within Palestinian society "in which the wanted individuals were hunted by the security forces, while the suspected collaborators were hunted by the wanted, who held them responsible for the death or capture of their comrades.[12]

Assassination is invariably linked to collaboration and its effects within the Palestinian community are two-fold. First, treacherous assassination provokes a fierce reaction against both collaborators and those who recruit them and second, it rends the fabric of the moral community and destabilises Palestinian society. Assassination facilitated by widespread collaboration invites fierce retaliatory response, incurs additional civilian casualties and makes it more difficult to forge peace.

Assassination is prohibited because its treacherous aspects either undermine the local community where it is practiced and/or breach the fragile trust that endures between nations in wartime. While these are important arguments, they only address the means associated with assassination. Assassination may also be accomplished without the assistance of collaborators or without any violation of trust during wartime. Shorn of treachery and its evil consequences, assassination is nothing more than a "named killing." This is by no means trivial, for it stands in contrast to all other forms of killing during war as victims of assassination are identified by name, sought out and killed. But is naming names enough to condemn assassination? Repudiating named killings requires a moral argument that invokes self-defense during wartime. Assassination not only runs afoul of calculations of expected utility; it is also difficult to defend as a form of self-defense.

2.   Assassination: Named Killings and the Problem of Self-Defense During War

If one has a right to kill in self-defense during wartime, why not a corollary right to assassinate, not by treachery but simply by naming and hunting down an armed adversary? As attractive as the argument might seem, assassination is not easily justified as a form self-defense, and is confounded by the justification of self-defensive killing in general and killing during war in particular.

A.   Killing in Self-Defense

Paradigm cases of self-defense pit two individuals against one another, an attacker (A) and a victim (V). Additional players include bystanders (B) who can intervene at relatively little cost. To justify V's right to kill A, as well as B's obligation to intervene and also kill A, A must be "materially non-innocent," that is, he must pose an immediate and otherwise unavoidable grave or mortal threat that cannot be eliminated by less violent means. Clearly, as many philosophers have pointed out, this is insufficient: moral conditions of fault, responsibility and intention are also required. A's action must be morally unjustified and without just cause (an unprovoked or disproportionate reaction, for example), A must intend to kill or gravely injure V, and A must be responsible for his action (un-coerced and without diminished moral capacities). Under these circumstances V may kill A because A is also "morally non-innocent" so that A's right to life is either lost, suspended or overridden by either V's right to life and/or his right to self-defense.[13]

As intuitively convincing as these cases may be, hard cases emerge when A is morally innocent (an innocent aggressor or IA.) Here the case for self-defense weakens. Lack of intent or diminished moral capacity, for example, may require V (or B) to disable rather than kill an AI even at some risk to himself.[14] In some cases soldiers may also be innocent aggressors, particularly when they are forced to fight or convinced they are fighting for a just cause. In other cases, they may not be aggressors at all, but armed victims defending themselves. If a theory of self-defense is to have any bite at all, A does not have the right of self-defense, only V. Why then may aggressors who happen to be soldiers kill victims who are soldiers? References to moral and material non-innocence do not seem to help.

B.   Killing Soldiers In Self-Defense

Ordinarily, soldiers may be killed in self-defense under circumstances that far outstrip those that constrain ordinary self-defense. Any soldier may be killed during armed conflict at any time whether armed or unarmed, whether posing a grievous threat or idly standing by, and whether innocent or non-innocent. Even when soldiers threaten one another materially, it seems clear that in many cases they are innocent aggressors. Many are conscripted, while soldiers on both sides are convinced of the justice of the their cause. Material and moral non-innocence no longer characterise aggressors. Nevertheless, we are certain that soldiers may legitimately kill one another during war. Why is this so?

To answer this question we often refer to the idea of collective or corporate non-innocence to explain a soldier's right to kill in self-defense and then reason from the domestic analogy. States fighting one another assume a status similar to individuals. Victim states attacked by aggressor states have the right to self-defense in the same way that ordinary victims do, an entirely coherent idea enshrined in Article 51 of the UN Charter. This tells us nothing, however, about how members of each state's armed forces assume the right to self-defense that only the state seems to possess. Here, one is inclined to look toward an argument that hinges on some limited form of agency or collective identity so that the justification for self-defense during wartime lies in the changing conception of the self. Just wars are waged by soldiers who defend their community against aggressors. Ordinarily, these aggressors are other nations not specific individuals. Nations threaten one another so that the moral and material conditions that justify self-defense apply to states not to soldiers. But soldiers are those who have to fight and kill. How can their roles be justified? The answer emerges when we view the citizen/soldier as an extension of his community. When the community is threatened it is as if the soldier himself is also threatened. This is a bit of a stretch but it partly restores the conditions necessary for an individual to kill in self-defense. However, the conditions are only vaguely restored for the soldier is not threatened in the same, concrete way the community is.

A vague justification that leans heavily on an individual's identification with his or her political community might be all that is possible to justify his role in the fighting because killing during war can never attain the degree of specificity that characterises ordinary self-defense. So the soldier who fights can only do so when his individuality is subsumed by the collective identity of his community. He fights to protect his community, not himself. The same transformation occurs on the other side as well, rendering individual soldiers amorphous, fighting each other not as individuals but as agents of their respective polities. As agents they act not in their own name but in the collective name of their community.

A collective or agency driven account of a soldier's right to kill in self-defense does not, however, explain the moral innocence that we often attribute to soldiers of an aggressor nation. An invading German soldier shoots at a defending Pole in September 1939. The Pole shoots back and misses. The German returns fire and kills the defender. There are very few cases of clear cut aggression in human history but Germany's invasion of Poland is one of them. Nevertheless, every Allied soldier knew that his German counterpart has a right to self-defense even if his nation does not. But if the state is not innocent then its emissaries seem equally culpable. If soldiers gain their right to self-defense by their affiliation with the state, then they should lose it when the state is an aggressor.

One possible answer to this difficulty is the empirical observation that it is usually difficult to disentangle the claims of defenders and aggressors from one another, much less convince any soldier that his claim is not just. Nevertheless it is important to note that even defenders who have no doubt that they are facing an unjust aggressor, still believe that their adversaries command a right to self-defense. Part of the answer must be that the defenders attribute a certain moral innocence to enemy soldiers. But this just reverses the problem. If enemy soldiers are non-innocent then they have no right to self-defense. But if they are morally innocent, and this is a decisive factor, then enemy soldiers have such an overwhelming right to self-defense that the *defenders'* right to self-defense is now called into question. The idea of moral innocence does not help us understand a soldier's right to kill.

To solve this difficulty, Zohar suggests that any resort to individual morality to explain a soldier's right to kill during wartime only leads to confusion.[15] True, but the solution he proposes – a compromise between an individualistic and collective moral perspective – is only partially helpful. Rather than reconcile the two, Zohar is content to allow them a tense coexistence. The inability to reduce our intuitions about self-defense, whether personal or collective, to a single set of coherent principles is the singly most maddening aspect of the contemporary discussion of self-defense. Zohar's bifurcation captures an important aspect of moral reality, suggesting that soldiers may kill one another because each "participates" in the war effort as a member of a non-innocent "enemy people" yet still retain some measure of innocence as individuals. While this might clarify our intuition that enemy soldiers are both guilty and innocent, it does little to ease the friction between the moral status of the aggressor state (which in the eyes of the defender is always non-innocent) and the moral status of the attacking soldier (who may be innocent or non-innocent). These perplexities also confound our understanding of assassination.

C.   Assassinating Soldiers in Self-Defense

Despite the difficulty one encounters trying to establish the necessary and sufficient conditions that frame a soldier's right to kill in self-defense, one may defeat the argument for assassination by demonstrating that self-defense hinges on a single necessary condition, namely anonymity. Whether one chooses to describe the complex relationship between the state and the citizen or soldier in terms of agency or collective identity, each presupposes a firm measure of anonymity. Collective identity evokes the idea of peoplehood, a corporate concept that endows a large group of individuals characterised by a common language, history, culture and/or territory with ontological standing of its own. Apart from the aggregate interests of its members, political communities so characterised seek to perpetuate a variety of interests that include identity, self-respect, language, culture and norms. Collectives fight when threatened and members fight as embodiments of the whole, each substituting collective interests for self-interest. In the crudest sense the individual sacrifices his interests and identity to the state. Anonymity follows from this self-effacement and is an essential part of this process.

Agency, unlike collective identity, preserves the identity of the parties but renders the agent's identity irrelevant. It offers a better mechanism for understanding a soldier's right to self-defense because agents do not necessarily bear the guilt of corporate wrong doing. Collective identity, on the other hand, assumes the soldier's identification with the state so that the state's guilt might coherently devolve to the individual. Agency is a bilateral relationship between a principal and an agent, the former granting rights and authorities to the latter to undertake certain acts. A state, then, authorises certain individuals, i.e. soldiers, to kill on its behalf regardless of personal threat in the same way that a corporation authorises its agents to implement its business policy. In neither case are corporate agents responsible for actions undertaken in the corporate name unless, individually, they act illegally. Corporate agents may not commit fraud nor may soldiers violate humanitarian law without incurring individual culpability. Otherwise, their identities, interests and attributes are irrelevant. Agents have names of course, but they do not act in their own name and attributing responsibility to them by name only creates confusion and misguided culpability.

When the principal is the state, the individual is authorised to kill members of another state who belong to its army regardless of the level of personal threat. A state's right to wage war is a matter of international law, independent of a state's right to compel its citizens to act in certain ways, an authority granted by positive law. When a state determines that certain interests are threatened (including its national honor) it may call upon the armed forces to implement policy. Each state, aggressor and defender alike, authorises certain groups of individuals – its soldiers – to kill one another. We may be tempted to speak in terms of rights, the right to self-defense and the right to kill in self-defense, or in terms of moral and material non-innocence but these only tend to complicate the issues by forcing the counterexamples described earlier. Nations go to war for a wide variety of reasons many of which are rarely grave, existential threats. When they do, they command the authority to compel their citizens to behave in certain ways and, in general, their citizens usually do. Soldiers confronting an adversary simply know that they are authorised to kill enemy soldiers and that enemy soldiers are authorised to kill them. Killing soldiers is not murder (for the homicide is legal) but nor is it personal self-defense.

Whether driven by agency or collective identity the individual soldier necessarily remains depersonalised. He either loses his personal identity or finds it set aside as he goes about his business of soldiering. The difficulty of assassination is its need to re-personalise the state of war and move individual identity, culpability and responsibility to center stage. Once named, victims of assassination must be morally and materially non-innocent aggressors. Often they are not and under these circumstances assassination violates the conditions of killing in self-defense.

3.   Overriding the Ban on Assassination

As "murder by treachery" assassination must bring more good than harm to merit justification. "Ticking bombs" provide such an example. As "named killing" assassination is only justified when the victims are morally and materially non-innocent. Terrorists, but not all terrorists, meet these criteria.

A.   Ticking Bombs: The Argument from Necessity

In conventional war and under rare circumstances, a belligerent may appeal to "supreme necessity" to defend unjust means of warfare. In the most famous instances, nations without any alternative means to avert an existential threat may successfully invoke supreme necessity to defend massive destruction of civilian populations.[16] Similarly, although on a more restrained scale, jurists in Israel, for example, defend torture to elicit information by the same reference to necessity.[17] "Ticking bombs", immediate and mortal threats to innocent civilian lives are the classic example. To meet such threats, Israeli authorities defend the use of torture or "moderate physical pressure" to elicit vital information when no other means are available. Aptly termed the "necessity defense" it is localised version of the argument from supreme necessity and exempts a person from criminal responsibility if he acts "in order to avoid consequences which could not otherwise be avoided and which would have inflicted grievous harm or injury [and] provided that he did no more harm than was reasonably necessary [nor] disproportionate to the harm avoided.[18] The necessity defense is not unique to Israel although its use there is one of the rare instances where justifications for individual actions are drawn on to defend political or military policy.[19]

Necessity in this case is not "supreme" necessity because there is no existential threat to the entire community and while this fact alone may be sufficient to defeat the necessity defense without further argument, it seems reasonable to allow one to invoke the necessity defense commensurate with proportionality. Assassination, then, may be defensible in rare cases of overriding necessity.[20] While this would forbid obliterating Palestinian cities to raise the probability of preventing a terrorist attack, it might allow a banned practice like assassination, whether a named killing or murder by treachery, to eliminate a reasonably certain threat to innocent civilians.

It is important to keep in mind, however, that the necessity defense cannot legalise assassination. It only provides a defense for illegal acts. Extenuating circumstances only offer grounds for mitigating punishment. The necessity defense is not, nor can it be, grounds for a blanket endorsement for illegal forms of warfare. On the contrary, it reinforces the rule prohibiting assassination with the hope that violations will be rare and defenses solidly grounded.

If assassination is ever to be defensible, then, it must meet the general conditions that the necessity defense demands. First, assassination is a measure of last resort taken in the face of an immediate and otherwise unavoidable mortal threat to innocent civilians. This restricts the illegal act to one of absolute necessity, limits its use and arrests the slide toward those forms of assassination that have no strategic value - such as retribution - or unnecessarily harm civilians. Assassination therefore must be primarily interdictive and not aim toward punishment. Second, it must be certain that that the victim is a key figure whose death will achieve the desired results. This demands knowledge that the suspect is not only preparing an attack but is so instrumentally involved that only his death can prevent it. Third, one must be fairly certain that assassination would accomplish its strategic goal and therefore leave little chance that the mission itself and/or subsequent retaliation would take more lives that the assassination saves. Finally, it must be remembered that costs can be contained only if assassination is used on rare occasions. This attenuates, but does not entirely dissolve, the moral repugnance associated with assassination. Once widespread, the value of assassination is defeated by the cost to mutual trust and the fierce and inimical resistance it engenders if and when facilitated by collaborators and informers.

B.   Assassinating   Terrorists: Self-Defense   or   "Punitive" Assassination?

Named killings can be justified in self-defense if the aggressor is morally and materially non-innocent. This suggests three categories to consider. At one extreme are those soldiers fighting in a conventional war who are materially and morally non-innocent and, as such, they *cannot* be justifiably assassinated. As nations fight one another, the material threat that soldiers pose to one another is generally irrelevant as their identity and individual welfare is subsumed by the collective. Moreover, any soldier's commitment to his cause and willingness to respect humanitarian law grant him a firm measure of moral innocence. Material and, in particular, moral innocence contribute to feelings of dishonor and revulsion often associated with wartime assassination independent of its effect on subsequent peace making efforts.

Opposite conventional soldiers are international terrorists who are neither materially nor morally innocent. Qaeda terrorists, for example, target civilians in clear and willful violation of humanitarian law leading some to suggest that they may be readily assassinated in self-defense. This immediately raises questions about assassinating any terrorist. "If the United States can fire a missile at an al Qaeda leader in Yemen," asks the Washington Post, "why shouldn't Israel aim one at Yasser Arafat in Ramallah, or Russia target exiled Chechen leaders in Turkey?" The relevant differences, the Post points out, are "fundamental:" Al Qaeda lacks affiliation to any national cause that can provide any basis for *casus belli* or self-defense, has no political leaders to speak of, nor seeks political compromise or accommodation.[21]

These differences imply that joining a national cause bestows a special status on combatants, an assumption that just war theory and international law support. This has two implications when considering assassination. First, Qaeda terrorists, in the absence of national affiliation, are simply bands of individuals threatening others. In many ways this makes them nothing more than criminals and while this deserves further attention the important point is that Qaeda terrorists are always a material threat. Their operatives cannot claim, as ordinary soldiers sometimes can, that they are materially innocent. Second, justice and innocence in war depends upon a recognised political cause that Al Qaeda does not possess thereby undermining any claim of moral innocence. As a result their operatives are both materially and morally non-innocent and may be killed under the conditions inherent in justified self-defense. Given that the fight against international terrorism is also generally free of the corrosive effects of collaboration, there should be little compunction about hunting down Qaeda militants who are planning military operations against civilians in other nations.

Somewhere between conventional soldiers and international terrorists are those like Palestinians and Chechens. Looking at the utility of assassination it is clear that Chechens and Palestinians cannot usually be assassinated without the assistance of local collaborators, without harming civilians, without precipitating a vicious response, and without jeopardising the trust necessary to subsequently make peace. However, there is also no doubt that their moral non-innocence is tempered by their national cause. In other words, it is not only costly to assassinate these terrorists but it is also true that they do not represent the same kind of material and moral threat that characterises international terrorists. The question remains whether a national cause is sufficient to make a combatant morally innocent in order to preclude assassination. The answer is no. Moral innocence requires a just cause *and* just means. One generally assumes that soldiers party to a conventional war will fight by just means and respect humanitarian law. Their innocence, therefore, hinges on the perceived justice of their cause. Combatants fighting in violation of humanitarian law, however, cannot lay claim to moral innocence. Thus a Palestinian or Chechen terrorist is less non-innocent than an Qaeda terrorist although not sufficiently so to shield him from assassination when there are no overriding utilitarian considerations. This assessment may change, however, if terrorists pursue conventional means of fighting by targeting combatants, for example, and by making an effort to limit civilian casualties when they do so.

Assassinating terrorists, however, is not the same as punishing terrorists for prior misdeeds. Defensive assassination targets individuals in order to prevent imminent harm. Punitive assassination targets those accused of crimes committed in the past. At first glance, punitive assassination is nothing more than "extrajudicial execution." Like torture, it is unequivocally banned by UN conventions without regard for "a state of war or threat of war, internal political instability or any other public emergency."[22] In theory, few dispute this prohibition. Most nations support the ban on extra-judicial execution with a clear understanding that it grossly infringes upon civil rights and dangerously undermines law and order. In practice, however, the issue is more complicated. While arrest and trial are preferable to extra-judicial execution, governments headed by the Palestinian Authority or Taliban do not readily extradite suspected terrorists. This leaves nations like Israel or the US with little choice but to arrest suspects themselves. This creates no ground, however, for execution or punitive assassination. While law enforcement officials may legitimately use lethal force if threatened with grievous harm, they have no right to execute suspects when "operational difficulties," as Israel's Chief of Staff once tried to argue, "make it too dangerous to capture and bring suspects to trial."[23]

Yet the argument for punitive assassination cannot be dismissed without considering the larger place of punishment in warfare. Nations wage war to punish aggressors as well as to repulse them. The Americans not only wage war to dismantle terrorist infrastructures but to punish terrorists like bin Laden for what they have done and to compel the states harboring terrorists to hand them over for justice. States refusing this call may be attacked as agents hostile to the interests of the United States. This is the logic for attacking Afghanistan. Not only is the US set to ferret out terrorism but to punish the Afghan government for abetting terrorism in the first place.

Punishing an aggressor state by sanction, territorial loss and/or the ravages of war remains an integral part of the international order. Lack of a judge leaves nations free to pursue justice and exact punishment. Extending this right to pursue individuals creates two distinct categories of extra-judicial assassination: one domestic and one international. Domestic extra-judicial assassination is ruled out as an affront to law and order, but international extra-judicial assassination is a different issue. If a criminal state may be punished, why not some of its citizens?

In many ways this brings us back to the issue of self-defense. Because war is directed against states, and soldiers are only its agents, then soldiers themselves do not bear the guilt of the aggressor state. Thus soldiers may not be punished for fighting. They may be killed in the course of the war, but they may not be punished following capture and may not, if the arguments above are correct, be assassinated. Instead, they may only be punished for personal misdeeds. Most often, the state to which they owe their allegiance is the agent of their punishment. However, this is not always true. In fact, the closest analogy to terrorists are war criminals, that is, participants in an armed conflict who violate humanitarian law. War criminals are judged by other states, usually the victors. But the point is that they are judged; a suspected war criminal cannot be summarily executed but must be captured and tried. Ironically, he may be killed during hostilities even intentionally (e.g. by bombing a concentration camp) yet we recoil from hunting him down and killing him for his past deeds. The logic is the same of self-defense and assassination. Killing is permissible when soldiers are anonymous, once named they may only be killed if materially and morally non-innocent. Terrorists actively targeting civilians and unaffiliated with a national cause are material and moral threats. Terrorists who admit their roles or whose criminal acts can be ascertained by other forms of evidence might be tried *in absentia* and executed. But this is no longer assassination, nor is it extrajudicial execution but the only sort of due process possible when hostile states harbor terrorists. Punishment in this way does what assassination can't: it circumvents the condition of anonymity that permits killing during war and allows named killing of specific individuals.

4.   Conclusion

Low intensity wars, limited conflicts, and struggles between asymmetrical forces bring alternative forms of warfare to the fore. Nations fighting guerillas or insurgents, but particularly terrorist groups intentionally targeting noncombatants, are faced with very difficult questions of appropriate response. The stronger power cannot, in good conscience, target noncombatants on the other side. The force of international law and the customary norms of conduct incumbent upon peace loving nations of the world community are just too strong. On the other hand, stronger nations always face the risk of a response that is perceived to be disproportionate leading to cries of injustice from the other side and expressions of sympathy from some in the world community, precisely the response terrorists seek when they target civilians in the first place.

In this context, assassination has much to offer. It avoids the pitfalls of disproportionality, nondiscrimination (by targeting only the terror suspect) and the fear of violating noncombatant immunity. Yet it meets with particular outrage and rightly so. Apart from the harm it poses to civilians and civilian communities as collaborators are recruited to facilitate assassination, assassination impinges upon the relationship between combatants, a category often overlooked in contemporary discussion of ethics and war. When combatants are legitimate, in the narrow sense that they belong to some military hierarchy and generally adhere to humanitarian law, assassination of a adversary prompts a particular outrage because it undermines the very nature of self-defensive killing together with some of the basic institutions of trust that operate during wartime. When adversaries are criminals then assassination smacks of extrajudicial execution, a violation of basic international norms that nations in good standing in the world community can no more violate than noncombatant immunity. In either case, the stronger adversary faces a difficult dilemma. Most often,it cannot respond without accusations of disproportionality, nondiscrimination and harm to civilians. When it tries to minimise these by resorting to tactics like assassination it runs up against similarly well entrenched institutions of war and peace. This places stronger adversaries in a firm quandary that may be resolved partly by the judicious use of assassination but more likely means that grossly asymmetrical national conflicts cannot be solved or readily addressed by military means.

Notes

1. J.M. Spaight, *War Rights on Land* (London: Macmillan, 1911):8 (emphasis added).

2. Emer de Vattel, *The Law of Nations or the Principles of Natural Law*, translated by Charles G Fenwick, (Geneva: Slatkine Reprints, Henry Dunant Institute, 1983 [1758]): Book III, chapter 8, para. 155.

3. See, General Orders 100 (*Lieber's Code*), (1863: Article 148), *US Army Field Manual* (US Army 1956: Field Manual 27-10) and L.C. Green, *The Contemporary Law of Armed Conflict* (Manchester: Manchester University Press, 1993):197. An executive order (Executive Order 12333,

1981) prohibits intelligence services from assassinating terrorists and others.

4. International Committee of the Red Cross, *Protocol I to the Geneva Conventions of 12 August 1949, and relating to the Protection of Victims of International Armed Conflict, 8 June, 1977.* (Geneva, International Committee of the Red Cross, 1977, accessed November 18, 2002): Article 37, http://www.icrc.org/; internet. Protocol 1 extends the prohibition against perfidy, already codified in the 1907 Hague Convention (Article 23b) to non-international conflicts.

5. International Committee of the Red Cross. *Commentary, Protocol I to the Geneva Conventions of 12 August 1949, and relating to the Protection of Victims of International Armed Conflicts, 8 June 1977.* (Geneva, International Committee of the Red Cross, 1977, accessed November 18, 2002): http://www.icrc.org/; Internet. Paragraph 1500.
1. Ibid.

6.ibid.

7. Michael L. Gross, "Fighting By Other Means In The Mideast: A Critical Analysis Of Israel's Assassination Policy. *Political Studies* 50, (2002): forthcoming.

8. Guy Bechor, "Liquidating the Liquidations," *Yidiot Aharonot* (Hebrew) 27 November 2000. Amos Harel, "Security Brass: Targeted Killings Don't Work, No Military Solution To Terror," *Haaretz* 19 December, 2001.

9. Gross, "Fighting by Other Means."

10. Yizhar Be'er and Saleh 'Abdel-Jawad, *Collaborators in the Occupied Territories: Human Rights Abuses and Violations* (Jerusalem: B'Tselem, (1994); Andrew Rigby, *The Legacy of the Past: The Problem of Collaborators and the Palestinian Case* (Jerusalem: Palestinian Academic Society for the Study of International Affairs, 1997).

11. Saleh Abdel-Jawad," The Classification and Recruitment of Collaborators" in *The Phenomenon of Collaborators in Palestine Proceedings of a Passia Workshop* (Jerusalem: Palestinian Academic Society for the Study of International Affairs, 2001):18.

12. Beer and Abdel-Jawad, 164.

13. Judith Jarvis Thomson, "Self-Defense and Rights" in *Rights Restitution and Risk: Essays in Moral Theory* (Cambridge: Harvard University Press, (1986).

14. Phillip Montague, "Self-Defense And Choosing Between Lives, *Philosophical Studies* 40 (1981):207-219. Jeff McMahan, "Innocence, Self-Defense And Killing In War*" Journal Of Political Philosophy* 2 (1994):193-221; Seumas Miller "Killing in Self-defense" *Public Affairs Quarterly* 7 (1993): 325-339.

15. Noam Zohar, "Collective War And Individualistic Ethics: Against The Conscription Of "Self-Defense, *Political Theory* 21 (1993):606-622.

16. See Walzer's defense of Britain's bombing of Germany in 1943 (Michael Walzer, *Just and Unjust Wars: A Moral Argument with Historical Illustrations* (New York: Basic Books, 1977): 255-63.

17. PCATI (Public Committee Against Torture in Israel) v The State of Israel 1999, HC 5100/94, para 8-13.

18. Israel's Penal Law, section 22, cited in Landau Commission (para. 3.11), "Commission of Inquiry into the Methods of Investigation of the General Security Service Regarding Hostile Terrorist Activity," *Israel Law Review*, 2, 3(1989):146-188.

19. For a review of the necessity defense in other nations see David Cohen "The Development of the Modern Doctrine of Necessity: A Comparative Critique," eds. Albin Eser and George P. Fletcher *Justification and Excuse: Comparative Aspects*, volume 2, (Dobbs Ferry, N.Y.: Transnational Juris Publications, Inc., 1987): 973-1001.

20. Gross, "Fighting by Other Means."

21. A Strike in Yemen, *The Washington Post*, 6 November, 2002.

22. UN High Commission on Human Rights, *United Nations Principles on the Effective Prevention and Investigation of Extra Legal, Arbitrary and Summary Executions, Economic and Social Council, 1989/65,*

(accessed   on   November   18,   2002)   available   from
http://www.unhchr.ch/html/menu3/b/54.htm; Internet.

23. Gideon Alon, "Mofaz: IDF Jurist Approves Killings, *Ha'aretz*, 11
January 2001, quoted in Yael Stein *Position Paper: Israel's Assassination
Policy: Extra Judicial Executions*, (Jerusalem: B'Tselem, The Israeli
Information Center for Human Rights in the Occupied Territories,
2001):2.

Civil Disobedience and Military Ethics

Asa Kasher

1.   Introduction

About twenty years ago, I met, for the first time, IDF (Israel Defence Force) officers and NCOs who have refused to participate in military activity, in Lebanon, though the law of the state and the civil tradition expected them to do so. Those were the days of the 1982 Operation Peace of Galillee, later to turn into the Lebanon War, which lasted until 1985 in one form and until 2000 in another one.

About a year ago, I met the leadership of a newly established group of IDF reserve officers and NCOs who now refuse to participate in military activities, in some of the territories that have been controlled by Israel since the 1967 Six Day War, earlier governed by either Jordan or Egypt.

The issues under debate have significantly changed. In 1982, the major issue was whether the military operation waged by Israel could be described as a just war, according to any reasonable variant of the Doctrine of Just War (cf. Walzer, 1977; Regan, 1996). In 2002, the major issues were two: First, the political future of the territories beyond the "Green Line", the border of Israel before the Six Day War. Second, the proper political reaction to the Palestinian strategy of terrorist attacks on Israelis, in Israel and in the Israeli settlements in those territories (cf. Gross, 2002; Westhusing, 2003).

Under both circumstances, soldiers who refused to participate in military activities justified their acts of refusal on various grounds, including political opposition and conscientious refusal. We are presently interested just in those acts of refusal that have been defended or are defensible on grounds of *justified civil disobedience*.

The purpose of the present paper is to find out whether a philosophical conception of the nature and justification of civil disobedience, which was naturally applicable to circumstances of the type of the Lebanon War, is also applicable to utterly different circumstances, of the type we now face in Israel. Our affirmative answer will lead us to a negative evaluation of present acts of refusal *qua* civil disobedience, particularly when it takes place within the military framework.

2.   Civil Disobedience

Our starting points are several major components of Rawls'
conception of civil disobedience, as presented, discussed and defended in
detail in (the first edition[1] of) *A Theory of Justice* (Rawls, 1971, sections
55,57,59; for earlier presentations that Rawls used to a significant extent,
see his footnote on p. 364 and Bedau, 1961). Generally speaking, civil
disobedience is "a public, non-violent, conscientious yet political act
contrary to law usually done with the aim of bringing about a change in
the law or policies of the government" (*ibid.,* p. 364). Indeed, certain
conditions should obtain for such an act contrary to law to be morally
justified. The fully-fledged conception of civil disobedience consists of an
articulated presentation of the definition and a specification of conditions
that have to obtain for an act to be one of justified civil disobedience.
Several ingredients of the present conception are of particular significance.
     First, an act of civil disobedience is justified only if it is an
attempt to defend the democratic ideal of the state, when and where some
of its fundamental principles have been violated by the regime. Unpopular
traffic regulations and objectionable governmental taxing policies do not
usually involve violations of some fundamental principles of the
democratic regime. Sending conscripts or reserve troops to carry out
military missions, in which they jeopardise their life, for reasons that are
not confined to self-defence of the citizenry and its state, is usually an
example of such a violation.
     Secondly, an act of civil disobedience is in a sense, a symbolic
one. When one participates in a demonstration, carrying a banner that
manifests a stance, one performs a symbolic act, in the same sense of the
term. Demonstrations and acts of civil disobedience are intended to draw
the attention of some people, persuade them, motivate activities on their
part. Such acts are instrumental vehicles of expression.
     Thirdly, an act of civil disobedience involves a violation of the
law. Indeed, for an illegal act to count as one of civil disobedience the two
previous conditions should also obtain. Hence, the illegality of the act
should be compatible with its being a symbolic act performed in an
attempt to defend the democratic ideal. The Rule of Law principle is part
of that ideal, and acts of civil disobedience do not follow it. Genuine acts
of civil disobedience involve real rather than apparent violations of the
law. Therefore, even acts of justified civil disobedience are *prima facie*
punishable.
     In order to grasp the nature of the necessary preconditions that
have to obtain, for an act to be of justified civil disobedience, it would be

helpful to use the contract model, which anyway underlies much of the assumed theory of justice (cf. Wolff, 1977; Kukathas and Pettit, 1990). The question, for the contract analogy, would be as follows: You are party to a contract that is fair and reasonable. You fulfil your contractual duties and would very much like the contract to stay binding and effective. Some of the other parties to the contract go on breaching it, in a major way. What may be done under such circumstances? Particularly, on what conditions, would it be reasonable for you to breach the contract in an attempt to bring it about that the other parties do not breach the contract in a major way anymore?

Rationality requires of planned acts to be "most effective" and performed "at least cost". Since acts of civil disobedience have the objective of defending the ideal of democracy and enhancing its embodiment, they are required to be effective in their prospects of changing the situation in the right direction. Moreover, since acts of civil disobedience involve violations of law, which is a "cost" in terms of the democratic form of life, they are also required to involve the "least cost" in those terms. As will be presently shown, under current circumstances, these two preconditions of justified civil disobedience do not obtain.

3.   Democratic Infrastructure

The democratic ideal involves not just a conception of human liberties and rights, but also some established practices and suitable institutions that make it possible for the citizen to enjoy one's liberties and exercise one's rights. Those practices and institutions form the *infrastructure* of a democratic regime. Without such an infrastructure, civil liberties are bound to be very restricted and civil rights insignificant.

Consequently, in the affairs of a democracy, attention should be paid not only to the proclaimed adherence to some conception of civil liberties and rights, but also to the current conditions of the democratic infrastructure. Institution, maintenance and enhancement of a democratic regime all involve constant protection and development of the democratic infrastructure underlying the regime. Damage to an ingredient of a major element of the infrastructure could be more significant than that caused by infringement of some law, command or regulation.

There are two elements of the democratic infrastructure that pertain to the situation under consideration. Both are necessary elements of citizen protection in a democratic regime. Under usual circumstances, a citizen is always a possible victim of criminal attempts to render him or her unable to enjoy some liberty to the fullest extent prescribed by the fair arrangements of an (approximately) just state. Under belligerency circumstances, a citizen is always a possible victim of hostile attempts to kill him or his beloved ones, destroy their property, or oppress some or all of the citizens.

Facing the first, *internal* threat, a democratic regime provides its citizenry with various means of protection. One of them is the practice of the *Rule of Law*, as supported by an effective system of law enforcement. The end of such a practice is to create around each citizen a societal envelope in which one is able to enjoy one's liberties and exercise one's rights, at least to a very significant extent. The means of such a practice are (a) a legal system, which sets the formal confines of behaviour, according to the moral principles of democracy; (b) a system of professional law enforcement bodies, e.g., police forces and courts; and (c) a consensually practiced commitment of the citizens and the authorities to be law abiding.

Facing the second, *external* threat, a democratic regime renders its citizenry defence services, by another variety of means, including effective professional intelligence and military forces. Peace is, indeed, most desirable, being an effective if not the ultimate way of protecting the citizens from horrors of war, and it is, therefore, the moral duty of each regime and government to pursue it. However, as long as there is an external threat, on the life, welfare or independence of citizens, it is the moral duty of a democratic state to maintain an effective system of intelligence and military forces.

Accordingly, inflicting significant damage to the practice of the Rule of Law, which is a necessary element of the internal defence system of the citizenry, or to the effectiveness of the intelligence and military forces, which is a necessary element of the external defence system of the citizenry, is to significantly weaken the democratic regime.

4.   Damage to the Rule of Law

A premeditated violation of the law is often not only an endpoint of a process of planning, evaluation and performance, but also a starting point of a process of influence and propagation. An act can set a conspicuous example, enhance attitudes to behave in certain ways and diminish adherence to common practices.

An act of civil disobedience is, by its very nature, a premeditated violation of the law. When it is publicly presented as related to a politically debated issue, it is bound to create the danger of setting an example for apparently legitimate violation of the law on political grounds, of enhancing attitudes of disregard and even contempt towards principles and institutions of democracy, and of diminishing adherence to democratic practices of common decision making.

The political culture of Israel is by and large democratic, however it is not strongly so. A few years ago, it enabled an ordinary citizen to assassinate the prime minister and minister of defence Rabin. In the years that have elapsed since then, the attitude to use violence within the framework of an internal political debate has not disappeared. In certain respects it has even become stronger.

Hence a movement of civil disobedience, being a movement the practice of which involves violation of law on political grounds, contributes to a dangerous social drift that weakens the democratic defence system of the Rule of Law rather than strengthen it.

Notice the important difference between the 1982 situation and the present one. Before 1982, Israel had not experienced an organised violation of law, on political grounds, that led to a change of the government or its major policies. However, since 1995, Israel has already experienced a period of organised violations of the law, on political grounds, that led to the assassination of Rabin and to a major change of government and policies.

5.   Damage to Effective Military Defence

Military victory cannot be gained without troops and officers willing to participate in jeopardous combat activity. Thus, effective military defence is possible only when and where there are sufficiently many courageous citizens ready to face fatal danger in pursuit of military victory.

What are the roots of courage, that soldiers manifest in their behaviour in battle? Naïve answers ascribe courage to some general motivation, such as patriotism or military formalities and customs, or to some particular motivation, such as revenge. Although such mental and emotional forces can play a role in combat behaviour, they are neither necessary nor sufficient for manifestation of courage. Here is another explanation, as phrased by the former Prime Minister of Australia, the Hon Mr Paul Keating, at the Entombment of the Unknown Soldier at the Australian War Memorial, in 1993, with respect to the WWI ANZAC legend: "It is a legend of free and independent spirits whose discipline derived less from military formalities and customs than from the bonds of mateship and the demands of necessity". Military studies in different fields and states have shown that the same explanation holds for combat activity in general.

Comradeship is an essential value of military ethics. (It is one of the 11 values of the 1994 IDF Code of Ethics; cf. Kasher, 1996) The essence of comradeship is an attitude of mutual trust of utmost depth. The soldier entrusts his life in the hands of his comrades, when he is under enemy fire. In the life of a soldier, comradeship means he is never alone, in the battlefield (and elsewhere too), come what may. Hence, damage to the common sense of comradeship among troops and officers is a blow to the very ability of military combat units to act as such and accomplish their missions. Such a weakening of the military ability to gain victory in a war of self-defence is a weakening of the defence with which the state can provide its citizenry. It is, therefore, a weakening of the democratic regime.

Self evidently, Israel is in need of maintaining a strong military force. Acts of civil disobedience that take the form of refusal of reserve officers and NCOs to serve within the framework of their combat units cause damage to the necessary sense of military comradeship and thereby inflict damage on the democratic regime, which owes its citizenry an effective military force of self-defence.

Notice, again, the difference between the 1982 situation and the present one. In 1982 soldiers were puzzled by the refusal of some of their comrades to serve in Lebanon and tried to understand it on the background of a debate as to whether the ongoing war was just or unjust. Nowadays, soldiers have a sense of cracked comradeship, given the broad and justified depiction of the present war, held against homicide bombing and other terrorist atrocities, as a just war, regardless of what they think is the desired solution of the conflict.

6.   Minimising Costs

An act of civil disobedience is intended to be in support of the related democratic regime. Therefore, since it involves a violation of law, which as such inflicts damages on the democratic regime, it should be planned and performed with a manifest effort to minimise the inflicted damages.

Under the present circumstances, a refusal to serve in a military combat unit as a reserve officer or NCO is not an act that minimises damages. First, there is no reason to assume that citizens who are reserve officers or NCOs cannot perform acts of civil disobedience outside the confines of their military units and the military in general. In the Vietnam War period, acts of civil disobedience took different forms, not necessarily within the framework of military activity. Such alternative acts of civil disobedience do not harm in any way the necessary sense of military comradeship. Secondly, acts of civil disobedience can be performed on a distinctly individual level, dissociated from any movement or organisation that support or even preach disobedience. The contribution of an individual act of civil disobedience to a public attitude of diminishing the Rule of Law when political issues are under debate is less significant than that of an organised group that nurtures a conception of civil disobedience and enhances the apparent legitimacy of violating the law for political purposes. Finally, on some occasions, an act of civil disobedience can have more dangerous effects, even mortal ones. If a person refuses to serve within the framework of his combat unit, the unit is not going to be sent home and the mission is not going to be called off. The soldier who did not report is going to be replaced by another one. Since their missions are of a dangerous nature, it may happen that since one soldier refused to serve, it was another one who was injured or even fell in action. Acts of civil disobedience, which have to be non-violent, should never cast a shadow on anyone's life, all the more so, when their topic of protest has to do with matters of life and death.

7. Military Reaction

Whether a certain act of civil disobedience is justified or not, the question arises as to what is the proper reaction to it. When the act takes the form of a refusal to fulfil a reserve duty in a combat unit, the question arises within the framework of military ethics, as understood and expressed by the related military force, how should the commanders of an officer or an NCO who committed such an act of civil disobedience react towards him?

To be sure, this question should be addressed whether the soldier was indicted for his refusal or not. The realm of law and the realm of military ethics are different ones and should be kept apart from each other.

Legal reaction against a soldier who has refused to report for reserve duty in a combat unit is on a par with any other legal reaction against a citizen who violated some law. First and foremost, it is intended to serve justice, in the area of law enforcement, and is, therefore, grounded on the principles of the Rule of Law. Under consideration it has mainly the past refusal, which is a violation of the law. A typical result of the process it triggers is punishment of the culprit.

Military ethics, and as a matter of fact, professional ethics in general, is of an utterly different nature. First of all, its objective is not expression of justice, in the area of law enforcement, but rather improvement of behaviour of soldiers, according to the values and norms of military ethics. Whereas a legal reaction is against the soldier, a proper ethical reaction is for the soldier and with the soldier. Under consideration, an ethical reaction has the future behaviour of the soldier. Past behaviour is only a source of lessons to be drawn with respect to the future. A typical result of a process triggered by a proper ethical reaction, if it is successful, is never punishment, but rather improvement. Indeed, a rational ethical reaction should involve an attempt to maximise ethical improvement.

Consider, for example, the case of a reserve IDF major who told me that too many acts performed by reserve soldiers had been immoral for him to be ready to report for a reserve mission that might involve similarly improper behaviour on part of his troops. I assume that at least some of the acts that upset him were unethical, according to the values and norms of the IDF Code of Ethics. Clearly, indicting him and even sending him to jail, would not have convinced him to report for his reserve duty next time he is called and would not have changed improper, unethical behaviour of any troops. On the other hand, I would redefine his assignment, at least for the time being, to be in charge of an ethical improvement project of troops of several combat units. His duty would be to collect data about unethical behaviour, analyse it and, most importantly, suggest ways for improvement of soldier behaviour in a way that enables the troops to accomplish their missions in an ethical way or at least a more ethical one. This is a better ethical reaction, since, first, it is reasonable to assume that given such an assignment a responsible officer won't refuse to serve in his combat unit and carry out his assigned ethical improvement project, and secondly, it is also reasonable to assume that such an officer will be able to improve the behaviour of at least some of the troops on circumstances of some kinds and render it ethical.

8.   Conclusion

On grounds of certain philosophical conceptions of civil disobedience, democratic infrastructure and military ethics, we tried to show that acts of civil disobedience that take the form of refusal to serve in reserve combat units cannot be justified under the present circumstances of Israel.

On the other hand, on grounds of the same conception of military ethics, we tried to show that the reaction to acts of refusal to serve in such units, when they are meant as acts of civil disobedience, should be ethical rather than legal, improvement-oriented rather than punishment-oriented.

Notes

1. In a restatement of his theory of justice (Rawls, 2001), Rawls does not discuss civil disobedience.

Bibliography

Gross, Emanuel, "Self-Defense against Terrorism – What Does it Mean? The Israeli Perspective", *Journal of Military Ethics* 1:2, 77-90, (2002).

Kasher, Asa, *Military Ethics*. Tel Aviv: MOD Publishing House. [Hebrew], (1996).

Kukathas, Chandran and Pettit, Philip, *Rawls, A Theory of Justice and its Critics*. Stanford: Stanford University Press, (1990).

Rawls, John, *A Theory of Justice*. Cambridge, MA: Harvard University Press, (1971).

Rawls, John, *Justice as Fairness, A Restatement*. Edited by Erin Kelly. Cambridge, MA and London, UK: Harvard University Press, (2001).

Regan, Richard J., *Just War: Principles and Cases*. Washington, DC: Catholic University of America Press, (1996).

Walzer, Michael , *Just and Unjust Wars*. New York: Basic Books, (1977).

Westhusing, Ted, "Taking Terrorism and ROE Seriously", *Journal of Military Ethics* 2:1, 1-19, (2003).

Wolff, Robert Paul, *Understanding Rawls*. Princeton: Princeton University Press, (1977).

* The views expressed in the present paper are personal and not official in any way.

Part III

Representations of War

The Exclusion of American Nurses from
The Imagery of Liberation

Deborah A. Gómez

I have undertaken a project concerned with American nurses who served during World War II and provided medical care to the inmates during the liberation of Nazi concentration camps. The "uncovering" (the term used in official records) of the camps presented a unique medical situation that was generally outside the experience of the medical personnel—all of the inmates had interacting pathologies in an extreme environment that required urgent action, and it is thus surprising that so little has been written about their strategies for providing medical care.[1]

The liberation of the camps appears to have been well documented: British Army and American Army Signal Corps cameramen took numerous photographs and shot reels of film.[2] Photojournalists, including Margaret Bourke-White and Lee Miller, recorded the unimaginable.[3] Images of liberation are generally of the initial period: the discovery of the camps, the survivors listless with hunger and disbelief, uniformed military personnel distributing food, Germans being forced at gunpoint to bury the thousands of dead who lay in piles on the ground, the U.S. 42nd Rainbow Division medics looking in disbelief at the dead in train cars, and in the crematoria.[4] Military doctors are seen administering medication, spraying DDT, starting intravenous lines, or looking in disbelief at the hundreds who lay at their feet. Photographs show German doctors compelled to treat those they had previously ignored and German nurses forced to wash and cleanse typhus patients. They show civilians working for the army carrying deloused patients to receiving tents of the various evacuation hospitals.[5] Photographs of General Eisenhower and twelve U.S. Congressmen inspecting the recently liberated camps of Dachau, Buchenwald, and Nordhausen were also widely published in carefully constructed shots intended to add credibility to horrific scenes of death and brutality.[6]

Liberation imagery has appeared in museum exhibitions, in documentary films, in historical texts, in articles written by and about military medical personnel, and in official publications such as that published by the U.S. Medical Department.[7] Yet, surprisingly left out of this history and visual narrative is a record of the critical and sustained role played by American nurses. Within traditional hierarchies of medical care, the female arena of nursing and their heroic efforts in the camps has been marginalised. For those who were not the beneficiaries of their care, their work has largely been ignored and unrecognised. As part of official reports they received little comment or acknowledgement.

The photographic and filmic record of liberation occupies a unique position in the documentation and presentation of the camps.[8] Unlike survivor and perpetrator testimonies that would gradually be made public in the following decades, the camera provided visual evidence of the atrocities that was immediate and widely publicised.[9] Though news of the camps had appeared in the press, such as in the American Protestant press, as early as 1942, photographs provided visual evidence that challenged those who sought to minimise or distort the nature of the camps and initiated a traumatic and on-going discourse.

Liberation imagery in many ways structured the perception and shaped the memory of what occurred in the German concentration and extermination camps.[10] At General Eisenhower's request, the U.S. government arranged for American editors and publishers to visit the recently liberated camps.[11] For three weeks in the spring of 1945, pictures of camp victims were widely published in daily newspapers in England and the United States.[12] Scenes of a brutal environment unlike anything previously covered by war reportage appeared in the popular press and percolated into the common consciousness.[13] This imagery shaped not only initial understanding of what happened, but seemed to establish a chronology and indeed, created a gendered and moralising tale.

Victorious Allied soldiers were portrayed forcibly entering the camps, looking in saddened disbelief, distributing food, and moving patients to receiving areas. Official delegations to the camps included U.S. Congressmen, editors, and chaplains. They were invited as witnesses and appear in photographs looking at the dead in the crematoria, in piles on the ground, being buried in mass pits, and facing the dazed survivors. Official photographs of their presence in the camps were recycled repeatedly.[14] What imagery exists of women shows them outside the immediate area of the camps away from the dead and dying, setting up tents, sitting quietly, or talking to survivors. And yet American nurses were there and worked in the immediate aftermath at the height of the medical crisis. Generally nurses were given charge of entire wards, had extensive and prolonged personal contact with the internees, and were thus witnesses to the consequences of the barbarity of the Nazis.

Understanding liberation imagery is a complex process. The imagery appears to offer itself as a complete record of the phenomena of the camps. Media imagery provides a unique perspective through which we can examine and reconsider the social, military, medical, and gendered history of war.

Liberation studies often focus on the early period—the discovery of the camps, the shock, the grateful survivors, and the mass burials—and not on the subsequent weeks in which medical, nutritional, and emotional support was critical in determining survival. What has been published, either by the U.S. Medical Department or in articles written by doctors who worked in the camps, rarely mentions, let alone describes, the crucial and sustained role American and indeed British nurses played.[15]

American nurses worked in evacuation and field hospitals, generally the first medical units assigned to the camps. American nurses I have interviewed who worked in the camps following liberation have repeatedly characterised the extreme emaciated condition of the patients they encountered: they had lowered bodily and mental processes, were prostrate, apathetic, had grossly impaired digestive functions, œdema of the feet, dry gangrenous toes, and depressed peripheral circulation. Severe diarrhoea, the result of tuberculosis infection of the gastrointestinal tract, was very common, caused anaemia, and often led to an aggravated dehydrated state.[16] The extreme crowding and poor lighting, language differences, and the general suspicion with which the internees regarded the medical personnel compounded an already difficult examination process. The primary problem was however, typhus, which appeared to be universal and opportunistic—a consequence of the physical burden of malnutrition and severe diarrhea.[17]

Prior to the arrival of medical personnel in the camps, a decrease in food led to severe malnutrition and incidents of cannibalism amongst the internees.[18] Crowded conditions, unburied corpses, insufficient clothing and blankets, inadequate toilet facilities, and human excreta from those too ill or weak to leave their bunks, soiled and infected the main rooms. Needless to say, these conditions led to louse-borne diseases, including typhus.[19]

Victor Maurer, the Swiss representative of the International Red Cross, attempted to inspect Dachau on 27 April 1945. Though the German Commandant refused to allow him to do so, he nonetheless was able to find out from the prisoners that approximately 15,000 inmates had died of typhus in the previous four months. Maurer negotiated with the Germans and arranged for the sentries to remain in the camp towers in order to keep the prisoners under control and from spreading the contagion to the surrounding population.[20] Within twenty-four hours of liberation DP Team 115 arrived at Dachau and began an aggressive campaign to save as many lives as possible.[21]

Typhus patients need copious amounts of water and protein, and the lack of water prior to liberation inevitably increased the death rates.[22] Once the camps were liberated internees circulated more freely and thus unknowingly facilitated the spread of the disease. Because the patients were filthy, heavily infested, covered in sores and scabies, and severely malnourished and dehydrated, it was impossible to determine initially with certainty if they had the typical petechial typhus rash. Most had tuberculosis.[23] It was also difficult to determine if the dysentery was bacterial or due to malnutrition. Selective autopsies revealed that typhus had flourished in their tubercular and malnourished bodies. The hearts of these patients was generally so pale and soft; a finger could easily penetrate it.

Of the situation, one American nurse at Dachau was overheard saying, "There is no disposition except death." [24]

Some nurses were sprayed with DDT prior to entering the camps at least once, others everyday. Some wore protective masks. One strategy was to wash their hands thoroughly and constantly. At Gusen the army removed most of the dead and set up a triage and delousing system before sending the patients to the nurses. In other instances the nurses went in and cleansed the huts with the assistance of corpsmen. It appears that none of the nurses however, contracted typhus.

Stations were set-up and American military and local civilians were enlisted in the delousing process. It proved to be slow and rapid re-infestation from other patients or clothing left in the huts was common. Some wards bathed and cleansed the inmates—others were washed with a creosote solution by civilians in "human laundries," and deloused prior to entering their barracks. Photographs of this phase of the recovery period were widely circulated. These pictures show German nurses and doctors forced to wash the patients at the cleansing stations. Photographs also show British doctors and medical students wearing full-protective clothing and American doctors and corpsmen, often with facemasks, transporting the patients. Though they worked alongside them, images of nurses are almost non-existent.

One of the most-attended photographic exhibitions of the camps was co-sponsored by Joseph Pulitzer's newspaper *Saint Louis Post-Dispatch* and the U.S. government. The exhibition, "Lest We—Or They— Forget," displayed enlarged photomurals taken at Bergen-Belsen and Dachau and was supplemented with a documentary of film footage taken by the U.S. Army Signal Corps.[25] Approximately 25,000 people filed into the Kiel Auditorium to view the photographs. The writer Susan Sontag saw a display of those photographs in a Santa Monica bookstore and wrote, "Nothing I have seen—in photographs or in real life—ever cut me as sharply, deeply, instantaneously. Indeed, it seems plausible for me to divide my life into two parts, before I saw those photographs (I was twelve) and after."[26] This exhibition, and a similar one in England, was important in shaping the public's understanding of liberation and yet missing from this exhibition were images of female medical personnel.

What imagery exists of nurses is often anecdotal and social: two memorial albums—commemorative volumes that recorded the history of evacuation hospitals from their official activation, training, through their participation in the major European Theatre of Operations—include photographs of nurses posing before a tent, washing their hair, playing with a puppy, preparing to go on a hike, having a picnic, holding up a Christmas greeting to the folks at home, or being serenaded by a group of American soldiers.[27] Their ornamental appearance is deceptive, for it was these very women who worked alone in the barracks for twelve-hour shifts, who were exposed to typhus-carrying lice generally without protective clothing or masks, who were haphazardly re-inoculated prior to entering the camps, who worked with German medical personnel initially reluctant and resentful, who communicated with their patients despite the language barriers, calmed them and treated them to the best of their ability and with what they had at hand. They worked in the camps with initiative and great professionalism after already having served at the height of the war as part of evacuation hospitals that struggled to maintain pace with the army's great push eastward.

War photography, whether taken by photojournalists or military photographers, reflected and impacted American perceptions about the war and in particular the nature of the enemy they were defeating. Though the Signal Corps photographic assignments accounted for less than three percent of their total activity, by 1943 they received more commendations for those activities than all their other responsibilities combined.[28] Still pictures were important for tactical and administrative information, for the maintenance of historical records, and for distribution to news media.

Understanding their mission and coordinating their efforts with the Public Information Office appears to have been a constant source of confusion. Weekly team activity reports filed by Signal Corps photographers reflect the failure to assign specific objectives or even to define zones of activity and responsibility and hint at the conflicting interests between their Signal Officer, the War Crimes Board, and SHAEF.[29] These reports indicate that sometimes photographers received notice from the War Crimes Board about the existence of the camps and assignments to document U.S. Army and medical personnel working in the camps as well as visits of official delegations. Their photographs documented the U.S. Army entering the camps, often after sustained fighting in which they participated. The photographs, and film footage, appeared to provide a complete visual and chronological record of the liberation of the camps, the response to the medical emergency, and the ultimate transportation of the patients to recovery or hospital stations.

In combat zones, film was generally processed in rear collecting points and then sent to the Signal Corps Photographic Laboratory at the Army War College in Washington, D.C. There the film was processed and culled for its intelligence, strategic, tactical, or historical importance. Those pictures that were not destroyed were catalogued, indexed, captions were written, and finally the photographs were filed, cross-referenced, and distributed by the Still Picture Library. By 1944 the Signal Corps had taken 50 percent of all still pictures published in newspapers, magazines, and books.[30] Photographs published in newspapers and journals were intended to reach mass audiences, both public and military, and necessarily reflected the censorship policies, editorial biases, military tactics, contemporary photographic technology, the photographic assignment, issues of national diplomacy, and the aesthetics and sensibilities of the individual photographer. Signal Corps photographs are housed at the National Archives Research Administration. In that entire collection only a couple pictures of nurses working in the camps exist.

Liberation imagery, whether taken by military photographers or photojournalists, carefully edited out the nurses. This exclusion reflects, I believe, a paternalism that sought to show the public that they protected women from exposure to such a horrific environment.

Photographs of female medical personnel working in the camps are extremely rare. Though cautioned against taking photographs, some nurses did so and preserved images of themselves more as visitors in a strange environment than as medical personnel working in a concerted effort to preserve life. Nurses played a vital role in the recovery period following liberation. They were present and active in the camps from the earliest days following liberation and yet their work remains generally unknown.

Holocaust photography and film are important historic documents and have often been considered as credible evidence. The inclusion of film and photographs by the prosecution at Nuremberg, however, reveals the challenges and problems with the presumption that the camera functioned as an unbiased witness as was argued by Justice Robert H. Jackson.[31] Liberation imagery necessarily focused on those who survived and their appalling situation. Images of American G.I.'s, medical personnel, and official delegations witnessing form one chapter in the visual catalogue of masculine participation in the liberation process. The pictorial record of women can be divided into several categories: the dead, the survivors, German civilians forced and reluctant to view the atrocities, and female perpetrators. Though caption information was notoriously incomplete, they tended to describe women as either victims or "female fiends." Missing from this war narrative are the American and British nurses.

I hope that this project will shed new light on the complex process of liberation, the nature of medical care given, as well as document women's observations and experiences.

The memorial album of the 120th Evacuation Hospital is dedicated to those who perished at Buchenwald:

Those whom fate spared from murder lived by the sheer force of faith and the hope of liberation. Into their emaciated bodies and tortured souls, we of the 120th Evacuation Hospital tried to inject the medicines of recovery.

American nurses played a critical and sustained role in that recovery and it is to them that this paper is respectfully dedicated.

Notes

1. See for example: Marcus Smith, *The Harrowing of Hell: Dachau* (Albuquerque: University of New Mexico Press, 1972); Michael Selzer, *Deliverance Day: The Last House at Dachau* (London: Sphere, 1980); Yaffa Eliach, *The Liberators: Eyewitness Accounts of the Liberation of the Concentration* Camps (Brooklyn, NY: Center for Holocaust Studies, Documentation, and Research, 1981); Maurice Goldstein, editor, *The Liberation of Nazis Concentration* Camps (Brussels: International Committees of Camps, 1985); Brewster S. Chamberlin, *The Liberation of the Nazi Concentration Camps 1945: Eyewitness Accounts of the Liberators* (Washington, D.C.: United States Holocaust Memorial Council, 1987); Robert H. Abzug, *G.I.'s Remember: Liberating the Concentration* Camps (Washington, D.C.: National Museum of American Jewish Military History, 1994); and Sam Dann, editor, *Dachau 29 April 1945: The Rainbow Liberation Memoirs* (Lubbock, TX: Texas Tech University Press, 1998).

2.   The United States Signal Corps published various reports regarding
their activities during the war. These can be found in the U.S. National
Archives and Records Administration, College Park, Maryland (NARA):
War Department, *Summary Report on Photographic Activities of the
Signal Corps since 4 August 1941 in the Fields of Motion Pictures &
Visual Aids* (Office of the Chief Signal Officer, 26 February 1943): RG
319; James V. Clark, *Signal Corps Army Pictorial Service in World War
II. 1 September 1939 to 15 August 1945* (Historical Section, Special
Activities Branch, Office of the Chief Signal Officer, 16 January 1945):
RG 319. *'Photo by the Signal Corps': The Story of the 166th* (SPC,
Office of the Chief Signal Officer): RG 407; *Army Pictorial Service
Annual Report for the Fiscal Year 1 July 1944 to 30 June 1945* (Office of
the Chief Signal Officer, 21 July 1945): RG 30; War Department, *History
of Signal Corps Research and Development in World War II. Volume XV.
Photographic Equipment* (Washington, D.C.: Army Service Forces,
December 1945): RG 319; Donald O. Wagner, *Army Pictorial Service
During Demobilization, 15 August 1945 to 31 December 1945* (Historical
Section, Special Activities Branch, Office of the Chief Signal Officer, no
date): RG 319. Also see NARA, RG 407 for the records and weekly
reports of the 161st SPC, 162nd SPC, 163rd SPC, 164th SPC, 165th SPC,
167th SPC, and 168th SPC; George R. Thompson and Dixie R. Harris,
*The United States Army in World War II. The Signal Corps: The Outcome.
Mid-1943 through 1945* (Washington, D.C.: Office of the Chief of
Military History, 1966). For general histories of combat photography see:
Frank P. Lieberman, "History of Army Photography," *Business Screen
Magazine* (30 December 1946): 16-17; Susan D. Moeller, *Shooting War.
Photography and the American Experience of Combat* (New York: Basic
Books, Inc., Publishers, 1989); and Peter Maslowski, *Armed with
Cameras. The American Military Photographers of World War II* (New
York: The Free Press, 1993).

3. Widely circulated photographs taken by Lee Miller include: *Rainbow
Soldiers Open a Death Train Car, 30 April 1945* and *Rainbow Medics
Examine a Corpse on the Death Train, 30 April 1945*, Photographer: Lee
Miller, Collection: Lee Miller. Reproduced in Sam Dann, editor, *Dachau
29 April 1945. The Rainbow Liberation Memoirs* (Lubbock, TX: Texas
Tech University Press, 1998): 80-82. For works on Miller's career as a
photographer see: David E. Scherman and Antony Penrose, editors, *Lee
Miller's War: Photographer and Correspondent with the Allies in Europe,
1944-1945* (Boston: Little Brown, 1992); and Jane Livingstone, *Lee
Miller: Photographer* (New York: Thames and Hudson, 1989). Margaret

Bourke-White's photographs of Buchenwald originally appeared in *Life* magazine and were subsequently published in her book *Dear Fatherland, Rest Quietly. A Report on the Collapse of Hitler's "Thousand Years"* (New York: Simon & Schuster, 1946). Also see: Margaret Bourke-White, *Portrait of Myself* (New York: Simon & Schuster, 1963); Sean Callahan, editor, *The Photographs of Margaret Bourke-White* (Greenwich, CT: New York Graphic Society, 1972); Jonathan Silverman, *For the World to See: The Life of Margaret Bourke-White* (New York: Viking Press, 1983); Vicki Goldberg, *Margaret Bourke-White. A Biography* (New York: Harper & Row, 1986).

4. Other photographers who covered the camps for *Life* magazine included Dave Scherman (Auschwitz); John Florea (Nordhausen) William Vandivert (Gardelegen), and George Rodger (Bergen-Belsen).

5. Examples of press coverage photography include: *New York Times* (18 April 1945); *San Francisco Examiner* (19 April 1945): 4; *The Washington Post* (19 April 1945): 2; *Miami Herald* (21 April 1945): 1; *Illustrated London News* (28 April 1945): detachable four-page supplement; *Miami Herald* (28 April 1945): 1,2; *New York World Telegram* (30 April 1945): 1, 2; *Time* (30 April 1945): 40, 43; *Baltimore Sun* (1 May 1945): 2; *Chicago Herald American* (1 May 1945); *New York Journal American* (1 May 1945): 14; *San Francisco Examiner* (1 May 1945): 14; *New York Sun* (2 May 1945): 8; *Miami Herald* (4 May 1945): 1; *Chicago Tribune* (6 May 1945): 7; *Miami Herald* (6 May 1945): 11; *Miami Herald* (6 May 1945): 11; *New York Journal American* (6 May 1945): 5; *New York World Telegram* (10 May 1945): 17; *St. Louis Post Dispatch* (13 May 1945): 2a; *St. Louis Dispatch* (15 May 1945); Joseph Pulitzer, *St. Louis Dispatch* (18 May 1945): 1; and Joseph Pulitzer, "Report on German Murder Mills," *Army Talks* (10 July 1945): 7-11.

6. U.S. Signal Corps photographers documented the Congressional tour of the camps. These photographs can be seen at the NARA, RG 111: Records of the Office of the Chief Signal Officer. Also see Kevin Mahoney, ed., *The Year of 1945 Liberation* (Washington, D.C.: United States Holocaust Memorial Museum, 1995): 148-168. Also see "'Ike' at Scene of Atrocity," *Washington Post* (16 April 1945): 4. For the use of this tour to add credibility to press coverage of the camps see David S. Wyman, *The Abandonment of the Jews: America and the Holocaust, 1941-1945* (New York: Pantheon Books, 1985): 323-326.

138   Deborah A. Gómez

7. For the activities of the Medical Department of the U.S. Army in the
European Theatre of Operations see: Office of the Surgeon General,
Preventive Medicine in World War II (Washington, D.C.: Office of the
Surgeon General, Department of the Army, 1955); Clarence McKittrick
Smith, *The Medical Department: Hospitalization and Evacuation: Zone of
Interior* (Washington, D.C.: Office of the Chief of Military History,
Department of the Army, 1956); Graham A. Cosmas and Albert E.
Cowdrey, *The Medical Department: Medical Service in the European
Theatre of Operations* (Washington, D.C.: Center of Military History,
United States Army, 1992).

8. Hannah Arendt, *The Origins of Totalitarianism* (New York: Meridian
Books, 1958); Cornelia Brink, "Looking at Photographs from Nazi
Concentration Camps," *History & Memory* 12 (Spring/Summer 2000):
135-149; Greg Crysler, and Abidin Kusno, "Angels in the Temple: The
Aesthetic Construction of Citizenship at the United States Holocaust
Memorial Museum," *Art Journal* (Spring 1997): 52-64; Marianne Hirsch,
"Surviving Images: Holocaust Photographs and the Work of
Postmemory," in *Visual Culture and the Holocaust,* Barbie Zelizer, ed.
(New Brunswick, NJ: Rutgers University Press, 2001): 215-246; Douglas
Lawrence, "The Shrunken Head of Buchenwald: Icons of Atrocity at
Nuremberg," *Representations* 63 (Summer 1998): 39-64; Walter Laqueur,
*The Terrible Secret: Suppression of the Truth about Hitler's "Final
Solution"* (New York: Penguin Books, 1982); Richard W. Ross, *So It Was
True: The American Protestant Press and the Nazi Persecution of the
Jews* (Minneapolis, 1980); Rachel Schreiber, "Seized Images:
Photography, Memory and the Holocaust," *New Art Examiner* (April
1997): 22-25; Barbie Zelizer, "Introduction: On Visualizing the
Holocaust," and "Gender and Atrocity: Women in Holocaust
Photographs," in *Visual Culture and the Holocaust,* Barbie Zelizer, ed.
(New Brunswick, NJ: Rutgers University Press, 2001): 1-12; 247-271;
Barbie Zelizer, "The Liberation of Buchenwald: Images and the Shape of
Memory," In *Cultural Memory and the Construction of Identity.* Dan Ben-
Amos and Lilian Weissberg, eds., (Detroit: Wayne State University,
1999): 100-135; and Barbie Zelizer, *Remembering to Forget: Holocaust
Memory Through the Camera's Eye* (Chicago: University of Chicago
Press, 1998).

9. As with medical personnel, photographers grappled with the
overwhelming nature of the task at hand and how to adequately respond.
Margaret Bourke-White, *"Dear Fatherland, Rest Quietly." A Report on*

the Collapse of Hitler's "Thousand Years," (New York: Simon and Schuster, 1946): 73-80; and Deborah Lipstadt, *Beyond Belief: The American Press and the Coming of the Holocaust, 1933-1945* (New York: The Free Press, 1986): 240-272; Andrew Sharf, *The British Press and Jews under Nazi Rule* (London: Oxford University Press, 1964).

10. For editorial manipulation of photographs by the editors at *Life* magazine see Moeller, 1989, 217-219.

11. Editors of the following newspapers were invited to tour the camps: *American Magazine, Chicago Sun, Collier's, Detroit Free Press, Fort Worth Star Telegram, Houston Chronicle, Kansas City Star, Life, Los Angeles Times, Minneapolis Star-Journal, New York Daily Mirror, New York Times, Reader's Digest, St. Louis Post Dispatch, This Week Magazine,* and the *Washington Star,* as well as various syndicated papers published by Hearst and Scripps-Howard.

12. Their tour was covered in the following articles: "M.P.s Will See Horror Camp Secrets," *Daily Mail* (21 April 1945): 1; "M.P.s View Hun Cruelty," *Daily Mirror* (24 April 1945); "American Legislators in Europe to Investigate Atrocities," *New York Times* (25 April 1945): 3; "Editors, Publishers on Way to Reich," *Los Angeles Times* (26 April 1945): 3; "Penna. Congressman Sees Evidence of Foe's Cruelty," "American Editors View Buchenwald Victims," *Boston Globe* (4 May 1945): 4; "Buchenwald," *Los Angeles Times* (4 May 1945): 3; and "Journey to a Shattered World," *Saturday Evening Post* (9 June 1945): 20.

13. "This was Nazi Germany-Blood, Starvation, the Stench of Death," *Stars and Stripes* (23 April 1945): 4-5; "Nazi Barbarism," *Philadelphia Inquirer* (26 April 1945): 14; "Horror, Starvation, Death in German Concentration Camps Revealed by Allies' Advance," *Stars and Stripes* (30 April 1945): 4; "Dachau-A Grisly Spectacle," *Washington Post* (2 May 1945): 3; "The World Must Not Forget," *New York Times Magazine* (6 May 1945): 8; "To Look at Horror," *Newsweek* (28 May 1945): 35.

14. In particular photographs of General Eisenhower at Ohrdurf (12 April 1945) was widely reproduced as were photographs of the American editors at Buchenwald that same month. "'Ike' at Scene of Atrocity," *The Washington Post* (16 April 1945): 4; "American Editors View

Buchenwald Victims," *Boston Globe* (4 May 1945): 4; "Buchenwald," *Los
Angeles Times* (4 May 1945): 3.

15. For the British experience see: R.F. Cordell and D.H. Forsdick,
"Symposium – Commemoration of the Liberation of the Bergen-Belsen
Concentration Camp and Medical Management of Disasters Study
Period," *Journal of the Royal Army Medical Corps* Vol. 145 (February
1999): 28-30; Imperial War Museum, *The Relief of Belsen, April 1945:
Eyewitness Accounts* (London: IWM, 1991); Brenda McBryde, *A Nurse's
War* (Essex, Great Britain: Cakebread Publications, 1993); Joanne Reilly,
Belsen: The Liberation of a Concentration Camp (London & New York:
Routledge, 1998); Joanne Reilly, ed. *Belsen in History and* Memory
(Portland, OR: F. Cass, 1997); and Roger Cowan Wilson, *Quaker Relief.
An Account of the Relief Work of the Society of Friends, 1940-1948*
(London, 1952).

16. United State Holocaust Memorial Museum interview with Dr. George
Tievsky. Record Group: 09.005.10.

17. Stanhope Bayne-Jones, "Typhus Fevers" (Introduction, note 6): 7:
164ff; Military Government Detachment E1-H2, 2d European Civil
Affairs Regiment, *Report to Chief Surgeon*, ETOUSA, (28 May 1945),
Subject: Typhus Epidemic, Köln, Germany (1945/1) File No. 350.05
ETOUSA, Center for Military History, Fort Lesley J. McNair.

18. Wilson, 1952, 226-229; Vella, 1984, 34-59l; Bishop-Spangenberg,
1995; 44-45 and Reilly, ed., 1997.

19. Franklin, 1945, 901-902; Hopping, Henderson, Shepard, et. al., 1945;
Davis, Juvera and Lira, 1945; Davis, 1947, 66-83; Lewis, 1985, 122-126;
Bishop-Spangenberg, 1995, 44-45; Zierler, 1995, 973-974; and
Schlossman, 1996, 737-739.

20. Smith, 1972, 97; Bridgman, 1990, 61-76; and NARA, Records of the
Office of the Surgeon General (Army), Record Group-112.

21. ETOUSA, *Periodic Report*, 1945, 5-7; *Essential Technical Medical
Data Report*, 1945, 3-4; Medical Section, Third U.S. Army, *Semiannual
Report*, 1945, 139; Proudfoot, 1956, 147-152.

22. Davis, 1947, 66-83.

23. For the activities of the 120th Evacuation Hospital and the tuberculosis hospital they set up to serve Buchenwald see NARA, Record Group-MDEH-120-0.1.

24. 116th Evacuation Hospital, *Semiannual Report* (1945/1): 7-8, NARA-Record Group: 112.

25. Joseph Pulitzer, *A Report to the American People* (St. Louis: St. Louis Post Dispatch, 1945). For a description of the reception of the exhibition see Robert H. Abzug, *Inside the Vicious Heart. Americans and the Liberation of Nazi Concentration Camps* (New York & Oxford: Oxford University Press, 1985): 134-137. For criticism on the Signal Corps documentary see James Agee, *Agee on Film: Criticism and Comment on the Movies* (originally published New York: McDowell, Oblensky, pp. 161-162; New York: Modern Library, 2000).

26. Sontag, 1977, 192.

27. *Buchenwald and Beyond: 120th Evacuation Hospital*, 1946?; Mihalich, 1945?.

28. "I get more kicks and commendations from the results of that service than from the results of all the rest of the Signal Corps activities put together." Quote from letter written by General Harry C. Ingles, Chief Signal Officer, (17 August 1944) to Colonel Terence J. Tully, Allied Force Headquarters, as quoted in Thompson and Harris, 1966, 540.

29. NARA-Record Group: 407.

30. *The Annual Report of the Chief Signal Officer*, 1944.

31. In his opening statement Justice Jackson made reference to the use of film as evidence, "We will show you these concentration camps in motion pictures [*Nazi Concentration Camps*], just as the Allied armies found them when they arrived...I am one who received during this war most atrocity tales with suspicion and skepticism. But the proof here will be so overwhelming that I venture to predict not one word I have spoken will be denied." International Military Tribunal, *The Trial of the Major War Criminals Before the International Military Tribunal* 42 vols.

(Nuremberg: International Military Tribunal, 1947-1949): 130. For the
dispute between Justice Jackson and prosecution counsel William
Donovan over the use of documentary evidence see Telford Taylor, *The
Anatomy of the Nuremberg Trials: A Personal Memoir* (Boston: Little,
Brown and Company, 1992): 146-149. For the impact of photographs and
films of the camps prior to the trials see Airey Neave, *On Trial at
Nuremberg* (Boston and Toronto: Little, Brown and Company, 1978): 63,
127.

Bibliography

American Magazine
Boston Globe
Chicago Sun
Collier's
Daily Mirror
Detroit Free Press,
Fort Worth Star Telegram
Houston Chronicle
Illustrated London News
Kansas City Star
Life
Los Angeles Times
Minneapolis Star-Journal
Newsweek
New York Daily Mirror
New York Times
New York Times Magazine
Philadelphia Inquirer
Reader's Digest
San Francisco Examiner
Saturday Evening Post
Stars and Stripes
St. Louis Post Dispatch
The Washington Post
This Week Magazine
Washington Star

Abzug, Robert H. *G.I.'s Remember: Liberating the Concentration Camps.* Washington, D.C.: National Museum of American Jewish Military History, 1994.

Inside the Vicious Heart. Americans and the Liberation of Nazi Concentration Camps. New York & Oxford: Oxford University Press, 1985.

Agee, James. *Agee on Film: Criticism and Comment on the Movies.* New York: Modern Library, 2000.

Arendt, Hannah. *The Origins of Totalitarianism.* New York: Meridian Books, 1958.

Bayne-Jones, Stanhope. "Typhus Fevers." *Report to Chief Surgeon, ETOUSA:* File No. 350.05. Center for Military History, 28 May 1945.

Bishop-Spangenberg, A. "A War of Starvation." *Nursing Times* 91 (1995): 44-45.

Bourke-White, Margaret. *'Dear Fatherland, Rest Quietly.' A Report on the Collapse of Hitler's 'Thousand Years.'* New York: Simon and Schuster, 1946.

Bridgman, Jon. *The End of the Holocaust: The Liberation of the Camps.* Portland: Areopagitica Press, 1990.

Brink, Cornelia. "Looking at Photographs from Nazi Concentration Camps." *History & Memory* 12 (2000): 135-149.

Clark, J.V. *Signal Corps Army Pictorial Service in World War II. 1 September 1939 to 15 August 1945.* (Office of the Chief Signal Officer, 1945): RG 319.

Cordell, R.F. and D.H. Forsdick. "Symposium – Commemoration of the Liberation of the Bergen-Belsen Concentration Camp and Medical Management of Disasters Study Period." *Journal of the Royal Army Medical Corps* 145 (1999): 28-30.

Cosmas, Graham A. and Albert E. Cowdrey. *The Medical Department: Medical Service in the European Theatre of Operations.* Washington, D.C.: Center of Military History, U.S. Army, 1992.

Dann, Sam, ed. *Dachau 29 April 1945: The Rainbow Liberation Memoirs.* Lubbock, TX: Texas Tech University Press, 1998.

Davis, William A., F.Malo Juvera, and P. Hernandez Lira. "Studies on Louse Control in a Civilian Population." *The American Journal of Hygiene* 39 (1945).

Davis, William A. "Typhus at Belsen. I. Control of the Typhus Epidemic." *The American Journal of Hygiene* 46 (1947): 66-83.

Eliach, Yaffa. *The Liberators: Eyewitness Accounts of the Liberation of the Concentration Camps.* Brooklyn: Center for Holocaust Studies, Documentation, and Research, 1981.

Chamberlin, Brewster S. *The Liberation of the Nazi Concentration Camps 1945: Eyewitness Accounts of the Liberators.* Washington, D.C.: United States Holocaust Memorial Council, 1987.

Crysler, Greg and Abidin Kusno. "Angels in the Temple: The Aesthetic Construction of Citizenship at the United States Holocaust Memorial Museum." *Art Journal* (Spring 1997): 52-64.

Franklin, Ann. "An Army Nurse at Dachau." *The American Journal of Nursing* 45 (1945): 901-902.

Goldstein, Maurice, ed. T*he Liberation of Nazi Concentration Camps.* Brussels: International Committee of Camps, 1985.

Hopping, N.H. and I.A. Henderson, R.G. Shepard, et. al. *Studies of Typhus Fever.* National Institute of Health Bulletin, No. 183. Washington, D.C.: U.S. Government Printing Office, 1945.

Lawrence, Douglas. "The Shrunken Head of Buchenwald: Icons of Atrocity at Nuremberg." *Representations* 63 (1998): 39-64.

Laqueur, Walter. *The Terrible Secret: Suppression of the Truth about Hitler's 'Final Solution.'* New York: Penguin Books, 1982.

Lewis, J.T. "Medical Problems at Belsen Concentration Camp." *Ulster Medical Journal.* (October 1985): 122-126.

Lieberman, Frank P. "History of Army Photography," *Business Screen Magazine* (30 December 1946): 16-17.

Lipstadt, Deborah E. *Beyond Belief: The American Press and the Coming of the Holocaust, 1933-1945.* New York: The Free Press, 1986.

Livingstone, Jane. *Lee Miller: Photographer.* New York: Thames and Hudson, 1989.

Mahoney, Kevin, ed. *The Year of 1945 Liberation.* Washington, D.C.: United States Holocaust Memorial Museum, 1995.

Maslowski, Peter. *Armed with Cameras. The American Military Photographers of World War II.* New York: The Free Press, 1993.

Moeller, Susan D. *Shooting War. Photography and the American Experience of Combat.* New York: Basic Books, Inc., Publishers, 1989.

Medical Section, Third U.S. Army, *Semiannual Report* (1945/1): 139, File No. 319.1-2.

Mihalich, Joseph J. *Five Stars to Victory: The Story of the 107th Evacuation Hospital.* ca. 1945. United States Holocaust Memorial Museum.

Neave, Airey. *On Trial at Nuremberg.* Boston and Toronto: Little, Brown and Company, 1978.

Preventive Medicine Division, ETOUSA. *Periodic Report* (January-July, 1945): 5-7.

ETOUSA. *Essential Technical Medical Data Report* (April 1945): 3-4.

Proudfoot, Malcolm. *European Refugees 1939-1952: A Study in Forced Population Movement.* Evanston: University of Illinois Press, 1956.

Pulitzer, Joseph. *A Report to the American People.* St. Louis: St. Louis Post Dispatch, 1945.

Reilly, Joanne, ed. *Belsen in History and Memory*. Portland: F. Cass, 1997.

Belsen: The Liberation of a Concentration Camp. London & New York: Routledge, 1998.

Ross, Richard W. *So It Was True: The American Protestant Press and the Nazi Persecution of the Jews*. Minneapolis: University of Minnesota Press, 1980.

Scherman, David E. and Antony Penrose, editors, *Lee Miller's War: Photographer and Correspondent with the Allies in Europe, 1944-1945*. Boston: Little Brown, 1992.

Schlossman, H.H. "Recollections of the Liberation of Buchenwald: 4/11/45."*Journal of the American Academy of Psychoanalysis* 24 (1996): 737-739.

Schreiber, Rachel. "Seized Images: Photography, Memory and the Holocaust." *New Art Examiner* (April 1997): 22-25.

Selzer, Michael. *Deliverance Day: The Last House at Dachau*. London: Sphere, 1980.

Sharf, Andrew. *The British Press and Jews Under Nazi Rule*. Oxford: Oxford University Press, 1964.

Smith, Clarence McKittrick. *The Medical Department: Hospitalization and Evacuation: Zone of Interior*. Washington, D.C.: Department of the Army, Office of the Chief of Military History, 1956.

Smith, Marcus. *The Harrowing of Hell: Dachau*. Albuquerque: University of New Mexico Press, 1972.

Sontag, Susan. *On Photography*. New York: Farrar, Straus & Giroux, 1977.

Taylor, Telford. *The Anatomy of the Nuremberg Trials: A Personal Memoir*. Boston: Little, Brown and Company, 1992.

Thompson, George R. and Dixie R. Harris, *The United States Army in World War II. The Signal Corps: The Outcome. Mid-1943 through 1945.* Washington, D.C.: Office of the Chief of Military History, 1966.

United States National Archives and Records Administration, College Park, Maryland. *Records of the Office of the Surgeon General* (Army): RG 112, RG 120.

War Department, Summary Report on Photographic Activities of the Signal Corps Since 4 August 1941 in the Fields of Motion Pictures & Visual Aids (Office of the Chief Signal Officer): RG 319.

World War II Operations Reports: 1940-1948 (The Adjutant General's Office): RG 407.

Army Pictorial Service Annual Report for the Fiscal Year 1 July 1944 to 30 June 1945 (Office of the Chief Signal Officer, 1945): RG 111.

Vella, E.E. "Belsen: Medical Aspects of a World War II Concentration Camp." *Journal of the Royal Army Medical Corps* (1984): 34-59.

Wilson, Roger Cowan. *Quaker Relief. An Account of the Relief Work of the Society of Friends, 1940-1948.* London: Allen & Unwin, 1952.

Zelizer, Barbie. *Remembering to Forget: Holocaust Memory Through the Camera's Eye.* Chicago: University of Chicago Press, 1998.

"The Liberation of Buchenwald: Images and the Shape of Memory." In *Cultural Memory and the Construction of Identity,* edited by D. Ben-Amos and L. Weissberg, 136-175. Detroit: Wayne State University, 1999.

ed. *Visual Culture and the Holocaust.* New Brunswick: Rutgers University Press, 2001.

Zierler, K. "Witness to the Liberation." *Maryland Medical Journal.* 44 (1995): 973-974.

Playing War in Computer Games: Images, Myths, and Reality

Martin Bayer

"Sometimes they will start a war – and everybody will join in the game." Adapting the famous quote of Carl Sandburg might seem suitable, according to both the increasing media coverage on computer (war) games and the actual number of games. This paper will examine how war has become some sort of interactive entertainment using today's computers. It will additionally address the myths connected to computer games and their users. Further emphasis will be placed on the distinction between (perceived) realism and reality, and how this may change the future perception of war.

Although having been despised for a long time, computer games have finally become part of our cultural possessions. The icons of the gaming world appear everywhere, the ubiquitous Lara Croft at the forefront. Computer games have already passed the cinema box-offices in terms of turnover. Successful games series like *Command & Conquer*, *Tomb Raider*, or *Warcraft* are selling millions of copies. The production costs for games rose up to $11 m (£7 m, €11.1), with teams of dozens of people producing them. However, a number of misperceptions and myths still exist: many people regard computer games as not too serious a business. Games are often described as mindless time-wasters, where hordes of aliens have to be shot down, played by lone male teenagers with spotty faces. To an increasing extent, computer games are associated with violence, though only a small proportion of the market share is similar or even more violent than children's fairy tales. However, violence in computer games is not only depicted in fantasy-like environments, but also in "realistic" settings of war. Due to the fast technological development, today's computer games offer a breath-taking audio-visual quality, soon equalling contemporary movies. Like in movies, this audio-visual quality is both presented and perceived as realistic and authentic. Of course, such a level of mainly graphical "realism" has often nothing to do with reality: virtual soldiers can carry tremendous amounts of kit without getting tired, virtual wounds can be healed easily, and virtual death is followed by the opportunity to play again. Nevertheless, both movies and computer games will shape the future perception of historical and contemporary wars, especially as the distinction between reality and virtuality will become increasingly difficult.

1.   Gaming Platforms

Computer games are played on several so-called platforms. The first breakthrough into the mass market could be achieved with the so-called home computers during the early 1980s. Relatively cheap computers like the *Commodore 64*, the *Commodore Amiga*, or the *Sinclair Spectrum* enabled ordinary people to play games at home. The graphics were pretty simple, as was the game design, but many of these early games were quite addictive. Many of these early games had been one-man projects; later on, a distinction between programming and graphical work occurred. Early war games such as *Blue Max* needed high levels of imagination on behalf of the players, as the representations of "tanks", "guns" and "planes" were restricted to only a couple of coarse pixels.

The solemn purpose of game consoles – as the name suggests – is for playing games. This specialisation enables easy handling (for example there is no need for learning a computer's operation system) and a powerful gaming experience for a modest price (in comparison to a standard PC, especially in the past) or additional mobility (handheld consoles, for example the *Game Boy Advance*). In some countries, such as Japan or the United Kingdom, consoles such as the *Sony Playstation*, the *PS2*, or the *Microsoft X-Box* are very successful, having a much larger market share than PC-based games; in other countries, the market is reversed. For a long time, most of the console games offered were simple and action-based. With today's consoles, more demanding games can be realised, too. *Medal of Honour: Frontline* is a recent and highly successful example of a next-generation console-based war game, set during the Second World War.

The PC is the platform of choice for many gamers, especially since standard office PCs provide astonishing capabilities for gaming: just a couple of years ago, PCs suitable for gaming were much more expensive than their office equivalents. Today, there is merely a distinction between them. Input devices such as keyboard or mouse offer wide-ranging possibilities for game designers, thus enabling greater complexity for the games. Additionally, specialised input devices such as joysticks, steering wheels or pedals can be attached to turn the gaming experience more realistic. The range of games offered on the PC platform is the widest, from adventures to role-playing games, and from shooters to strategy games and simulations. In the past ten years, PCs underwent a dramatic change. Every 18 months, the CPU power is being doubled. In the three years since 1999, the graphics power alone has increased tenfold. The development from the first 3D-egoshooter *Castle Wolfenstein 3D* of 1992 (published shortly before *Doom* took the fame) to the "successor" *Return to Castle Wolfenstein* hardly ten years later is just amazing: in the former game, lots of imagination was needed to regard the blocky blobs on the screen as German soldiers or as attacking shepherd dogs, whereas the latter offers high-resolution 3D-environments with game physics and stunning visuals. One has to bear in mind however, that back in 1992, the visuals of *Castle Wolfenstein 3D* and other contemporary games were regarded as "absolutely stunning", too. This development will continue until the visualisation will match the real world.

The oldest commercial platform for computer games are the so-called arcades, expensive devices set up in amusement halls or pubs, where the player has to pay a small charge for every game, usually lasting a couple of minutes. The grand days of the arcades are actually over, as low-cost platforms like consoles or PCs enable not only a better cost-benefit ratio for people playing games more frequently, but also a wider range of games. Most arcade games are simple action games. The war game aspect is however particularly interesting, as arcades may offer not only buttons and joysticks as input devices, but also mock-ups of real or fantasy weapons, like a sniper rifle in the "sniper simulation" *Fatal Judgement* ("the game that has all others in its sights", to quote the manufacturer's ad).[1] The Korean game manufacturer *Gamebox is* offering even more accurate replicas of historical or modern infantry weapons (called *Dreamgun*), for example the German World War II machine gun MG-34 or the British SA-80 assault rifle, all with "shock effect" to mimic the weapons' recoil.[2]

As the visual quality of modern high-end platforms is approaching "real life" quality, there is enough computing power to enrich today's games with physics and "artificial intelligence" (AI). The former describes the correct representation of physical events, for example a car being driven at high speed into a curve going into a skid. The latter, although being a slight misnomer, encompasses the more or less "intelligent" reaction of virtual objects to their environment, for example an enemy soldier, who does not wait to get killed but ducks down after being shot at or after "seeing" his opponent. To a certain extent, and one might add unfortunately, games are sold and bought with regards to their audiovisual quality, not unlike action movies: impressive explosions, more details, "realistic" weaponry, and fancy special effects do have some attraction. However, the main issue of a game is entertainment, and it is painful to see how many of today's games do fail in the primary objective, while some games of the mid-1980s, despite their technological limitations, still provide fascinating gaming experiences.

One brief outlook of the future might resemble some descriptions out of Ray Bradbury's science fiction novel *Fahrenheit 451*: in computer-aided virtual environments (CAVE), three-dimensional images are projected on up to six walls. The gamer, standing in the middle of this room, does not need to wear a clumsy VR (virtual reality) helmet, but only a pair of lightweight polarising glasses – a first step towards the *Star Trek* "holodeck". Thus, the player can move through the virtual environment without the need of a screen, a keyboard, or a mouse, making the whole experience much more realistic. Such CAVEs do already exist – the first had been developed in 1991,[3] and the author played *Quake II* in one in 2000 –, and it may be only in some years that the first game CAVEs are cheap enough to provide for a viable business model for amusement halls. However, remembering that some people already have problems to distinguish the virtual from the real world (although this phenomenon is still mostly connected to other media, such as TV and movies), such a technological development may lead to serious problems with reality for some unstable minds.

2.   Definition and Historical Context

To define computer war games, it might be easiest to start excluding what they are not: computer war games do not deal with fantasy environments ("dungeons and dragons") where the use of weaponry is enriched by magic spells and other supernatural powers, and where players battle against hordes of zombies, orks, dragons, and the like. Additionally, science fiction environments are also excluded from this definition, however "accurate" the fighting in space against alien races may be simulated. Thus, computer war games are about simulating or re-enacting historical or contemporary conflicts, including hypothetical events to some extent. Nevertheless, there is a grey area in this definition: while the hypothetic events displayed in *Operation Flashpoint: Cold War Crisis* might be regarded as connected to a possible reality, the zombies revived by mad Nazi scientists and leather-clad SS dominatrix in *Return to Castle Wolfenstein* are clearly not.[4] Another example for "what if"-cases is the recent ego-shooter *Iron Storm*: in this game, the First World War has just not ended in 1918, but continued for 50 years. It is very important that, after all, such games are entertainment, to which sometimes a (usual political) message has been added. Another aspect is the ongoing convergence of commercial off-the-shelf (COTS) computer games with professional military simulations.

Computer war games are set in a variety of historical contexts, throughout the history of mankind. The Stone Age and Classical Antiquity are represented by games such as *Age of Empires*, where the player can even develop his "race" from the former to the latter, i.e. to the Iron Age. In games set in the Middle Ages, such as *Stronghold* or *The Age of Kings*, building and battling castles is usually the centre of the game. In these games, a strong emphasis is build upon siege engines, which is far from being accurate: in reality, sieges were usually decided by starving out the opponent – an option being very boring and not entertaining at all if put in a game. The early modern period is addressed by games such as *Cossacks* or *Shogun*. As soon as firearms are introduced as weaponry, the guns' ranges often differ from real terms to balance the different units, thus producing a more challenging game. Of course, the modern period is most interesting for game developers, offering different weapon systems and all kinds of theatres of war. The First World War is relatively seldom represented, mainly as flight simulations such as *Dawn of Aces*. This is rather being surprising, as the main activities were shelling the trenches, storming against barbed wire entanglements, and being machine-gunned down. Nevertheless, the 3D strategy game *1914 – The Great War* is the exception proving the rule – and due to the covered activities, the main critique was that the game is boring and repetitive.

The "mother of all wars" for computer war games is surely the Second World War: it has all you want to have for such kind of entertainment. Firstly, there is a clear distinction between good and evil (although playing the evil side for some time may offer a special treat). Secondly, there are huge varieties of weapon systems, including planes, tanks, submarines, surface vessels, and all sorts of infantry weapons. Fighting can be done on the ground, in the air, and on and below the water surface. Thirdly, the theatres of war range from the desert of North Africa to the Atlantic, from the Pacific islands to South East Asia, and in the whole of Europe, from Norway to Italy, and from Great Britain to the vast steppes of the Soviet Union. Thus, players who prefer "exotic" environments are served, as are those preferring "local" environments, such as their own country or city. The list of games connected to the Second World War are endless. Recent examples include the successful *Medal of Honour* series (ego-shooters), the flight simulator *Il-2 Shturmovik*, or the strategy games *Sudden Strike II*, *Hidden & Dangerous II*, and *Combat Mission*, to name just a few.

The Cold War is seldom an issue for computer games, although for example the Vietnam War is well-represented in other forms of media. Firstly, most movies on the Vietnam War were produced some time ago, when computer games were still pure science fiction.[5] Second, most proxy wars are obviously not interesting for a game. Third, the main actors of the Cold War did not fight each other directly (at least, not on a large scale). Thus, games using the Cold War as a background usually do so on the basis of hypothetical events. The story of the highly realistic ego-shooter *Operation Flashpoint: Cold War Crisis* is based on a Soviet rogue general invading the fictitious East-European country Everon during the mid-1980s after Gorbachev has become President. Games covering the contemporary world often use a similar approach, for example *Conflict Zone* or *World War III* offer fictitious enemies like terrorist organisations, transnational companies or state alliances, challenging NATO, the UN or the West in general.

Like in the real world, terrorism is now a hot topic for games. Shortly after 9/11, a couple of simple, home-made games appeared in the Internet, for example *Bin Laden Liquours*, where the player could kill Osama bin Laden. With an increasing number of games, such as *Splinter Cell*, the *Rogue Spear* series, *Soldier of Fortune II*, and *Land Warrior III*, the fight against terrorism can be pursued at the home front.

4.   Computer Game Genres

Nearly all genres of computer games (except sports and racing) are suitable for covering war as their main subject. In adventures – used seldom for war games – the player is using a pre-defined character to solve a set of puzzles, eventually accomplishing the main objective, often by interacting with other people (i.e. virtual characters). Prime examples for the main objective would be rescuing a princess or nothing less than saving the world. Usually, adventures are single-player games only. One of the war games of this genre is the recent 3D action adventure *Prisoner of War*, where the player, being a U.S. Air Force officer held captive in various POW camps in Nazi Germany War, has to solve puzzles to get himself free. However, as this would obviously not be enough to make a "higher goal", he also has to find information about Nazi Germany's programme to develop "weapons of mass destruction" – thus, he ultimately saves the world.

Role-playing games (RPGs) are to some extent similar to adventures. The player also has to solve a set of puzzles, but in RPGs, the fighting element is much more important. Additionally, the player does usually not only control one pre-defined character, but a whole set of characters whose abilities (for example use of specific weapons, sneaking, or lock-picking) can be improved throughout the game. Most role-playing games are set in fantasy worlds, but there are some war games, too, for example the *Jagged Alliance* series, where the player commands a group of mercenaries. A fascinating "real life approach" might become the new RPG by the U.S. Army, *America's Army: Soldiers* that is to be published soon. In this game, the player can develop a career inside the U.S. Army and does learn a lot about this organisation and possible career prospects – the emphasis on "educational" aspects is not surprising, because *Soldiers –*

like *America's Army: Operations* – is a "recruitment game" distributed without any charge, with the ultimate aim to attract new recruits.

Simple action games – also called "shoot'em ups", many of whom are using arcades as their platform – have come somewhat out of fashion. Regarding war games, the content of killing as many waves of enemies in as short a time as possible does not appeal to many people. Secondly, it regularly led to *Indizierung* ("indication") in Germany – the third-largest games market worldwide – due to the glorification of war and violence. An example is the old C-64 game *Commando Libya*, where the player's only task was machine-gunning waves of "Ghaddafi's children" charging from the top to the lower end of the screen. One recent example is *Beach Head 2000*, where the player constantly fires his all-purpose gun against tanks, ships, planes, helicopters, and individual soldiers alike. A statement by the developer (like in "the old days", just a single individual) says that he does not want to glorify war, but just wanted to bring the fun of the original *Beachhead* to today's graphical levels.[6] Thus, no classical background story is provided, it is just faceless enemies without any affiliation to a country or a cause.

Some might regard "fun games" as a separate genre, where war is put into a comic or "funny" kind of setting. One group of games lets the player use virtual plastic war toys for warfighting, for example *Airfix Dogfighter*, a flight simulation of plastic models set in kitchens, gardens, or living rooms. The successful *Army Men* series let the player command plastic toy soldiers in similar environments, where household items such as hotplates may become threatening for its protagonists. Other games put the war theme into a "cute" context: pigs fight each other in a World War I environment in *Hogs of War – Born to Grill*, pigs fight hamsters in *S.W.I.N.E.*, or the comic-style worms of the same-named series blow each other into pieces. A third strand of games uses war (or the context of war) for "non-violent" (or "less-violent") fun. Most of these games are advertisement games, such as *Sol Bombers* where the player has to steer a B-17 bomber to hit remote islands with bottles of beer, or an advertisement game for the British bookmaker *Ladbrokes*, published before the Football World Cup qualifier in Munich in September 2000: one commanded a World War II *Lancaster* bomber that dropped balls onto German football players at Munich's Olympic Stadium. In the latter case however, public outrage (in the United Kingdom) led to the withdrawal of the game after the first few days.

A very important genre for war games is simulation. The mastery of complex technology is prominent; the actual war fighting may be even regarded as less important. Nearly all kind of equipment has already been simulated (with an emphasis on flight simulations), from tanks (*Armoured*

Fist) to submarines (*Aces of the Deep*), and from helicopters (*Gunship!*) to planes (the *Combat Flight Simulator* series). There is however a distinction between highly accurate and "action-oriented" simulations. The former group, consisting of games such as *Falcon 4.0* (an F-16 simulator) need considerable time on behalf of the player until he is able to "master" the machinery. Players favouring these games are somewhat disregarded as obsessed and freakish anorak-types. The games of the latter group put an emphasis on the "fun" element, which is, regarding combat simulators, the actual fighting. The equipment is not simulated to its full complexity, leading to a less steep learning-curve. An example of such action simulations is the *Comanche* series, sporting the RAH-66 helicopter. While some more realistic simulations do also include the possibility of malfunction (for example torpedo duds or missiles missing their designated targets), less complex games may lead to a certain kind of (mis)perception: in this case, precision weapons do always hit their target, which is not the case even with the most sophisticated systems available to the military. Gamers may recognise "their" hardware in media reports on actual conflicts and wrongly apply their "experience" to reality, for example the near-invincibility in some games. Furthermore, the suffering caused by war (common to most games) is not taken into any account, resulting often in a "clean" way of chivalrous if not heroic fight "man vs. man", especially in historic flight simulators. An important aspect is the convergence of professional simulators with COTS simulation games. Microsoft's *Flight Simulator*, for example, is being used by the U.S. armed forces for theoretical flight training, providing enough realism for the task, combined with cheap license fees, especially in comparison to "professional" simulations.

One of the popular genres in contemporary gaming are the so-called strategy games. There are many non-violent strategy games, where the player has to develop a city's infrastructure (the *SimCity* series) or to organise a theme park (the *Theme Park* series), to name a few. Nevertheless, many strategy games focus on military content. To dispel a common misunderstanding at the very beginning: despite their name, most strategy war games are not tackling the strategic but the tactical level of warfare. Single tanks or soldiers (or at maximum a group of them) are commanded, leading in some cases to a frantic micro-management. There are two big strands, the first (and older) consists of "turn-based", the second (and more popular) of "real-time" strategy games (RTS). The former may be described as the continuation of chess by other means. The whole genre is based on board and pen-and-paper games. Two (or more) armies fight each other, whereas each player may carry out a certain number of moves during each turn, for example moving a tank to a certain position, and, if there are enough "action points" left, firing, repairing, or rearming it. Some of these games go into a very deep level of simulation, for example *Eastern Front*: all infantry weapons, tank version, or truck types of the historical conflict at a certain time and place are included, as are many hampering factors such as the terrain type, its height, the overall visibility, or the weather. Less accurate but more playable are games like the *Panzer General* series, whose first instalment was put on the index in Germany, as the player had to wage a war of aggression.

Since the early 1990s, real time strategy games became one of the most successful of all genres. The main distinction to turn-based strategy games is that all actions of the players (including the virtual ones) are done without having alternating turns, but at the same time. This leads to a faster pace which seems to appeal to many gamers. However encompassing the genre description may be, the approaches of the individual games are very different. In *Commandos II*, for example, the player must not lose a single of his only some special forces soldiers, while undertaking missions behind the German lines during World War II. Unlike most RTS games, he cannot "produce" more units and eventually crush the opponent by numerical superiority (the so-called "tank rush"). More typical examples of such RTS games are *Conflict Zone* and *Real War*, where the player can produce his units (also including soldiers) by building factories or barracks, and using resources like money or his "ability of command". In this respect, *Sudden Strike* uses a more realistic approach as the player may receive some reinforcements later in the game, but he cannot "build" new soldiers or equipment. Nearly all these games use the so-called isometric perspective (a view from above at an angle), usually accompanied with several zoom levels. The number of units represented may range from only a handful – as in *Commandos* – to several hundreds – as in *Sudden Strike* – leading to different kinds of demands on the player.

A very prominent genre is the ego- or first-person-shooter (FPS). The player sees the virtual 3D-world "through the eyes" of his character, while holding a weapon (seen on the lower part of the screen) and blazing his way through numerous opponents. The player has just to move his character over weapons and ammunition to supply himself with the hardware needed, which are practically scattered in the maze's rooms. If the hero becomes wounded, "health packs" can be picked up for some instant relief. *Castle Wolfenstein 3D* was the first of these games in 1992, but it was one year later the genre's breakthrough came with *Doom*, as normal office-PCs became powerful enough for being used for "real" gaming (i.e. beyond text-based games). Although the first representative of ego-shooters was a war game, it took some years to see another example, while science fiction- or fantasy-based environments dominated the genre. In the recent years however, war games conquered ego-shooters with a vengeance. Until the mid-1990s, both the environment and the level objectives were quite simple: find the exit and kill everything that is moving. Since then, the genre has developed tremendously, giving way for complex scenarios and cooperation. As with simulations, there are on the one hand more realistic ego-shooters such as *America's Army: Operations* or *Operation Flashpoint*, and on the other hand action-oriented games such as *Medal of Honour* or *Frontline 1942*. The former put emphasis on the "realistic" experience of fighting, with its needs, among others, to hide, wait, save ammunition, and proceed in a militarily tactical way. The second group of shooters put emphasis on the action: there is lots of ammunition available, opponents to be killed are numerous, the player can carry many weapons and may be healed instantly, while tactics like jumping and circle-strafing (moving sideways around an enemy while shooting) make sense, unlike in the real world. Many of today's ego-shooters are multiplayer games, where two parties of four, eight, or sometimes more players each fight against each other. A well-known example is *Half Life: Counterstrike*, a multiplayer game developed by gamers from the original *Half Life*. In this game, a group of terrorists is fighting against a group of policemen. To be successful in this virtual version of "cops and robbers", the players need to communicate extensively and train their tactics.

Although they do not represent a genre as the ones described above, the increasing number of (massive) multiplayer games needs to be mentioned. While until the mid-1990s, most games were played alone, this has tremendously changed since then. Today, most games would just not sell if they were offered without a multiplayer option. Despite all the efforts to develop better "artificial intelligence", men seem to prefer to play with each other, while winning against another real person provides for a much higher drive. Multiplayer games are played in company or private networks – so-called LANs (local area network) – as well as online on the Internet. While most games allow only for a small number of players to join in, there are also a couple of massive multiplayer games, such as *Warbirds* (a World War II flight simulator) or *World War II Online*, where hundreds if not thousands of gamers can play together. Although multiplayer games stirred up quite some hype recently, they will not completely displace single player games from the market. Especially for casual gamers (i.e. people who like a game from time to time) it is not always easy to find a suitable opponent; additionally, many online games are infested with cheaters, people that use forbidden means to enhance their capabilities, for example they may see and shoot through walls. A similar exuberant hype appeared about mobile gaming shortly ago. However, there is still no viable business model, and the huge technical constraints (for example, the small resolution of the displays, the devices' slow CPU, or the low bandwidth) have not been fully overcome to date.

5.   The Gamers and their Motivation

"'One cannot play war' ...grandpa says!" was the marketing campaign's slogan for the strategy game *Sudden Strike*. Obviously, the desire to play war is as old as war (and thus man) itself. Playing war in computer games is just the transfer of an existing desire to a new medium. The two most obvious questions for somebody without any game experience are "who is playing such games, and why?" Regarding the former one, the media succeeded in further entrenching existing prejudices. Unfortunately, most media members of the non-specialist press writing about computer games seem to have a negligible experience in actually playing these games. With the increasing discussion on violence and games, *Counterstrike* has become synonymous for both "excessive and senseless violence" (according to the media) and badly researched media coverage.

Despite the fact that playing computer games has become quite normal, some myths regarding the gamers still exist (or reappear). First of all, computer games are regarded as nothing serious and thus for children only. In reality, the average age of gamers steadily increases, being now in the mid-twenties. An increasing number of mature people have computer experience, and there are surely not only kids' games available on the market. Many war games are intended for an older audience only, and, due to the content and the complexity, do not attract younger players. However, as with other forms of media, the access of younger audiences to games unsuitable for them is indeed a problem.

Computer games are often associated with a male audience only. Although the overwhelming majority of war gamers are indeed male, this prejudice is not true for computer games as such, where – as with the Internet usage ratio – parity has been reached between female and male users. Nevertheless, some war games like *Age of Empires* do also attract female users. The publishers have finally discovered this huge market laying fallow. However, the first approach of making computer games attractive for women was to transfer the *Barbie* franchise on the computer. But as a female game developer said: "It's a lie we all dislike violent games. But we don't want to be represented by women such as Lara Croft. Why are there no strong female characters like Marge in [the movie] *Fargo*?"[7] – the latter being a pregnant policewomen and arguably the only sane character in this movie.

The next prejudice is that all gamers are loners and freaks. Although there are indeed some weird people (as within any other group), the majority consists of "normal" people. As mentioned above, multiplayer games become increasingly important. "LAN parties" with up to several thousand participants are about gaming *and* communication. Gamers also communicate in Internet-based user groups and chat rooms, and there are countless websites set up by individuals or groups to improve the community. "Hardcore gamers" – who play quite a lot, in contrary to "casual gamers" – join online clans such as the many virtual *War Birds* squadrons. While some clans are mainly virtual, many of them are set up by friends, and the participants meet regularly in "real life".

The last prejudice is that gamers are a small minority who do not know what to do with themselves. The recent market data however proves this assumption wrong: In 2001, the U.S. gaming industry's turnover amounted to $ 9.4 bn (about £ 6.0 bn/€ 9.5 bn), thus exceeding the takings of the U.S. box offices to 12.7%.[8] The market magazine MCV estimates that the British game market will reach £ 2 bn (€ 3.2 bn) in 2002.[9] Such figures cannot be caused by a small minority, making the games industry an important player of the economy.

Overall, it is very hard to describe the fascination of computer games to somebody who has never experienced a good one by oneself. It might be compared to telling somebody who never has read a book before how wonderful a certain book was. Of course, "the gamers" are no homogenous group. Thus, their motivations are manifold and depend on the preferred genre. People who like to play simulations will find the "mastering" of high-tech equipment (or historical technology) fascinating. Even more so, computer games enable the virtual realisation of dreams and fantasies, for example to fly a plane. In games, it is possible to save the world. Or, as the actor George Clooney put it, regarding his role in the war movie *The Thin Red Line:* "Everybody wants to be a World War II hero." Cooperation and team spirit are important for multiplayer games. Being able to successfully set up tactics and strategies is fascinating for people into strategy games. An attractive presentation (visual effects or sounds) may be interesting for some other people. For many gamers, the competition as such and the thrill of the game are huge incentives. Others just try to get over stress or to work off aggression. After all, war may be considered as the ultimate challenge, to kill or to be killed. Indeed, there is no single answer why people play computer games nor war games in particular.

6.   Realism vs. Reality

As with the movie industry, the desire for "absolute" realism is high. However, *what kind* of realism is desired? To approach this question, a short case study might be useful: "You don't play – you volunteer"™ is the marketing slogan for the World War II shooter *Medal of Honour*. Interestingly, this project was initiated by Steven Spielberg and his *Dreamworks Studios* after producing the war movie *Saving Private Ryan*. This movie set new levels of (perceived) realism and tried its best to involve the audience in the action, using audio-visual effects, news-style camerawork, and realistic depiction of massive violence. Spielberg wanted to create an interactive experience as close to the movie as possible. The developers did their very best, and both *Medal of Honour: Allied Assault* and *Medal of Honour: Frontline* provided an astonishing level of audiovisual quality. Both games are highly successful and very playable. As with the movie, the games' most stunning sequence is the invasion of the French Normandy coast on 6 June 1944. In this level, *Medal of Honour* becomes realistic in both a fascinating and frustrating way: the player's only task is to survive. He cannot defend himself actively, but only by ducking down and running to the next covering. While doing so, the player passes scenes of wounded soldiers, of panicked soldiers refusing to move, and of bodies blown up – and it is very likely that he is to be killed by one of the numerous bullets coming in from far away. It is the re-enactment of the re-enactment (in *Saving Private Ryan*) of the Omaha Beach landing. Usually, game developers do not willingly expose their audience to such high levels of frustration: the Omaha Beach level has to be restarted several times, as surviving it is just a stroke of luck. This is where the "real realism" stops. Most war games, although they claim to be "realistic", offer quite strange definitions of "realism". This should come as no surprise, as games are intended to entertain, to be fun, and the utmost level of realism can only be boring, frustrating, disgusting, or a mixture of all these factors. To quote the producer of *Medal of Honour: Allied Assault*: "We are putting our focus into authenticity, not necessarily total realism. We want the game to be as enjoyable as possible, and try not to sacrifice fun at the expense of accurate physics or ballistics."

To distinguish between "realism" and reality, some aspects of simulated and real warfighting need to be examined. Like in action movies, weapons are very prominent in war games. Developers announce on their websites that they were using original historical weaponry for making their virtual counterparts "authentic". Today, gamers can expect that the different weapons in the game sound like the real ones, as the sounds of loading, cocking and shooting have been sampled. The distinction to reality starts usually with the use of these weapons. Firstly, in many games, the player can carry an impressive amount of kit. For example, in the aforementioned game *Medal of Honour*, he may carry a pistol, a sniper rifle, a machine pistol, an automatic assault rifle (which were quite heavy during the Second World War) and a bazooka, accompanied by over 1,200 rounds of all calibres involved and a couple of hand grenades; no soldier would be burdened with this weight. Games like *Operation Flashpoint* or *America's Army* are the exception, where the player is limited to a primary weapon and an optional secondary sidearm, with only a reasonable amount of ammunition. Of course, this limitation changes the whole character of the game: if a soldier is only equipped with an assault rifle and 60 rounds of ammunition, he may not engage a whole enemy company. In action-oriented shooters however, firing thousands of rounds (!) in each level is no exception. For example, the magazine *Playstation Planet* wrote in its review of *Medal of Honour: Frontline*: "Without a doubt, *Medal of Honour* is the best and most realistic war game you can buy ... You'll be so busy pulling the trigger, you won't notice what time it is." So much for realism.

The way these weapons are used is also significant. In most first-person-shooters, the weapon chosen is being shown in the lower part of the screen, whereas in the middle of the screen a crosshair provides the weapon's aiming point. In many games, the player can fire his weapon and exactly hit the object in the crosshair, even consecutive times. Similar to Western movies, the weapons are more or less fired from the hip, and there is also no recoil to be taken into account. The most realistic games so far are *Operation Flashpoint* and *America's Army: Operations*. Here, the weapon may be fired from the hip, but hitting something is highly unlikely. In order to take a proper aim, the player needs to look through the weapon's sight, thus restricting his view. Even more so, not only is each shot being followed by recoil, but also the player's breathing is taken into account: like hunters or soldiers need to learn, the player has to choose the right moment to pull the trigger.

Speaking of the soldier, human movements and behaviour are far from being adequately simulated. Usually, there is no fatigue, and the soldier may run and run and run without getting tired. Often, movements are very restricted for the sake of an easy interface and high playability. Nevertheless, it is somewhat odd when a soldier cannot just look around the corner without exposing his full body. When moving around in the game, many "natural" ways are blocked, for example a soldier may not cross through a hedge, as he is just not allowed to do so. Additionally, in games, war is always "action" – but in reality, most of the time the soldier spends is waiting or doing repetitive if not boring tasks like cleaning his weapons, or guard duty. In "recruiting games" like *America's Army*, this may lead to a wrong perception of life in the military on behalf of the gamer, which will be rapidly and completely cured if he should eventually enrol for military service. An interesting side issue may be called "racial equity", as *America's Army* is the first game where the player can chose from different skin colours to fit Asian, Afro-American, Latino, or Caucasian background.

Prominent aspects of "wargaming" are how wounds and death are depicted. There are three different ways of depicting wounds in games. The first one is not to show any, as being used in *Medal of Honour*. Soldiers may walk slower or limp, but there are no pools of blood, no severed limbs, and no nasty wounds. Interestingly, this approach seems to be the one favoured by most gamers, as they play the game not to wound or kill somebody, having fun watching the other's suffering, but to succeed in the missions by communicating and jointly acting with their team members. Most *Counterstrike* players thus switch off the option to depict blood and gore. The second strand, taking *America's Army: Operations* as an example, depict a paintball-like red blob on the uniform if a soldier has been hit. The third strand depicts violence and wounds in a "realistic" way. However, there are huge differences between the games. *Operation Flashpoint* offers some position between the second and third way by virtually soaking the uniforms with blood where the hit(s) occurred. On the other extreme, *Soldier of Fortune II: Double Helix* provides for one of the goriest gaming experiences in "real-world" environments.

Not only the depiction of wounds, but also their effects and their treatment are interesting aspects: In most games, the player can instantly improve his quality or even completely heal himself by using "health packs" which can be found throughout game. In action-oriented shooters, it is quite normal being hit by 150 bullets – no problem, as long as there are enough health packs; of course, there are also no long-term effects. Games like *Operation Flashpoint* do not provide such treatments: if the player is hit, he is highly restricted (depending on where he took the bullet) and can be happy to survive. Another "arcade issue" is that often the higher rank an enemy has, the more hits he can take, which does not really correspond to life.

After the "health level" of a virtual soldier has reached 0%, he dies. Often, the player is not restricted in his movements or his speed although being badly hit; even with 1% of his strength, he may run and jump around. In most games, people who are killed literally just "drop dead"; a couple of seconds later they vanish – especially in action-oriented games, it would probably be just too ridiculous to walk on these piles of corpses, as in a single level (lasting maybe a quarter or half an hour) killing 100 or more enemies is not uncommon. Of course, the ultimate difference to reality (and the most obvious one) is that there is always the possibility to restart a game, which will provide no problems as long as there is a clear distinction between real and virtual world.

Interestingly, taking prisoners (i.e. not wiping out the enemy) is not an objective to most games. Quite seldom, like in *America's Army: Operations*, missions include the possibility of taking an enemy prisoner. In most games however, enemy soldiers neither give up nor flee. Even if outnumbered, they just keep on fighting until the last one of them could be killed. This "total war"-approach of killing everybody may have its parallel in the "blood rage" occurring in real warfare; the non-existence of surrender and POWs (except the friendly ones the player may have to liberate) is surely strange. There is no way of negotiating, no other possibility than to kill the opponent, the more the better, and in some games it is even necessary to destroy all enemy units to complete a level.

Civilians do not appear in most war games, similar to many war movies. If they are depicted, they might be mad Nazi scientists (who are to be killed anyway), but not normal people inhabiting the fighting zones. This is even stranger in scenarios of urban warfare, if one remembers the contemporary problems with civilian casualties, or the high number of civilians killed in all conflicts since the 20th century. Some games try to give an explanation for this; for example, in one mission of *Medal of Honour: Allied Assault*, set in a half-destroyed French town, the briefing says that all civilians have been evacuated beforehand. Of course, as there are no civilians, there is also no need to bother about other social issues or civil-military relations.

"Collateral damage" has become a hot topic recently, and the influence of the media on the outbreak and course of wars (for example regarding popular support for a campaign) is well known. In war games however, these issues do hardly matter, with the exception of the game *Conflict Zone*. If the player chooses the "good" side (an organisation similar to the UN), civilians have not only to be spared but protected and eventually evacuated from the war zone, and collateral damage has to be avoided. If the player chooses the "evil" side (a conglomerate of rogue states and transnational organisations), he may use media for propaganda purposes.

Logistics, an enormous part of any military activity, is seldom important in any war game. In many strategy games, new units can be produced and repaired. To an increasing level, real-time strategy games try to add a realistic aspect, for example by not offering reinforcements or the fast production of additional forces. However, tanks and other weapons often do not run out of ammunition or fuel, and even if this aspect is regarded at all, there may be just a penalty, for example the loss of "action points" during a turn.

Precision regarding both small arms and larger weapon systems is another issue. Only the most proficient simulations include the possibility of malfunctions. In most cases, a locked-on missile will always hit its designated target. In some team-based shooters, for example in the recent *Conflict: Desert Storm*, the hit ratio of the friendly soldiers is exaggerated, and enemy equipment can be destroyed in nearly arcade-like fashion. One might argue that one is more likely to believe the reports on the successful use of precision weapons in real conflicts if one has "used" the same equipment with a similar positive outcome.

However, the convergence of COTS games and military professional simulations will continue. The U.S. Army has already developed the aforementioned *America's Army: Operations* as a "recruitment game". More than 700,000 people downloaded the free game in the first couple of weeks, while several millions of CD-ROMs were distributed. Furthermore, two other games are in production for the U.S. Army by the games developer *Pandemic Studios*. One of them, *Full Spectrum Warrior* is a tactical MOUT (military operations in urban terrain) fighting game, which will be published as a commercial game, and which will be used – in a slightly adapted version – to train infantry soldiers.[10]

7.   Conclusion

Overall, most computer war games are not realistic, despite their stunning audiovisual quality. The latter will surely continue to improve, soon providing near-lifelike or even better quality with standard home-PCs or the coming generation of game consoles. Although games such as *Operation Flashpoint* and *America's Army: Operations* prove that it is possible to produce a both gripping and (relatively) realistic war game, any further "improvements" in realism are probably undesirable, as such games might only become overly complex, boring, and frustrating. Furthermore, the majority of gamers do not long for a realistic depiction of violence, wounds, and death. Any virtual "experience" of war is destined to be a very limited one, even if future visual application systems are taken into account. This is by intent and to no surprise, as the idea of gaming is entertainment and fun. However, one may ask the question, to what extent a violent activity such as war can be regarded as such at all? Firstly, one has to remember that the majority of computer games are not violent or even war games, even if reports in the media present another image. Secondly, war always was and continues to be a dominant human activity with its very own fascination. As with all other forms of media, war will also play its role in computer games.

Media attention on violent computer games is especially high after incidents such as the Columbine High School killings in 1999 or the Erfurt massacre in 2002. Games such as *Counterstrike* are depicted as "killer trainers", especially since the military does use adapted versions of COTS war games for their own training. The assumption for many people is that if the military – being in the "real business" of killing – is using such games, there must have been some influence on the killers, either by reducing the human threshold to kill another of its own species by habitualisation, or by just improving their aiming and shooting skills. The former U.S. military psychologist Dave Grossman has particularly attacked arcade video games with mock-up models of weapons in his argument that this is indeed the case.[11] However, one has to take into account that all these young killers had both access to and training with real guns. Additionally, although several armed forces are using COTS computer games for training purposes, these games are neither intended to reduce the threshold to kill (the military has much better means for doing so) nor to improve other skills than communication, co-operation, and team spirit, all of which are definitely of "dual use" and positive for any civilian career, too.[12]

With the continuing high speed of technological development, one cannot foresee the development of interactive entertainment and experiences in the near future; both the "holodeck" and the "mind link" are still science fiction, but as entertainment and war are large markets, we may live to see their very application. Additionally, the possible influence on the perception of historical and contemporary events through modern media (including their wide range of possibilities of both faking and mimicking reality) should not be underrated. For the younger and the coming generations, movies such as *Saving Private Ryan* and corresponding games such as *Frontline 1942* and *Medal of Honour* may represent the view of events they will trust in most. The responsibility of media producers thus may even increase. Nevertheless, one should not have too high expectations of the level to which computer games will provide their users with explanations of the causes of wars and the motivations of their protagonists. This lack of explanation and the presentation of both clear-cut distinctions between good and evil and easy (military) solutions may be less due to the usual tendency of games to simplify, but more a derivation of the political reality. Even if real war as such will not be regarded as a "normal" kind of activity or even fun, truth will become an increasingly precious value.

Notes

1. The successor to the 'police simulation' *Silent Scope* has now, of course, an anti-terrorist theme; http://www.konami.co.uk/home/games/action/fjudge/index.asp

2. http://www.dreamgun.com. However, the manufacturer could not confirm if the real SA-80's jamming problems were accurately simulated.

3. CAVE™ was developed by the Electronic Visualisation Laboratory of the University of Illinois, Chicago http://www.evl.uic.edu/research/vrdev.html

4. On the other hand, the locations are representation of historically correct sites, adding to extensive research on Himmler's ideology and plans towards setting up the SS as the future European elite.

5. Just recently, the strategy game *Platoon* has been published, mainly using the movie franchise for its name.

6. The original *Beachhead* was an arcade and C-64 game, the latter having been set on the German index.

7. Roundtable 'Women and computer games', Games Developers' Conference 1998, Long Beach, USA

8. Market research institute NPD, http://www.spiegel.de/netzwelt/technologie/0,1518,druck-208698,00.html

9. MCV, 23.09.02;

http://www.mcvuk.com/link.asp?newsId=342http://www.mcvuk.com/link.asp?newsId=342

10. http://www.pandemicstudios.com/games/fsw/index.html

11. See also his website, http://www.killology.com

12. The U.S. Marine Corps used an adapted version of *Doom* since 1993, while for example the British Army uses an adapted version of *Counterstrike*.

Bibliography

1.   Books

Der Derian, James. *Virtuous War – Mapping the Military-Industrial-Media-Entertainment Network.* Boulder, Col.: Westview, 2001.

Fritz, Jürgen & Fehr, Wolfgang. "Gewalt, Aggression und Krieg – Bestimmende Spielthematiken in Computerspielen." In: *Handbuch Medien: Computerspiele – Theorie, Forschung, Praxis,* edited by Jürgen Fritz and Wolfgang Fehr. Bonn: Bundeszentrale für Politische Bildung, 1997.

Grossman, Lt. Col. Dave. *On Killing – The Psychological Cost of Learning to Kill in War and Society.* Boston: Little, Brown & Co, 1996.

Grossman, Lt. Col. Dave. *Stop Teaching our Kids to Kill.* Boston: Little, Brown & Co, 1999.

National Research Council et al, ed. *Modeling and Simulation – Linking Entertainment and Defence.* Washington, D.C.: National Academy Press, 1997

Poole, Steven. *Trigger Happy – The Inner Life of Videogames.* London: Fourth Estate, 2000.

Thompson, Clive. "Violence and the Political Life of Videogames." In: *Game On – The History and Culture of Videogames,* exhibition catalogue, edited by Lucien King, 22 – 31. London: Laurence King, 2002.

2.   Articles

Anderson, Craig A. & Dill, Karen E. "Video Games and Aggressive Thoughts, Feelings, and Behaviour in the Laboratory and in Life." *Journal of Personality and Social Psychology,* April 2000, Vol. 78, No. 4, 772-790, http://www.apa.org/journals/psp/psp784772.html

Albrecht, Harro (2002), "Blut und Spiele." *Die Zeit,* 19/2002

Büttner, Christian. *Zum Verhältnis von phantasierter zu realer Gewalt,* 1996, <http://www.bpb.de/snp/referate/buettner.htm> (10.07.2002)

Eng, Paul. *A Play for Better Soldiers – The Rise of Computer Games to Recruit and Train U.S. Soldiers,* abcNews.com 21.08.2002,

<http://abcnews.go.com/sections/scitech/DailyNews/wargames020821.ht ml> (25.08.2002)

Fritz, Jürgen & Fehr, Wolfgang, *Computerspiele zwischen Faszination und Gewalt*, online, 1996

hag. *Spiel mit dem Terror*, heise news 20.08.2002, <http://www.heise.de/newsticker/data/hag-20.08.02-000/> (22.08.2002)

Meves, Helge. *Das falsche Spiel mit der Gewalt – Computerspiele und die Gewalt in der Gesellschaft*, telepolis 29.07.2002, <http://www.telepolis.de/deutsch/special/game/12973/1.html> (31.07.2002)

Osunsami, Steve. *Simulated Sniping – U.S. Army Recruits Teens With Internet Game*, abcNews 31.10.2002, <http://abcnews.go.com/sections/wnt/DailyNews/army_game021031.html > (02.11.2002)

Rötzer, Florian. *Üben für den Krieg im Irak – Wartainment: Computerspiele für den Krieg und zur Anwerbung*, telepolis 06.10.2002, <http://www.telepolis.de/deutsch/special/game/13367/1.html> (07.10.2002)

Streibl, Ralf E. *Krieg im Computerspiel*, 1996 <http://www.bpb.de/snp/referate/streibl.htm> (20.06.2002)

Streibl, Ralf E., *Spielend zum Sieg!*, 1996, http://www.bpb.de/snp/referate/streibl2.htm (20.06.2002)

Villanueva, Lt. Col. Frank & Huber, Maj. Al. "Out of the Box – Using COTS Products to Build Collective Skills." In: *Training and Simulation*, June/July 2002, 40 – 45

Willmann, Thomas. *Death's a Game*, telepolis 17.06.2002, <http://www.telepolis.de/deutsch/kolumnen/wil/12679/1.html> (19.06.02)

Willmann, Thomas. *Ganz anders als Krieg sollte ein gutes Spiel immer Spaß machen*, telepolis 26.07.2002, <http://www.telepolis.de/deutsch/special/game/12928/1.html> (31.07.02)

Woznicki, Krystian. *Krieg als Massenkultur*, telepolis 24.08.02, <http://www.telepolis.de/deutsch/inhalt/co/13059/1.html> (30.08.2002)

Wright, Kathryn. *Does Media cause Violent Behaviour? – A Look at the Research*, womengamers.com, 06.10.2000, <http://www.womengamers.com/articles/gameviolence1.html> (02.11.01)

Contemporary British Cinema and the Re-imagining of World War Two: A Virtual/Humane Sensibility to War and a 'New' Grammar of Heroism

Christopher Macallister[1]

The UK continues to have an appetite for war. Since the end of the Cold War, in alliance with the United States or alone, Britain has used military power in Iraq, Bosnia, Kosovo, Sierra Leone and Afghanistan. However, the UK now seems to want to engage in a very different kind of war to what was on offer up until 1991.

This chapter will explore Britain's virtual/humane sensibility to war through the re-imagination of the 'paradigm conflict' of World War Two by British cinema. The worlds created by films like *The English Patient (1996), Enigma (2001)* and *Charlotte Gray (2002)* reflect society's changed understanding of war. These stories are based on a different grammar of heroism to that which structured earlier films. A reading of the re-imagined landscape of WW2 reveals how the rules that script heroism have changed. The beliefs that underpin heroism are different because the gender roles and boundaries that are at the heart of Western notions of war have been turned upside down. No longer are men "virtuous warriors protecting beautiful souls" (women)[2]. Simultaneously, boundaries between the personal and the political have been erased and new rules apply.

This chapter will begin with an examination of what has become known as post modern, Virtual or humane war. Then there will be a discussion of World War Two's place in the collective imagination and why it functions as a 'paradigm' war that can act as a mirror for society's wider conceptions of warfare. This will be followed by an examination of the feminist turn taken by some scholars of International Relations. Here, war is read as a profoundly gendered activity whose meaning for society is built on understandings of the proper roles of men and women, and clear cut boundaries between the personal and the political. This chapter then presents a 'heroic' reading of *The English Patient, Enigma* and *Charlotte Gray* for the rules that their heroes have to live by. These reveal a WW2 of counter myths that challenge the gender roles and boundaries established by earlier recreations of the War.

1.   The Virtual and Humane Conception of War.

The Gulf War suggested that Western societies could insulate themselves from the costs of war and make it 'Virtual'[3]. This reached its apotheosis in Kosovo when NATO ended the campaign without a single combat casualty. Thus today in Western societies, including Britain, war should be waged in the name of humanitarianism, in a 'Humane' manner[4]. Britain and the West want to make the immense cruelty and suffering of 'Modern'/Total War a thing of the past. The harsh realities of war(pain, mutilation and death) are to be avoided at all costs. Not that long ago suffering was accepted as an inevitable part of war. Just twenty years ago British society bore the loss of five ships, and over one hundred dead in pursuit of victory in the Falklands. By the end of the 1990s in Sierra Leone and Macedonia the loss of a single British life was enough to set off a debate in the media about whether the price of intervention was too high. Hence, today war should ideally be conducted by air power supported by Special Forces and local proxies.

With the rejection of the price of Modern war, Britain has also rejected one of the concepts that made Modern war possible: heroism. Not just the Homeric heroism of a warrior, but the heroism of Modernity that sustained the British war machine through two world wars. The qualities that were required of a hero in Modern war were the ability to endure hardship and suffering, and the willingness to sacrifice your physical and emotional well being for a greater cause e.g. your nation[5]. Already individualistic, Homeric heroism had become outdated. Indeed, on the Modern battlefield it was something of a liability[6].

However, today even Modern heroism is redundant[7]. As the West has rejected the harsh realities of war there is no need, or desire, for its citizens to endure suffering or sacrifice themselves. Neither, do courage, or risk taking, have a place in war as these qualities, by their very nature, court death. The West and Britain have rejected heroism. Thus the reality of war is now left to a small class of 'supermen' special forces: paratroopers, marines, and the SAS. In a society that social theorists like Beck see as obsessed with risk and how to avoid it[8], the common soldier, a figure society could identify with, is safely out of harms way.

2.   World War Two: Britain's 'Paradigm' War.

These new Virtual and Humane understandings of war have grown out of the events of the recent past. However, they also give society a different lens for how the more distant past is viewed, and how defining moments in Britain's collective past are re-imagined and can thus in turn affect the present. In Britain the Second World War is just such an event. It has become a model or paradigm of what a war is, and should be. In the British consciousness it has become a benchmark against which other conflicts are contrasted, and understood.

Whenever Britain has gone to war since 1945: at Suez (1956), over the Falklands (1982) and in the Gulf (1990), WW2 has been invoked. This is reflected in both the public rhetoric of politicians and the discourse of the general public[9]. Indeed polling data about the public understanding of the Gulf War showed how British society had to fall back on WW2 when it came to making sense of a new dictator and the war he threatened.[10]

In particular it is the Second World War's clear-cut position as a conflict between good and evil that still resonates. It was the 'Free World' against Nazism in a struggle for the course of History. Hence when the memory of WW2 is invoked, Hitler and the authoritarian nature of his regime feature prominently. It was a 'good' war that 'we' can be proud of having fought.

Therefore, in the collective imagination World War Two can function as both a discrete historical event, and the very definition and essence of what War is about: it is an ideal type of war. Thus, contemporary representations of WW2 have the potential to say something about the British understanding of war today. Indeed, as resource they are far more useful as commentary on society today than as a historical document about events that occurred fifty years before they were made.

Film plays a part in the creation of this collective imagination, especially films that identify themselves with the British story. *The English Patient, Enigma* and *Charlotte Gray* all do this. While they may not be fully financed from British sources, they use British creative talent and narratives that revolve around British characters to contribute to the collective imagination.

3. War Gender and Identity

In a reflection of current sensibilities, the re-imagining of WW2 is based on a new moral grammar that makes heroism and the hero superfluous. The key to understanding this new grammar can be found in the perspectives opened up by two groundbreaking feminist contributions to International Relations and security studies[11]. These are Jean Elshtain's focus on the strict gender roles war that underwrite war[12]. And Cynthia Enloe's concern with debating the boundary between the personal and the political realms, a boundary that war has traditionally upheld[13].

Elshtain puts forward the thesis that war is a profoundly gendered activity: Men and women have traditionally had distinct roles. Women are part of a treasured homeland that men protect: 'beautiful souls' protected by 'just warriors'[14]. This is where heroism comes in. It is the ethic that sustains the just warrior and is thus firmly part of the masculine world.

Cynthia Enloe insists that even in International Relations the personal is political.[15] The position of heroism in British culture, with its element of personal sacrifice to protect a public good, is at stake in how the dichotomy between the personal and the political is resolved. For heroism to have meaning the public good must be put before personal needs and desires.

Recent British WW2 films call into question the orthodox positions on these issues: traditional gender roles are turned upside down, heroism as a virtue is doubted and the personal is elevated above the political. In doing so they create a new heroic grammar at odds with both earlier films and traditional understandings of war. In the world of *The English Patient, Enigma* and *Charlotte Gray* gender roles are reversed, heroism mocked, and the personal is raised above the political.

4.   A 'Heroic' Reading of: *The English Patient, Charlotte Gray, and Enigma*

This journey into the version of WW2 created by these three films will uncover the rules that create a moral grammar for heroes and heroic behaviour. This strategy will utilise the approaches of IR scholars who have treated fiction as a site of the political: Shapiro, Weber and Weldes[16]. They have gone outside International Relations to draw on post modern/cultural theorists: Foucault, Barthes and Hall[17].

Therefore, the films will be read for the ideologies that underwrite the explicit story of the narratives. What are the implicit premises that govern the lives of the characters when it comes to heroism? My reading of the films will focus this question on the three key issues that underpin heroism: gender roles, the respectability of heroic acts, and whether the personal or political takes precedence.

I focus on *The English Patient (1996), Charlotte Gray (2002)* and *Enigma (2001)* because they interweave personal and domestic concerns with the dangers of the frontline. All three films force their characters to deal with the dilemmas that arise as the war challenges their identities, and makes them choose between the personal and the political. Because these films juxtapose the private and public spheres they present a more holistic vision of war than other films that concentrate on the home front e.g. *Land*

Girls (1998) and *The End of the Affair (1999)*. To provide a guide rail through the heroic reading that follows, I begin with a brief summary of each film's story. The next three sections then zoom in to look at key moments where these films reveal the heroic rules of the game. The focus is on how these films script gender roles, the respectability of heroic acts, and whether the personal or political takes precedence.

A.   The films: a synopsis.

The English Patient tells the story of an aristocratic Hungarian explorer, Count Almasy (Ralph Fiennes) and his doomed affair with Katherine (Kristin Scott Thomas) the wife of a fellow explorer. These events, set in the Libyan deserts, are told in flashback at the end of the War. Here we find Almasy in a make shift hospital in Northern Italy being cared for by a Canadian nurse, Hanna (Juliette Binoche). He is bedridden and burnt beyond recognition following an air crash. He claims to have forgotten his identity and is known simply as the English Patient. Over, the course of the film, Almasy tells his story. How he was caught up in the war and how his personal affairs became part of the struggle for North Africa. His recollections are assisted by the allied spy Caravaggio (Willem Dafoe), another victim of the war who has been captured and tortured by the Germans as a direct result of Almasy's actions.

Enigma is set at the British code breaking station Bletchley Park during the crisis point of the battle of the Atlantic. Jericho (Dougary Scott), a brilliant but unstable code breaker, has been recalled as the Germans have suddenly switched to new indecipherable code. Rumours of a traitor are rife and Jericho's former girlfriend (part of the clerical staff) has disappeared. The movie then follows Jericho's attempts to crack the code, find the traitor and discover the fate of his ex lover. In this, he is assisted by his missing lover's friend, Hester (Kate Winslett), while he is pursued and hampered by a shadowy spymaster/MI5 officer Wigram (Jeremy Northam).

In *Charlotte Gray* the titular heroine joins the British secret service, SOE, and is parachuted into occupied France as a liaison operative with the French Resistance. While there, she attempts to find her missing boyfriend Peter Gregory, an RAF pilot who has been shot down over France. Her personal quest runs parallel to her involvement in the internecine war within French society, the resistance movement, and London.

B.   The manly warrior is reduced to a passive victim.

From Homer's Iliad onwards, the 'proper' role of men in war has been as active rational 'warriors', defending the domestic, passive world of women and family. In *The English Patient, Charlotte Gray,* and *Enigma* this gender divide is turned upside down. Men, far from being heroic warriors, are reduced to passive bodies and minds. They are physically and emotionally weak, and it is the women in these stories who drive the narrative forward.

In the cinematic world of these films men are regularly reduced to helpless, prone bodies. In *The English Patient* the eponymous hero Almasy spends half the story as a living corpse. He is totally dependent on his nurse, Hanna. Indeed, she holds his life in her hands, and eventually euthanises him. The supporting male character, Caravaggio, also has his body turned into a site of victim hood as the Germans torture him after capture by getting a female, civilian nurse to sever his thumbs. The male body as a site of victimhood is normal in this world.

Important also is how Almasy is made passive through his role as a downed pilot, how we first see him in the film's opening sequence. The pilot who has been torn out of the sky here functions as a symbol of helplessness and passivity. He is the vigorous, male warrior reduced to victim. This theme recurs throughout the literature of flight, from Saint Exupery[18] to Richard Hillary[19] and on to J G Ballard[20]. Ballard can still be found using this motif in his latest novel: *Super Cannes[21]*. The downed aviator as victim is a role that links Almasy to one of the male leads in *Charlotte Gray*: the RAF pilot Peter Gregory. It is the loss of his aircraft over France that makes this former Battle of Britain pilot a helpless figure. He is then reliant on Charlotte Gray to come and rescue him. Though we never see his injuries in the film (the novel does however depict Peter as a wounded body[22]) without a plane he is as passive as the bedridden Almasy.

Emotionally, the male characters are if anything even more broken. *Enigma*'s hero, Jericho, is constantly on the verge of breakdown. This, however, is not due to the stress of combat. His breakdown is the result of an extended one-night-stand coming to an end. Suddenly it is the male who is left distraught by the idea that they were used for sex. He has to be rescued by another woman, Hester. She is rational, stable and in control. Again, this theme of the emotionally distraught man is extended to the Spymaster Wigram. For all his cool detachment, we discover he is as distraught over a relationship with a woman (the same one Jericho is obsessed with) as Jericho is.

Neither is Almasy any better. He is similarly unable to handle a relationship. His lover Katherine is the one in control; she keeps a 'stiff upper lip'. So, it is she who begins their affair, and she who ends it. Just as

Charlotte Gray finds herself looking into the 'puppy dog' eyes of Peter to tell him he is no longer needed.

With all this mental and physical weakness, it is no surprise then that women, Charlotte Gray, Hester, Katherine and Hanna, are the individuals who pull the narrative strings. By contrast, when the 'Modern' sensibility prevailed, WW2 films were primarily about "men proving their masculinity"[23]. Thus, if one was damaged, giving in and letting wounds get the better of oneself was not possible. For example, in *Reach for the Sky* (1956), our hero Douglas Bader (here played by Kenneth More) has his body turned into a site of potential victim hood when he loses both legs. Bader, however, is not held back from being a manly warrior. He commands fighter squadrons in the Battle of Britain, is shot down, captured and makes repeated escape attempts.

Alternatively, if one was doomed to end up as a victim, it was best to make sure that one's own well being was sacrificed for a greater good. In *A Town Like Alice* (1956), set during the Japanese occupation of Malaya, a group British women prisoners encounters two Australian POWs. It is not they who save the men. Rather, one of the Australians (Peter Finch) risks himself to get the women food. He caught and savagely punished. He becomes a victim. The difference between him and Almasy is that his mutilation has a point to it. His suffering 'buys' food and time for the women.

However, in the 'real' world of the 1990s, it is the cinematic universe of *The English Patient, Charlotte Gray,* and *Enigma*, not *A Town Like Alice* that makes sense. The soldier as victim has become an acceptable role that society is sympathetic to. Gulf War Syndrome turned the manly warrior into a prone body confined to housing estates. Physical victim hood is complemented by a similar psychological state. In recent litigation, former service personnel have taken the government to court for emotional trauma suffered through their duties[24]. Thus, the manly warrior prefers to be part of the victim society.

In conclusion, in the 'real' world manly warriors have always found themselves as prone bodies with disturbed minds. What is new is that this aspect is now being narrated to British society. It has now become part of war's representation and part of war's politics, but without the gloss of perseverance or sacrifice.

C.   The heroic ethic is questioned.

In the world of the WW2 counter myth the heroic ethic is itself portrayed as deviant. The self-interested survival of Catch 22's captain Yossarian[25] is no longer satire, it is now the norm. Heroism is depicted as a misguided activity through two processes. Firstly, heroic acts are questioned, and shown as pointless to the extent that they are actually mocked. Then, the 'heroic geographies' of the desert, and the fighter pilot's sky, are robbed of their adventurous and heroic qualities. When the male leads in this re-imagined WW2 are actually able to do something heroic, their acts invariably end in failure. Heroic actions are shown as pointless, or indeed actually counter productive.

In *The English Patient* Almasy does get to perform a feat of heroic endurance as he marches for three days across the desert, to save his lover, as she lies injured. However, his moment of glory becomes irrelevant when he loses his temper and gets incarcerated by the British. Then, Almasy does not even get the heroic dignity of sacrificing himself for his cause (individualistic as it is). When he's shot down, there is no cause as Katherine is already dead. Finally, he is denied a heroic exit. He lingers on for several years, and becomes director Anthony Minghella's narrative device. The sole of point of the bedridden Almasy's existence is to tell us his story and to make the other characters reflect on their lives. So it is not surprising that once this is done he is killed off.

In *Enigma*, the heroic moment fares no better. When Jericho tries his hand at heroism, in a pursuit of the traitor, the result verges on the farcical. Then, in case the audience has missed the point, the spymaster Wigram smugly tells us how ludicrous the whole situation is.

At the same time, it is not the case that women have replaced men as heroes. Charlotte Gray's time in occupied France is one fruitless act after another. In the film she fails to find her lover. She also fails to save two children from the Holocaust. Indeed, she contributes very little to the war effort.

In contrast to Charlotte, the story of her predecessor in the *Carve Her Name With Pride* (1958) identifies the lead character, Violette Szabo (Virginia McKenna) as a hero.[26] Here, the female agent has also been parachuted into France. Though Szabo is ultimately captured and killed, her actions in France were not in vain. Indeed, she is captured when, without a moment's hesitation she sacrifices herself for her comrades, holding a German patrol at bay until her comrades have escaped.

In these worlds then, what is so damning of the heroic act is not so much its failure, but the sense of irrelevance and cynicism that surrounds these acts. This is not even the world of Graham Greene and the anti-hero who does usually lose. The characters are not connected into a wider struggle between good and evil[27]. Thus the character's heroic actions don't have much point to them. As Greene would put it, these characters are just "Comedians"[28] playing at being heroes.

By questioning the point of the heroic act these counter myths also rob two traditionally heroic spaces, the desert and the sky, of much of their meaning. From Richard Burton's penetration of Mecca to T E Lawrence's escapades, the desert has been a 'space' where heroic adventure fantasies can be lived out. Even in the heat of Total war the desert gave WW2 a heroic, almost romantic character. Here, the Nazis found a chivalrous identity. Churchill himself eulogised their commander Rommel, 'the desert fox', while the war still raged![29] Similarly, even as World War Two loomed, potential participants like the author/pilot Richard Hilary saw the sky as a last heroic 'space'[30].

The cinematic universe of the counter myth will have none of this. *The English Patient's* opening sequence shows a gleaming biplane soaring over the desert. However, we are rudely awakened from our heroic idyll when a group of feral, semi naked German gunners blow the plane out of the sky. Indeed, this sequence is emblematic of the world of the counter myth, a world where heroism is denied. So, true to this world we never see *Charlotte Gray's* Pilot, Peter Gregory in his Spitfire. The film will not let us see him in a heroic role.

Once again, the new version of WW2 is in step with the 'real' world of the 1990's. The 1999 Kosovo war saw RAF pilots virtually accused of cowardice for flying out of the enemy's range. This scepticism about heroics was picked up again in the Afghan/al-Qaeda campaign. The elite Arctic and Mountain Warfare unit, of the Royal Marines had their mission turned into a farce.[31] The operation was supposed to be one of deadly combat with al-Qaeda with the Defence Secretary warning that "there may be casualties"[32]. Instead, the story became one of Britain's elite troops marching up and down hills, and blowing up empty caves, before they were laid low by the winter vomiting virus (the same virus had formerly struck down the young and the elderly on NHS wards). Again, what is not new is the 'reality'. Military operations have previously turned into farce and heroics have often been absent. What is new is that this story has begun to dominate representations of war.

D.   The end of sacrifice: why *The English Patient* is not *Casablanca*.

In the WW2 counter myth heroism is further eroded. The individual is put first and the whole point of sacrifice is questioned. However, this is another symptom of the new sensibility to war. In *Casablanca (1942)* Rick (Humphrey Bogart) and Elsa (Ingrid Bergman) agree that defeating the Nazis takes precedence over their own personal happiness. Their relationship takes second place to the dialectics of human history.

By contrast, Almasy in *The English Patient* sacrifices the public good for his own interests. Long before feminist scholars pointed it out, Modern war had already established the personal as political. The essential role of women in sustaining the war effort, and the massive civilian casualties made this unavoidable, though the politics of representation were reluctant to acknowledge this[33].

However, what *The English Patient, Charlotte Gray* and *Enigma* do is raise the personal above the political. The individual is everything in this cinematic world. Here, the needs of the one outweigh the needs of the many. In this world it is deviant to sacrifice oneself for a wider cause. What is normal is to put the priority on your personal well-being. This is what decision making should be based on.

The ethic of the 'individual first' dominates all three films. In *The English Patient* Almasy, and most of his fellow explorers despise the "world of nations". They want as little to do with the political world as possible. So, Almasy has no qualms about helping the Germans if it fits in with his personal desires. He is desperate to save his lover, whatever the wider cost.

His justification appears to be that in his (and perhaps the film's) opinion the Nazis are no better or worse than the British. Therefore, there are no higher, worthier causes and the personal can come first. Except that in the wider context of WW2, this is an incredibly selfish position. Whatever the moral shortcomings of Allied strategy in Europe, the Holocaust renders moral equivalence absurd. Indeed, the film seems to realise this, and takes the time to tell us that this ethic is flawed. The British ill treatment of Almasy can be put down to crass stupidity, while the deliberate torture and mutilation of Caravaggio by the Nazis is a blunt reminder of what they were and that the British were not the moral equivalents of the Nazis.

Enigma, too, is a film of personal priorities. The context may be the Battle of the Atlantic and the race to crack the U Boat codes, but Jericho is really driven by the quest to discover the fate of his missing lover. He compromises the wider hunt for a traitor to this end. Nor is he alone. The seemingly ruthless spymaster Wigram also turns out to be more concerned with his former lover's (the same woman Jericho is searching for) fate than he is with winning the war.

Also, the message that in war both sides are as bad as each other reoccurs when *Enigma* opens with the Nazis uncovering the mass grave at Katyn where some 10,000 Polish officers had been executed on Stalin's orders. The allies are not morally pure and have their own skeletons to keep hidden. Thus, we are presented with a morally relative world, which serves to legitimise putting the personal above the political. Once again, if there is no great moral cause, why should one sacrifice oneself for the political world?

Charlotte Gray upholds the message of this personal over the political through Charlotte's motivation for going to France. Her main reason for going to France is to find her boyfriend who has been shot down over enemy territory. From the point of view of the British war effort this seems both selfish and irresponsible. By contrast, Violette Szabo in *Carve Her Name With Pride* is motivated by the need to stop the Nazis. She does have a personal angle. Her husband died fighting with the Free French at Bir Hakeim, North Africa. Yet, she goes so far as to sacrifice her surviving family to the war effort. Her eventual death in Ravensbruck concentration camp leaves her daughter an orphan. Finally, in *Charlotte Gray* we again have the shadow of moral equivalence falling over the film. French collaboration is clear and the British are themselves playing off one resistance group against another.

It is not that personal concerns have never previously appeared in WW2 films. In films like *In Which We Serve* (1942), *The Battle of Britain (1969)* and *Carve Her Name With Pride* (1958), the personal world is very much in evidence, juxtaposed with the public world of combat. However, in these films the personal world serves to remind the characters and the audience, of what is at stake if we, Britain, lose. Individual wives and children symbolise the free world that has to be protected. Crucially, the male characters do not put their own loves and lives above the greater good. In these films we have heroes who, if necessary, give up their lives, and thus destroy their families for the wider cause.

Therefore, as the individual is placed at the centre of politics there is no room for the notion of sacrifice and the ethic of heroism is critically weakened[34]. In the 'real' world the ethos of the personal above the political has manifested itself through the paralysing fear of casualties that has come to dominate British military intervention. The loss of even one soldier in Sierra Leone or Macedonia was enough to prompt questioning of Britain's military role. Indeed, the military themselves have come to acknowledge that the biggest constraint on them is not military capability, but how many casualties the public will accept[35]. Whether the possible land invasions of Kosovo and now Iraq went/will go ahead depends on the public sensibility[36]. So, just as the happiness of Almasy, Charlotte Gray and Jericho was too precious to sacrifice to the war effort, the life of even a handful of Britons could be too high a price to pay for preventing another Rwanda or Bosnia.

5.   What is at Stake in how Cinema represents World War Two?

The changed British sensibility to war is being reflected in WW2 cinema. The change from the 'Modern' to the Virtual or Humane has cut across the boundaries between the 'real' and various forms of representation. There is no room for heroism in war, either on screen in the WW2 counter myth, or in the 'real' world. Both worlds are equally uncomfortable about the role of the manly warrior and the ethic of sacrifice. Normal people, ourselves or characters on screen like us, have no business being heroic. Yes, heroism can still be found in British society, as long as it is not too close to home. Thus, 'supermen' special forces, like the SAS, or the protagonists in the *Lord of the Rings* trilogy are allowed to be heroes. They are fantasy figures sufficiently removed from mainstream society, with its emphasis on avoiding risk or sacrifice and placing the individual at the "centre of the moral imagination"[37].

The 'reality' of War has become more and more alien to much of the English speaking world[38]. Fewer and fewer Westerners experience war as something that has any impact on their physical reality. With the end of the citizen soldier and the Modern conflict, war has become something done by professionals in far off places[39]. Only sudden acts of terrorism disrupt this notion of war. Though these resemble disasters more than 'proper' war, there is no sense of the flow or narrative of a campaign, no battles won, no territory gained. Instead, there is a series of random and staccato moments of destruction. These have the same senselessness as air crashes or earthquakes. Therefore, the gap between the political event and its representation is getting wider and what happens in this gap is ever more crucial. In the absence of more direct, overriding links, British society now encounters war almost solely through visual media. Britain is reliant on television and film to narrate war to it. Thus, the 'war event' has become another element in consumer culture and perhaps "qualitatively no different from the Olympic games"[40]. To rephrase Baudrillard's infamous remark[41], it is not that the Gulf War did not happen, rather, the Gulf War did not happen for much of Western society. The thousands of casualties feared by, among others, the CIA, did not materialise, and the 'reality' of war existed for Western society only in its representational form.

British society can interact with the international politics of globalisation, immigration and narcotics up close in their supermarkets and city streets. However, the politics of war can only be accessed through the aesthetics of the visual media that dominates war's representation. Therefore, for Britain and the West the 'moment of truth' isn't confined to the battlefield. The battle's representation forms a second 'site' where politics are done, meanings contested and events determined. Cinema, including the contemporary British WW2 film, is part of this second struggle. As it reflects popular sentiment, it feeds back and helps reinforce and assert the values that helped create it. British WW2 cinema is not the only media to play a role. News, documentaries and video games are all potential sites of the political. And like contemporary WW2, they have things to say about British understandings of war.

Notes

1. Thanks to Dr. Ruth Abbey and Dr Ian Manners for their feedback, and Kirsten Haack for comments and editorial input. Also thanks to Dr. Rob Fisher for organising the War, Virtual War 2002 conference at which a version of this paper was presented.

2. Elshtain, 1987, 4.

3. Ignatieff, 2002.

4. Coker, 2001, 2.

5. Ibid, 49.

6. Ibid, 106.

7. Ibid, chapter 3.

8. Beck, 1992.

9. Smith, 2000, chapter 7.

10. Shaw, 1997, chapter 12.

11. Sylvester, 2002, chapter 2.

12. Elshtain, 1987.

13. Enloe, 1990.

14. Elshtain, 1987, 4.

15. Enloe, 1990.

16. Shapiro, 1992, Weber, 2001, Weldes, 1999.

17. Hall, 1997.

18. In particular his crash in the Libyan Desert: de Saint-Exupery, 2000.

19. Hillary, 1997.

20. Especially his first volume of fictionalised autobiography: Ballard, 1984 and the short stories: *The Ultimate City* and *My Dream of Flying to Wake Island,* taken from Ballard, 2001.

21. Ballard, 2000.

22. Faulks, 1999.

23. Smith, 2000, 122.

24. *The Guardian,* March 5th, 2002.

25. Coker, 2001, 35.

26. *Carve Her Name With Pride* was based on a true story.

27. Hayim, 1997.

28. Greene, 1991.

29. For a good example of Britain's romanticized view of Rommel and the Afrika Korps see Young, 1950.

30. Hillary, 1997.

31. *The Guardian,* May 20th, 2002.

32. *The Guardian,* March 18th , 2002.

33. Elshtain, 1987, introduction.

34. Coker, 2001, 17 & 18.

35. Sir Charles Guthrie (then Britain's most senior military officer) *The Evening Standard*, April 1st , 1999.

36. *The Guardian*, May 25th , 2002.

37. Coker, 2001, 18.

38. Mann, 1987, 35-36.

39. Ibid.

40. Ibid.

41. Baudrillard made a series of remarks arguing that the Gulf War will/is/did not happen, beginning with: Baudrillard, *The Guardian*, January 11th, 1991.

Bibliography

Ballard, J. G. (2001), 'The Ultimate City and 'My Dream of Flying to Wake Island', in *J G. Ballard the Complete Short Stories*. London: Flamingo.

Ballard, J. G. (2000) *Super Cannes*. London: Flamingo.

Ballard, J. G. (1984), *Empire of the Sun*. London: Gollancz.

Baudrillard, J. (1991), 'The Reality Gulf' *The Guardian*. January 11th.
Beck, U. (1992), *Risk Society: Towards a New Modernity*. Trans. Ritter S. London: Sage.

Coker, C. (2001), *Humane Warfare*. London: Routledge.

Elshtain, J. (1987), *Women and War*. Brighton: Harvester.

Enloe, C. (1990), *Bananas Beaches & Bases: Making Feminist sense of International Politics*. Los Angeles: University of California Press.

Faulks, S. (1999), *Charlotte Gray*. London: Vintage.

Greene, G. (1991), *The Comedians*. Harmondsworth: Penguin.

Guthrie, C. (1999), 'Why NATO cannot simply march in and crush Milosevic', *The Evening Standard*. April 1st.

Hall, S. (1997), 'Introduction' in: Hall S. *Representation: Cultural Representations and Signifying Practices.* London: Sage.

Hayim, G. (1997), *Fighting Evil: unsung heroes in the novels of Graham Greene.* London: Greenwood Press.

Hillary, R. (1997), *The Last Enemy.* London: Pimlico.
Ignatieff, M. (2000), *Virtual War.* New York: Metropolitan Books.

Mann M. (1987) 'The Roots and Contradictions of Modern Militarism', *New Left Review,* 1987, Vol. 162.

de Saint-Exupery, A. (2000), *Wind, Sand and Stars.* trans. Rees W. Harmondsworth: Penguin.

Shapiro, M. (1992), *Reading the Postmodern Polity: Political Theory as Textual Practice.* Minneapolis: University of Minnesota Press.

Shaw, M. (1997), 'Past Wars and Present Conflicts: From the Second World War to the Gulf', in Evans M. & Lunn K. (eds.) *War and Memory in the Twentieth Century.* Oxford: Berg.

Smith, M. (2000), *Britain and 1940: History, Myth and Popular Memory.* London: Routledge.

Sylvester, C. (2002), *Feminist International Relations: An Unfinished Journey.* Cambridge: Cambridge University Press.

Weber, C. (2001), *International Relations Theory: a Critical Introduction.* London: Routledge.

Weldes, J. (1999), 'Going Cultural: Star Trek, State Action, and Popular Culture', *Millennium: Journal of International Studies,* Vol. 28, No. 1.

Filmography

A Town like Alice (1956)
Carve her Name with Pride (1958)
Casablanca (1942)
Charlotte Gray (2002)

Enigma (2001)
In Which We Serve (1942)
Land Girls (1998)
Reach for the Sky (1956)
The Battle of Britain (1969)
The End of the Affair (1999)
The English Patient (1996)

The 'Problem' (Not the 'Theorem') of War - On Pasolini's *Salò*

Jones Irwin

1. Introduction

From its inception, cinema maintained a special relationship with those human experiences which bring one to the limit of endurance or sanity: hallucination, dream, nightmare, amnesia, madness[1]. This might explain the perennial obsession of filmmakers with the phenomenon of war, and more generally with imagery of violence. The depiction of war in film has a long and complex history. Like film, war also introduces a systematic derangement of the senses. In his text, *War and Cinema*, Paul Virilio refers to both phenomena as involving a certain "psychotropic derangement and chronological disturbance"[2]. In this essay, I will concentrate on a paradigmatic film in this regard, a work which reflects the destructive aspects of both cinema and war, and their complex complicity, Pasolini's *Salò*.

Few philosophical or artistic works of the twentieth century come close to the intense vision presented by Pier Paulo Pasolini in his last film, *Salò*. With a screenplay adapted from the text of Sade's *One Hundred and Twenty Days of Sodom*[3] (and applied to 1940's fascist Italy), *Salò* has been severely maligned both for its supposed amoral nihilism and its cinematic grotesqueness. Such criticism, however, has singularly failed to address the complexity of Pasolini's philosophical intent in the film, preferring instead to opt for simple denunciation. The opening credits unusually include a bibliography referencing, amongst others, Blanchot, Klossowski, Lautréamont and Sade. My paper will seek to unpack this intellectual structure of *Salò* on the basis of the hypothesis that one of Pasolini's main reasons for making the film was to put forward a philosophy of the conditions of human life in the late twentieth century (with particular emphasis on the nature of war). Always more than a film director, Pasolini's celebrated poetry, art and critical writings, interpreted as an *oeuvre*, display an evolving vision of humanity which reaches some kind of catastrophic conclusion and synthesis in *Salò*.

At the heart of *Salò* lies a conception of war, both literal and metaphorical. In the literal sense, the film is an application of Sade's *120*

Days of Sodom to the context of the Second World War and in particular to the Italian Republic of Salò, created by Mussolini in the North of Italy in 1944. But through the use of an eighteenth century text, Pasolini is also seeking to offer a more generalised reflection on war and violence, which is not simply limited to 1940s Italy. Before looking at the specifics of *Salò* then, it is helpful to employ Carl Von Clausewitz's[4] paradigmatic theory of war as a philosophical backdrop.

2.   Reading Clausewitz - What is War?

War therefore is an act of violence intended to compel our opponent to fulfil our will[5].

Although more generally employed as a concept to describe relations between communities or nations, the concept of war might equally be applied to relations between individuals. In his famous text *On War*, Carl von Clausewitz describes what he terms the "trinitarian"[6] nature of war. In the first case, war is made up of the "original violence of its elements, hatred and animosity" (ibid.); in the second case, it is characterised by the "play of probabilities and chance" (ibid.); finally, in the third case, it is a means to a political end, and this is the aspect of war which is the most rational (ibid).

Pasolini's depiction of and meditation on war in *Salò* certainly addresses these different dimensions of war. Most particularly in this paper, however, I would like to focus specifically on the first element described by Clausewitz, the "original violence of its elements, hatred and animosity". For Clausewitz, these negative elements are characteristic of a state of war, where war is "an act of violence intended to compel our opponent to fulfil our will"[7] In such a state of war, what Clausewitz refers to as "absolute war"(ibid.), war must be waged with the "utmost violence".

The kind of relationship which is being described here, that of a violent submission of one will to that of another, and absolute submission through the utmost violence, bears striking similarities to the kinds of human relationship valorised in the work of the Marquis de Sade. Indeed, Sade has given his very name to such relationships – sadistic relations or relations of sadism. For Sade, the capacity to gain the submission of another's will is a sign of strength or superiority. One might say consequently (using Clausewitz's terminology) that for Sade, the highest kind of human life is one waged in absolute war, where human strength and superiority is exemplified through the submission of others' wills, through the utmost violence. Such a situation does not have to describe (although it can) a situation of explicit war, that is a formal war between communities or nations, but rather might be a description of the flow of life itself. War would not thus be a form of life but life would become a species of war, of absolute war, lived in the utmost violence.

This Sadean vision of a life as absolute war can certainly be said to have influenced Pasolini's conception of humanity and of existence. Here, I will look at this as evidenced in the detail of *Salò* itself.

3.   Pasolini at War – The Frame and Detail of *Salò*

Salò transposes the repetitive violence and tortures of the latter to 1940s Italy and Mussolini's Republic of Salò. As with Sade's novel, four powerful libertines (a duke, a bishop, a magistrate, and a banker) assemble their victims (eight male and eight female) in an isolated villa, having had these victims rounded up in the surrounding countryside by armed soldiers. Prior to this abduction, the film begins with a panoramic shot of an idllyic countryside, a peaceful and beautiful rural landscape, which acts as a fundamental contrast to the violence which will follow.   As the victims are rounded up, an ominous road sign pointing to Marzabotto signals what is to come; this was a town in the Republic of Salò where acts of the Resistance engendered a brutal fascist massacre (and this is the first of the intersections between fiction and reality which pervade the film).

The film itself is split into three circles of horror (imagery borrowed by Pasolini from Dante's Hell or 'Inferno'); a circle of 'mania', a circle of 'shit' and a circle of 'blood'. Each circle involves violent and increasingly gruesome actions performed by the libertines on their hapless victims. The actions of each circle are introduced and encouraged by three different female narrators (who tell lurid anecdotes to inspire the libertines), while a fourth woman provides musical accompaniment on the piano, until finally, and inexplicably, she jumps to her death from a window. In the final scene, all the victims are put to death through various and horrific methods of execution. Striking aspects of this descending series of circles are the general passivity of the victims, the involvement of some of the original victims in the acts of violence, and the inevitable destruction of the libertines themselves.

This clinical description of what takes place may seem out of place with the content, but it is an explicitly conscious style employed by Pasolini.   Although the camera lingers on every horrific detail, this focus seems more mathematical than voyeuristic. As Naomi Greene has observed, "everything speaks of formal precision and abstract lifelessness: dark and sombre colors (greys, blacks, browns); icy tile floors with geometrical patterns; and mathematical combinations – sixteen victims (eight female, eight male), four libertines, four middle aged women. More strongly than any words, the precise geometry and formal rituals of the film make it clear that no spontaneity or life, no *jouissance*, is possible; nothing can break the downward spiral of horrors, just as no one can escape the enclosed, windowless rooms of the infernal villa"[8].

This style can also be seen as somewhat of a parody of Fascistic aesthetics; the villa itself was styled after what Pasolini referred to as "the confiscated home of a rich Jew who had been deported", with its severe Bauhaus décor. It is clear that although the fictional and mythic elements of the film are important, that there is a powerful realist dimension, indeed autobiographical element. This description of *Salò* gives a sense both of its extreme character, certainly Pasolini's most extreme film, and one of the most extreme in cinema history, but also its artistic and philosophical complexity. For example, many critics have criticised *Salò* as a vile work of immoralism, with Pasolini eulogising sadism and cruelty. But the very fact that Pasolini explicitly refers to an autobiographical element seems to suggest that at the very least he is also signalling some reservations about fascist violence. His adored older brother Guido was in fact murdered in the Republic of Salò and one of the scenes is said to present this murder in a fictional setting. This is not to say that *Salò* is simply a work of lamentation but it is to point to certain contradictions or conflicting ideas and images at the heart of this work, which defy simple denunciation or categorisation.

Another powerful example of the complexity of the work relates to Pasolini's decision to depict fascism through an eighteenth century representation of libertinage in Sade's work. In mediating it through such a different historical period and thematic, Pasolini has been accused (most notably by the novelist and critic Italo Calvino) of turning the historical reality of fascism into a cinematic or aesthetic montage[9]. This problem is also complicated by several references in the film (albeit allegorical) to phenomena within neo-capitalist late twentieth century society. The famous scene, for example, when everyone at the banquet is presented as eating excrement, was intended by Pasolini as a metaphor or allegory for the commodification of food in capitalism. From Calvino's perspective, however, of the obligation for an authentic and historically accurate portrayal of fascism, this only serves to further confuse and complicate the moral problematic of fascism, as represented in the film. Here one might also refer to Pasolini's refusal to treat *Salò* simply as a *tragic* drama; rather such tragedy dovetails with an irreducible comedy or dimension of farce. Pasolini once described Sade as having turned Dante's poetics from marble into "papier-mâché" and Naomi Greene has noted how this conversion mirrors a certain comic reversal in *Salò*:

Pasolini may have been describing his own film, where horror may don a new mask or take a carnavalesque turn at any moment: here bloody executions turn into Grand Guignol as executioners perform a grotesque minuet amidst their victim's corpses. Steering a course between "seriousness" and "the impossibility of seriousness", *Salò* wavers between what Pasolini described as a "massacring and bloody *Thanatos*" and a "cheap Baubo" (Baubo, he added, was a Greek goddess known for her obscene and liberating laugh)[10].

On my interpretation, this aspect of *Salò* is not coincidental, but relates to Pasolini's conception of a new cinema semiotics which would go beyond what he regarded as the simplifications of neo-realist and traditional cinema (and I will return to this point below).

Salò is also cited as significant by many commentators because it is viewed as representing some kind of watershed for Pasolini; on Deleuze's terms[11], for example, this is expressed through its being a 'theorematic' rather than a 'problematic' film. However, this interpretation seems to me to be overly-literalist. In concluding this section on *Salò*, I would like to note this disagreement. First, in clarification of the very distinction as employed by Deleuze, the 'theorematic' refers to the use of cinema for the purposes of demonstrating a closed thesis where 'the theorem develops internal relationships from principle to consequences'(ibid.). Deleuze cites this 'theorematic' method as an aspect of the new cinema of the 'time-image' which moves away from the more 'metaphorical' traditional cinema (ibid). Primarily, the change takes place with regard to the relationship between the 'image' and 'thought'; in the old cinema according to Deleuze it was a question of the image as image of something, now it is a question of the 'thought of the image', the 'thought in the image' (ibid). This can also be described as the process by which cinema and the image are becoming-philosophical.

However, the 'theorematic' refers only to one dimension of this becoming-philosophical of cinema; the other important dimension concerns what Deleuze terms the 'problematic' or the 'problem' of cinema(ibid.). This also relates to 'the thought in the image' but here the thought is not assimilated into the deduction of a theorem but is rather the locus of an "unfathomable problem" (ibid). Here, the images of the film may be inherently philosophical and thoughtful but they do not become assimilated to a dialectic where a conclusion is reached in and through the film. The 'problematic' dimension rather emphasises the inconclusive nature of a film, the irreducibility of its philosophical significance. In general (at least in terms of the new cinema), both the 'theorematic' and 'problematic' aspects will be present in a kind of 'union' (ibid.), by which is signified the sense that there will be no ultimate theoretical closure to the film. An example of such a 'union' given by Deleuze is Pasolini's film entitled (ironically) *Theorem*. Surprisingly, however, Deleuze does not read *Salò* in the same way:

> In *Salò*, on the contrary, there is no longer a problem because there is no outside: Pasolini presents not even fascism in vivo but fascism at bay, shut away in the little town, reduced to a pure interiority, coinciding with the conditions of closure in which Sade's demonstrations took place. *Salò* is a pure, dead theorem, a theorem of death, as Pasolini wanted, while *Theorem* is a living problem[12].

It seems clear to this reader that Deleuze is overplaying the 'theorematic' dimension of *Salò*. If anything, *Salò* introduces a more complex 'problematical' dimension than Pasolini's previous films. One powerful example here might be Pasolini's introduction in *Salò* of Sade's eighteenth century problematic into the internal problem of Nazi-Fascism, and the additional introduction of the problem of 'neo-capitalist' commodification. This is an undeniable chronological problematisation which dovetails with a thematic problematisation and complication. Additionally, one might argue that if there is a 'moral' theorem of *Salò* that it is complicated (perhaps even undermined) by becoming intermingled with an 'aesthetic' problem which Pasolini sees as just as important in the film.

What I am arguing for here then, is (*contra* Deleuze) a 'problematic' rather than a 'theorematic' interpretation of *Salò*. This film does not present the viewer with a univocal reading of war and violence but rather an equivocal and ambiguous reading. In the next section, I will develop this hypothesis with reference to a new and influential reading of Sade which Pasolini explicitly invokes in *Salò*.

3.   After Sade – The Intellectual Context of Salò

Several *avant-garde* writers are cited in *Salò* - Maurice Blanchot, Pierre Klossowski, Philippe Sollers and Roland Barthes. The explicit unity between these authors can be described as their new reading of the work of Sade. Are we meant to consider Pasolini's interpretation as aligned to that of this new philosophical school? Here, I will concentrate specifically on the reading of Blanchot which, in its major themes, exemplifies the central tenets of the new reading of Sade.

As Blanchot observes in his essay on Sade, "Sade advanced himself as the means to a profound interpretation of human destiny taken in its entirety"[13]. In his analysis of Sade's thinking, Blanchot claims that there is a clear interpretation of human nature and destiny provided, although there are several stages to this interpretation. At the heart of Sade's vision lies an anti-humanistic conception of sadism: "For Sade, the equality of all human beings is the right to equal use of them all, freedom is the power to bend others to ones own will"[14]. As we already observed in relation to our analysis of Clausewitz, this conception of human relationships sees them as in a state of absolute war with each other, in a situation of the utmost violence. As Clausewitz noted, in such situations of war, the principle of moderation does not apply. The adverse effects on any moral conception of the human being (or human nature) are obvious here, but the implications for a philosophy of the person are even more fundamental. As Blanchot notes, once one accepts the Sadean interpretation of human nature, the very idea of a human individual, that is, of a human self, must also be problematised: "In leading a dangerous life, says Sade, what really matters is never to "lack the strength necessary to forge beyond the furthermost limits". One might say that this strange world is not made up of individuals, but of systems of vectors, of greater or lesser tensions"[15]

This Sadean conception of what one might term an "inhuman" condition, a condition of existence beyond or below the normal concept of human being, greatly influences the depiction of existence in *Salò*. What remains to be seen however, is Pasolini's own stance in relation to this Sadean inhumanity. Are we to take the vivid, candid depictions of cruelty in *Salò* as Pasolini's affirmation of the Sadean interpretation of existence or are we rather to see his work as implicitly critiquing and lamenting such a condition? That is, does Pasolini accept the Sadean version of a cruel humanity, in absolute war with itself, as the only, true conception?

What attracts Pasolini to Sade, aside from his simple extremism which is also a factor with regard to Pasolini's polemical style, is a complicated philosophy of violence and sadism. Sade depicts sadism in graphic technicolour, refusing to take the moral high ground, but simultaneously avoids a simple affirmation or romanticisation of a voluntaristic will to power. This enigmatic dimension of Sade's text is then employed by Pasolini to complicate the more standard readings of Nazi and Fascist violence. This complication is two-fold; it firstly undoes moral judgementalism concerning the specificity of Nazi-Fascism. In mediating Nazi-Fascism through the violence of eighteenth century libertines and contemporary capitalist violence, Pasolini generalises the question 'how could the Holocaust have taken place?' to the question 'how does violence and sadism ever take place?'. Thus in adapting the text of Sade, Pasolini inherits Sade's disavowal of moral judgement.

Similarly, from an aesthetic point of view, Pasolini can be said to inherit a certain aesthetic modernism from Sade (and perhaps even more so from Lautreamont's *Chants de Maldoror*, which is a very obvious precursor to *Salò*). That is, Pasolini refuses to present Nazi-Fascism in a 'realist' or 'neo-realist' perspective. Instead we get a presentation in a radical form of the new cinema of the 'time-image', with its especial emphasis on formalism, mannerist detachment and camera consciousness. Even a high modernist such as Calvino can only baulk at such dreadful lack of seriousness. This would then be the very Sadean inheritance which *Salò* proudly displays. Pasolini's arrival on the scene of Italian cinema places him exactly at the cusp of the changeover from a neo-realist perspective in film to a more ambivalent and problematical understanding of the status of the cinematic image. Pasolini, perhaps more than any other director, is the motor of this aesthetic change. A paradigmatic example of a new cinematic style is the stylistic procedures which the new revolutionary directors use. Pasolini here refers to several important stylistic procedures used by both himself and others such as Godard, Antonioni and Rohmer (although it is significant that each director is more famous for the use of one style most especially). This is not intended as an exhaustive list but Pasolini refers to three procedures particularly (and one can add also his and others' use of the 'commentary' and also the 'insert');
1.   Insistent or obsessive framing, which makes the camera await the entry of a character into the frame and then continues to frame the space when the character has exited
2.   The alternation of different lenses on the same image
3.   The excessive use of the zoom.

It is perhaps the intensive use of the zoom which is most strikingly associated with *Salò*, particularly in the massacre scene which concludes the film. Here, some of the libertines watch this horror through binoculars, which then become one with the camera, symbolising a certain complicity between the libertines enjoying the violence and both the film directors use of these images and the film viewer's voyeurism in being drawn to watch these horrors.

What is perhaps most striking about this scene is the aestheticisation of extreme violence through Pasolini's use of music and gesture. At times, it is like watching ballet rather than a massacre. There is a specific kind of 'formalism' or 'mannerism' at work here. In this scene it is expressed amongst other things, through the use of the immobile 'tableau', the plan tableau or tableau-shot. This is another of Pasolini's favourite styles, not commented on by Deleuze, but very linked with the latter's idea of the 'simulacrum'[16]. For Deleuze, the 'simulacrum' banishes the real, replaces the real. In a 1971 interview Pasolini refers to his motivation for the tableau shot as seeking "forms of stylistic crystallisation that would confer guarantees of stability and 'form' upon uncertainty and chaos"[17]. In another of his phrases, this is 'reality which has nothing to do with realism' (ibid) and is also evidenced in his constant use of allegory and myth, particularly in the later films. Through the use of allegory and myth, particularly as it relates to ancient myths (such as *Medea* and *Oedipus*, both Pasolini films), and through his constant adaptation of literary texts (such as the *Decameron*, *Canterbury Tales* and *Arabian Nights*), Pasolini is putting his new semiotics into practice and trying to create distance between his work and that of neo-realism. Although neo-realism is also part of the 'time-image' revolutionary cinema, Pasolini sees his own work as radicalising neo-realist aesthetics beyond itself. If as one commentator has observed, neo-realism is more definable as a 'moral attitude'[18] than as a semiotics, then it is also clear that Pasolini's cinema subverts such a morality or moralism[19], most especially in *Salò*. Here one also sees how Pasolini's semiotics complements his more general philosophy.

In his text 'Lutheran Letters', Pasolini refers to a certain 'sin of the fathers: "The sin of the fathers is not only the violence of power, Fascism. It is also this: the dismissal from our consciousness by us anti-Fascists of the old Fascism, that fact that we comfortably freed ourselves from our deep *intimacy* with it"[20]. *Salò* can be seen as a film which expresses the horrors of war through a complex depiction of Fascism, but which retreats from a simple moral denunciation of such violence. This moral reticence (which is both filmic and philosophical) is not based on a position of amoralism as such but is rather located in an unease concerning the 'intimacy' between humanity as such and Fascism. On one level, *Salò* appears to be very much a film of its time. Pasolini is indicting all the Italian opponents of Fascism as somehow complicit, in their very humanity, with this horror. And contemporary post-fascist Italian society in 1975 remains guilty: "the sin of the fathers is….secondly and above all, the acceptance(all the more guilty because unconscious) of the degrading violence, of the real, immense genocides of the new Fascism"[21].

But in *Salò*, Pasolini has also given us a work which transcends its time. It is a film which foregrounds, above all through its aestheticism, a possible complicity between film and the imagery of war and violence. This complicity, *Salò* seems to suggest, might be *de jure* and not *de facto*. Through its disorientation of our senses, film can be said to reflect the derangements of war. More to the point, it appears to make these

derangements aesthetic, almost beautiful. This would be Pasolini's
'problem'(although not his 'theorem').

Notes

1. cf. Sadie Plant *Writing on Drugs* (London, Faber, 1999), 30-50.

2. Paul Virilio *War and Cinema: The Logistics of Perception* (London, Verso, 1989), 21.

3. Marquis De Sade *120 Days of Sodom* (London, Arrow Books, 1990)

4. Carl von Clausewitz *On War* (Harmondsworth, Penguin, 1968)

5. Clausewitz, Chapter 1 Section 2.

6. Ibid., 24.

7. Ibid., 5.

8. Naomi Greene *Cinema as Heresy* (London, Duckworth, 1974), 199ff.

9. Ibid., 215.

10. Ibid., 213.

11. Gilles Deleuze *Cinema 2: The Time-Image* translated by Hugh Tomlinson and Robert Galeta (London, Athlone Press, 2000).

12. Deleuze, 174.

13. Maurice Blanchot 'Sade' in *Lautréamont et Sade* (Paris, Editions de Minuit, 1949), 71.

14. Ibid., 41.

15. Ibid., 66.

16. cf . Deleuze , Chapter 6.

17. quoted Greene, 140.

18. Marcia Landy Italian Film (Cambridge, Cambridge University Press, 2000), 281.

19. "That's why, in the anxiety of my sins, I've never been touched by real remorse" Pasolini, *Roman Poems* (California, City Light Books, 1986).

20. Pasolini *Lutheran Letters* (New York, Carcanet, 1987), 16.

21. Ibid., 17.

Part IV

Whither Peace?

Peace and Virtual Peace: Challenges to War

Edward Horgan

An entry in Franz Kafka's diary in 1914 reads "2 August. Germany has declared war on Russia – swimming in the afternoon."[1] HG Wells observed that "Human history becomes more and more a race between education and catastrophe."[2] George W Bush tells the world that "either you are with us, or you are with the terrorists." 2001[3]

We are living in dangerous times. This paper will challenge the concept of international relations by asking whether the nation-state and the concept of the international provide the most appropriate framework to ensure an acceptable level of peace and security for humanity. It will examine the confused and sometimes chaotic state of international relations since the end of the Cold War and will suggest that there appears to be a logjam in the development of societal structures at the level of the nation-state that needs to be broken if a catastrophic flood of human conflict is to be avoided. The role of communities, including states, has been given predominance over the role of individuals. It will query in particular the level of power that has been evolved to the state, without commensurate controls on how states use that power.[4] It will suggest that the state may be the problem rather than the solution. Since individuals are the roots, foundations and building blocks of communities, and the very substance of society, it will be suggested that it is in the context of the sovereignty of the individual, individually and collectively, rather than in state-centric, or international relations frameworks, that progress towards a more perpetual peace may be found. The proliferation of weapons of mass destruction, varying from hijacked aircraft to nuclear intercontinental missiles, makes it imperative that comprehensive and sustainable peace replaces, rather than alternates with, war.

The end of the Cold War should have produced a better environment for the promotion of global peace and justice. Yet the wheels started to fall off the "New World Order" wagon almost immediately.[5] The Gulf War in 1991 brought the world its first example of virtual war broadcast by CNN into our living rooms.[6] It also brought examples of selective use of the denial of human rights, the preservation of freedom and state sovereignty, as justifications for war.[7] The sovereignty of the state of Kuwait, an important oil resource for the west, but not noted for its democracy or freedom, was restored. The human rights of the people of

Iraq were more violated than defended; the Shia Muslims in southern Iraq
and the Kurds of northern Iraq were used when it suited western interests
to infringe Iraqi sovereignty under the guise of protecting human rights.[8]
The same criteria were denied to their Kurdish brethren across the border
in Turkey. Tens of thousands of Iraqi children have died as a result of UN
imposed sanctions on Iraq.[9] French writer, Jean Baudrillard, went so far as
to suggest that the Gulf War did not actually happen.[10] A much more
critical analysis is needed into the real reasons and justification for wars
such as the Gulf War, and of the long-term consequences of such wars.
The taking of human life for any purpose other than the protection of
human life, in a justified and proportionate way, must be challenged. The
ultimate human right is the right to life of an individual.

A summary of the problems of international security during the
first half of the 1990s include:

1.   The inappropriate intervention in Somalia, abandoned in 1993
when 18 Americans were killed in a fire-fight.[11]
2.   In 1994 in Rwanda, UN peace-keepers evacuated foreign
nationals when the Hutu government began killing its opponents.
However, the international community stood by helplessly, unwilling, but
arguably not unable, to prevent the murder of nearly a million Tutsis.
France intervened not to protect the victims of this genocide, but to rescue
the perpetrators.[12]
3.   In July 1995, the Dutch government sent in peace-keepers to
protect the civilians of Srebrenica but instead its troops delivered them up
to execution and deportation by the Serbs.[13]

Michael Ignatieff highlights the dangers of states that see
themselves as the world's policemen, making war with apparent impunity:
"(b)ut war without death – to our side – is war that ceases to be fully real
to us: virtual war."[14] Peace, on the other hand, is often seen as the opposite
to, or absence of, war. Seventeenth century philosopher, Baruch Spinoza
defined peace more challengingly: "Peace is not an absence of war; it is a
virtue, a state of mind, a disposition for benevolence, confidence,
justice".[15] This conflicts with the Hobbesian presumption that war is the
natural state of man in the state of nature. Although Hobbes did believe in
an active state of peace, his Leviathan approach to peace contrasts with the
Kantian liberal approach. The second half of the 1990s saw the Yugoslav
wars of disintegration combined with the US/NATO response afflict the
peoples of Kosovo. The sovereignty of Yugoslavia was initially cited by
the international community as the main excuse for non-intervention in
1991, and cited by Serbia as its excuse for intervention in Kosovo in 1999.

[16] While a quarter of a million people were losing their lives, the most basic of human rights, democracy was being flouted by President Tudjman in Croatia, the Dayton Accord in Bosnia,[17] and by political participants on all sides in Kosovo and Serbia. Marrak Goulding, retired Under Secretary General of the UN in charge of peacekeeping, also confirms the selective use of human rights abuses by the West as justification for military intervention.[18] New states sprung up like mushrooms claiming sovereignty in the wake of the collapse of communism[19].

In South-East Asia, Indonesia took some steps towards democracy in 1998/99, but this was followed by the bloody re-birth of East Timor, and the risk of further disintegration of Indonesia.[20] Following the disasters of Somalia and Rwanda, Africa was perceived as almost a no-go area for Western military intervention. The slaughter continues in central and western Africa, with a combination of peacekeeping and partisan military intervention by regional African forces, neighbouring states and the UN. The Middle East conflict, having boiled over periodically since 1948[21], deteriorated following Ariel Sharon's provocative visit to the Dome of the Rock. Some Palestinians resorted to suicide bombings against mainly civilian Israeli targets, while the Israeli US-equipped or supported forces responded with arguably disproportionate military force. The political and social structures resulting from these conflicts and interventions show little signs of creating peace and stability for the future.

The relative impunity with which the US, its western allies, waged virtual war in the Middle East and in the Balkans, combined with the perceived powerlessness of the Palestinian people and the hopelessness of their refugee population, created the impetus for a new kind of war. The example of Palestinian suicide martyrs' perceived or virtual success against Israel was extrapolated from the regional to the global, when on September 11th 2001 Islamic suicide hijackers killed almost three thousand people in New York and Washington. The US responded, not against Saudi Arabia, from which most of the hijackers came, but against Afghanistan, whose people became victims of their undemocratic government's support for Al Qaida terrorist led by Osama Bin Laden. The importance of strategic energy resources may also be a factor in the use of US military action to protect US economic interests. Jean Baudrillard attracted further criticism by suggesting in an article "The Spirit of Terrorism" in Le Monde on 11th November 2001, that the attack on the World Trade Centre Twin Towers was a reaction to the hegemonic power of the US and its western allies.[22] In the short-term the forces of the hegemonic alliance appear to have won but the price or the permanence of victory has yet to be fully assessed. In the meantime, the threat, or the perception of the threat, of nuclear warfare had receded from most people's minds. The Cold War balance of terror appears to be over. However, India and Pakistan have renewed the reality of the nuclear threat to each other and to the world at large, with the renewal of their periodic conflict over disputed Kashmir.[23] The interconnectedness of modern conflicts, as well as political and social interaction (the complex interdependency suggested by Robert Keohane and Joseph Nye[24]), in areas as diverse as Kashmir, the Middle East, East Timor and New York, is of such intensity that any attempt to establish global peace on a piecemeal basis only is likely to fail. Likewise, it must be questioned whether nation-states pursuing their own national interests, separately or in alliances, can form the basis of a solution to the problems of global conflict and peace.

This now leaves us with the question, how does humanity progress beyond the impasse of increasingly interconnected conflicts? Virtual war is a reality for those that can afford it, virtual terrorism a virtual reality for those who cannot. The prospects for virtual peace are receding. All this is developing at a time when the risks of the catastrophic use of weapons of mass destruction are increasing. A more permanent peace is no longer just an option, it is now, arguably, an imperative. Instead of further tinkering with existing structures and systems in international relations, it may now be necessary to look at human interaction in a more holistic way, taking nothing for granted in the quest for survival, not just peace. Philip Bobbitt suggests that: "The modern state came into existence when it proved necessary to organise a constitutional order that could wage war more effectively than the feudal and mercantile orders it replaced."[25] In the meantime, relationships between states are considered to be akin to the natural state of man, a state of war. The state is the supreme sovereign and beyond it the international system is in a state of anarchy. In archaic English, *beyond here be dragones*. While some idealists may view the United Nations as a super-national or supra-national structure, realists insist that it is an organisation of states, with no executive power over states and answerable, not even to a majority of states, but to an effective cabal of self-appointed founding states who exercise a monopoly of power within the UN.[26] John Hillen cites Brian Urquhart in support of his contention that the underlying structure of the United Nations may be fundamentally flawed, particularly towards undertaking tasks which it has assumed in the areas of peacekeeping and peace-enforcing.[27] Hedley Bull deals more prosaically with the concept of world order, in his *Anarchical Society: a study of order in world politics*. He downplays the role of international organisations such as the United Nations in this world order.

...to find the cause of such order as exists in world politics, one must not look to the League of Nations, the United Nations and such bodies, but to institutions of international society that arose before these international organisations were established.[28]

Those who agree with Bull have probably increased in number in the early years of the twenty-first century. Michael Ignatieff queries the inevitability of human conflict but suggests that the state may be at least part of the problem: "... there is nothing in our natures that makes ethnic or racial conflict unavoidable. ...It is the disintegration of states, and the Hobbesian fear that results, that produces ethnic fragmentation and war."[29] The belief of Hobbes and others that "the natural state of man was a state of war" and that this maxim applied equally to the relationships between states has arguably coloured much of the theory of Realism.[30] The undue amount of power and authority that is evolved by a state's citizens to the state, and the anarchy or lack of superior authority, or effective collective security mechanisms, above the state makes it almost inevitable that such unrestrained power will be abused not just by some states some of the time, but by virtually all states some of the time. With the possible exceptions of Switzerland and Britain, the US has the longest and most consistent history of freedom, democracy and constitutional order.[31] Yet its reputation internationally is blighted by its activities in pursuit of US national interests, especially in Latin America, and South-East Asia in the past, and more recently in Central Asia and the Middle East. If a more permanent and just system of global security is to be achieved, then a system or societal structure will have to be created which will exercise a mollifying influence on key actors on the international stage, especially the most powerful nation-states. However, since a single all powerful global or world government would be likely to be subject to similar if not greater abuses of power as has been the case with nation-states, then global government, with sovereignty at global level, is also unlikely to be the answer.

Ferdinand Tönnies' studies of communities and society (Gemeinschaft und Gesellschaft) divides human interaction into the more personal community and more rational or organised association or society. Yet for Tönnies: "... the end and meaning of any social order was peaceful relationships among men".[32] While some of Tönnies' theories may be outdated in the twenty-first century, the study of human interaction from the individual to the global needs to be re-examined to help chart safer ways of ordering human behaviour and society interaction, to avoid catastrophic conflict. The wisdom of dividing human interaction into separate and distinct categories and levels of activity may also be mistaken or inappropriate for a future in which humanity must learn to coexist in a world of limited resources, in which the luxury of isolation or separation is no longer feasible for most. Living individuals are the essence of reality from the perspective of humanity. Beyond that, social structures for the ordering of society, such as families, communities, states, *et al*, are simply, or complicatedly, mental constructs to enable individuals to achieve some order and understanding in human interaction. Tönnies work supports this view of social relationships: "As social facts they only exist through the will of the individual to associate."[33] This raises the issue of state sovereignty that has come to be accepted as a fact of political life, and whether this is a natural development, or even a desirable development, for the well-being and survival of humanity. Hobbes describes the commonwealth (Leviathan) as: "... a creation of man ... an artificial man" and sovereignty as "an artificial soul." However he assigns total discretion and power to the sovereign or monarch.[34] With Rousseau on the other hand, the sovereign means: "not the monarch or the government, but the community in its collective and legislative capacity." However, in Rousseau's social contract the individual effectively abrogated his/her sovereignty, which evolves to the state.[35] The difficulty with these concepts is that once the individual's sovereignty evolves to the state, there is a danger of individuals losing control over that sovereignty to the detriment of the majority of individuals. Even in democracies the tendency is for states to fail to allow sovereignty to evolve further up the social chain, or devolve back down, except at election times. This results in the continuation of the power and sovereignty blockage at state level, with anarchy on top. Functional governance at a level beyond the state, as in the European Union (EU), has the potential to break this logjam, provided that the EU does not evolve into a modern but old-fashioned super-state. So far the EU has succeeded admirably in breaking the cycle of wars that devastated Europe for centuries, by its cooperative common-interest approach. The creation of a European super-state risks reinventing boundaries and the insider/outsider syndrome, except at a larger and potentially more dangerous level.

While it is a reality also that individuals will all die in the relatively short-term, some political philosophers in the past, including Kant, have held that the laws of nature or "providence" would ensure that humanity as whole would survive in the medium and longer-term, in spite of self destruct tendencies within particular individuals and groups.[36] The reality of weapons of mass destruction must now make such a theory at least questionable. Humanity can no longer presume on its survivability. Peace must be positively created and war must be positively eliminated. Communities can become part of this positive process, provided they remain focused and controlled by their *raison d'être*, individuals.

Communities, including the state, must come to be visualised as convenient mental structures for imagined society to live within, like houses in a cold climate, rather than something to die for.[37] Individuals are the reality. Communities are part of the mechanisms through which individuals perceive reality. The state and its evolutions, such as the EU and the UN are part of what Benedict Anderson calls imagined communities.[38]

The issue of boundaries or points of differentiation between communities must be critically examined. Boundaries are deemed important for the creation of identity bonds within communities. In an increasingly global society these bonds or differentiation become more problematic than advantageous and may enhance the propensity for conflict. Samuel Huntington argues that: "(i)n the emerging era, clashes of civilizations are the greatest threat to world peace, and an international order based on civilizations is the surest safeguard against world war."[39] His, arguably flawed, thesis has belatedly created a convenient rallying point for those who seek to unite the west against the rest. With the advent of globalisation the elite at international level now appear to be substituting the questionable concept of western civilization instead of nationalism, as a myth to justify wars of resource manipulation on behalf of global elite interests. A functional and inclusive EU could become a blueprint that communities could use to develop peace, as the EU has achieved within a Europe of diminishing boundaries. The concept of the other, insider/outsider, considered essential for the development of communities of common interest, must be queried as counterproductive in this age of developing globalisation, whereby avoidance of conflict and deepening co-operation are arguably becoming prerequisites for survival. Communities such as nation-states should not disappear, but should have their power and sovereignty curtailed, and their more functional roles enhanced. A more holistic view of humanity, with *gemeinscahft* and *gesellschaft* intermingling from the individual to the global, would visualise communities at all levels as *collectivities* of sovereign individuals, rather than simply the raw material of such communities. This would establish a safer basis or foundation on which to build a comprehensive system of peace and justice. Peace without justice is arguably just a temporary ceasefire.

In discussing theories of international relations, R.B. J. Walker refers to political theories so caught up in, or mesmerised by, the contradictions of the modern state, that they create "... conditions under which alternatives to the present have been rendered implausible or even unthinkable." It is these alternatives that political scientists must now seek out and test. The concepts of the national and the international, including the United Nations, must be challenged. Kjell Goldmann defines internationalism as:

a set of beliefs to the effect that if there is more law, organisation, exchange, and communication among states, this will reinforce peace and security. ...That for example is Hedley Bull's usage when he distinguishes between the "realism" of Hobbes, the "universalism" of Kant, and the "internationalism" of Grotius.

This exclusive state-centred approach to peace and security has signally failed to achieve acceptable results over the past decade. Those who seek solutions to the problems of peace for global society with the United Nations, must consider that if the state is a significant part of the problem, then the association of states, which is the most the UN can claim to be, is unlikely to provide comprehensive solutions. Ignatieff suggests that: "(w)e live our lives in language and thus in representation". To overcome the critical problems facing humanity, we may need to begin by overcoming given language constructions, the divisive boundaries of communities and the flawed structures of society. But we must learn to build without destroying. Nation-states, and the international community, must be made responsible and responsive to the needs of humanity's individuals, present and future, but not past. Justice can never be achieved for the slaughtered of the past regardless of how many we slaughter in the present. The future lies only with peace. Paul Hirst is pessimistic for the future. "It is almost impossible to see the present world order as sustainable in the long run, it is so unfair and environmentally destructive."[40] However, his prognosis is that there is little prospect for either peaceful or revolutionary change. This suggests that catastrophic change may be inevitable.

This paper concludes that neither the complacency of Kant nor the pessimism of Hirst offers a safe way forward. Peace, security and survival for humanity can only be achieved by a combination of recognition of the risks, use of human ingenuity to overcome the almost insurmountable obstacles, and new approaches to both the old and the new problems of human survival. Crisis management is no longer enough. Root, trunk and branch changes are necessary in the structures that individuals have put in place to order humanity's existence in the past. We need a new social architecture. It is as if we have built a complex house with all the right materials, but on a flawed foundation, and with no roof. We have been putting up umbrellas to keep out the rain, shoring up the foundations and using scaffolding to support the cracked walls. It could come tumbling down at any time. All our efforts over the past three hundred years have gone in to strengthening the central levels of the building at the expense of the base and the top. To misquote Bill Clinton,

"Its the nation-state, stupid". The replacement of the nation-state and the international (including the United Nations) is neither likely to be possible nor wise, but the power they exert must be ceded, or removed, and transferred vertically and laterally.

Individuals are the roots and foundations, the very source of existence for all levels of humanity. The structures of society should have no existence independent of the individual. The term "imagined communities" coined by Anderson is equally applicable to the *gemeinschaft* and *gesellschaft* of Tönnies. Communities can become part of the solution, provided they are used towards cooperation and togetherness rather than competition and exclusion. A globalised world of over six billion people cannot sustain the Westphalian concept of sovereign armed states confronting each other from within fortified borders. Power, sovereignty and democracy have evolved upwards to the disadvantage of human individuals. Individuals must regain control over the concepts of human ingenuity, of which the nation-state is but one. War and peace must no longer be seen as part of the balancing mechanisms in human society. They are not two sides of the same coin. Peace must be positively created and developed to the exclusion of war. If humanity can create ingenious weapons of mass destructions, surely it can create peace. War is no longer acceptable as "politics by other means". War is – the acceleration of the natural process of death for individuals, by other means. It is inherently unnatural and inhuman. While Francis Fukuyama had a very optimistic, and simplistic view of the end of history there is an alternative view which is a doomsday one. We need to learn to live together, to work together, and to achieve peace and harmony together, or we will all "melt into the air" together, physically or metaphorically as in the prophetic words of Karl Marx. Virtual war is likely to lead to virtual extinction. Virtual peace is the only alternative. There is virtually nothing in between.

Notes

1. Max Brod, ed., *The Diaries of Franz Kafka 1910-23* (London, Penguin, 1972), 301.

2. Lucian Ashworth, *Creating international studies: Angell, Mitrany and the liberal tradition* (Aldershot, Ashgate, 1999), 1, citing H. G. Wells.

3. Statement by President George W Bush in his Address to Congress on September 20th 2002.

4. Louis Fisher, *Presidential War Power* (Lawrence, University of Kansas Press, 2000). Fisher suggests that Presidents Bush (in the Persian Gulf) and Clinton (in Haiti and Bosnia) violated: "... the letter and the spirit of the Constitution." side-stepping congressional approval by asserting United Nations authority for military actions beyond US borders.

5. US President George H W Bush proclaimed the "New World Order" in Kuwait, following the US led victory over Iraq in 1991.

6. Michael Ignatieff, *Virtual War, Kosovo and Beyond*, (London, Picador, 2000), 5. Ignatieff who coined the term "virtual war" argues, however, that the Gulf War was "... in retrospect the last of the old wars: ...Soldiers were committed in full expectation of casualties".

7. This is reminiscent of the questionable claim that World War One was justified in defence of the neutrality of small nations such as Belgium, while Belgium was itself involved in gross breaches of human rights in central Africa.

8. Interview of Bernard Dorin, former French Ambassador to Iraq, by *Iraq Kurdistan Dispatch*, March 2002, "If the situation you described (Turkish attack of Iraqi Kurds) ever occurred, then the Kurds, as usual, would only have themselves to rely on."

9. Denis Halliday stated in an interview with Matthew Rothschild, in *The Progressive,* Madison, Wisconsin, that "Four thousand to 5,000 children are dying unnecessarily every month due to the impact of sanctions."

10. Jean Baudrillard, translated by Paul Patton, *The Gulf War did not take place* (Bloomington, Indiana, 1995).

11. Ten years previously, the US was forced to withdraw its forces from Lebanon after a suicide bomb attack killed 241 US Marines in Beirut.

12. Linda Melvern, *A People Betrayed: The role of the West in Rwanda's Genocide* (London, Zed Books, 2000).

13. Michael Ignatieff, *Virtual War, Kosovo and Beyond*, (London, Picador, 2000), 7.

14. Ibid. 5.

15. Charles Hauss, *International Conflict Resolution: international relations for the 21st century*, (London, Continuum, 2001), 30.

16. Misha Glenny, *The Balkans, 1804-1999: Nationalism,War and the Great Powers* (London, Viking, 1999), 633. Glenny suggests that "Milosevic and Tudjman were acting in harmony at the expense of both Yugoslavia and Bosnia".

17. Edward Horgan, *Assisting or hindering democracy? International intervention and the democratisation of Bosnia and Herzegovina*, (Irish School of Ecumenics, Dublin, 1999), Unpublished M.Phil. dissertation.

18. Marrak Goulding, *Peacemongering* (London, 2002), 343. Goulding speaks of: "... blatant cases of double standards by the West: it spent hundreds of millions of dollars on stopping comparatively minor violations of human rights in Kosovo, but did nothing to stop the murder of 800,000 people in the Rwandan genocide;"

19. Bosnia, Chechnya and Kosovo are examples of states, or would-be states, where issues of ethnicity, nationality, and sovereignty have been most pronounced and least resolved.

20. Following 400 years of Portuguese colonisation, East Timor was technically independent for a brief period in 1975, before it was annexed by Indonesia, brutally suppressed for 25 years with the support of the USA, UK and Australia.

21. Arab/Israeli wars since 1948 include, Sinai War 1956, Six Day War 1967, Yom Kippur War 1973, expulsion of Palestinians from Jordan 1970, Lebanon's Civil War and Israeli invasions 1970s/80s, Interfada 1990s.

22. Jean Baudrillard, "The Spirit of Terrorism", *Le Monde*, 11 November 2001. "They have succeeded in making their own deaths into an absolute weapon against a system that lives on the exclusion of death, whose ideal is that of zero casualties."

23. Arundhati Roy, *The Algebra of Infinite Justice* (London, Flamingo, 2002). Roy's book illustrates the terror of the threat of nuclear conflict combined with the fascist tendencies in Indian and Pakistani nationalism, and the failures to address the real problems afflicting most of India's one billion people.

24. Chris Brown, *Understanding International Relations* (London, Palgrave, 1997), 42-45.

25. Philip Bobbitt, *The Shield of Achilles: War, Peace and the Course of History* (London: Penguin, 2002), xxv.

26. France has a population of about sixty million and permanent membership of the UN Security Council, while India, with a population of over one billion has the same legal status in the UN as Liechtenstein with a population of thirty thousand.

27. John Hillen, "Peace(keeping) in Our Time: The UN as a Professional Military Manager" in *Parameters*, Autumn (1996), 17-34. Hillen says that: "The Charter had been based on the concept of an extension of the wartime alliance into peacetime. The "United" in United Nations came from the Atlantic Charter of 1941 and referred to nations united in war, not in peace.

28. Hedley Bull, *The Anarchical Society: a study of order in world politics* (London, Palgrave, 1977), p. 318. Bull concludes that: "…such prospects as there may be for order in world politics lie in attempts to arrest this (states system) decline rather than to hasten it."

29. Michael Ignatieff, *Virtual War, Kosovo and Beyond* (London, Palgrave, 2000).

30. Bertrand Russell, *History of Western Philosophy; and its connection with political and social circumstances from the earliest times to the present day* (London, Simon & Schuster 1945), 535. Russell suggests that Hobbes' social contract whereby individuals choose a sovereign to exercise authority over them in the common interest, is really "an explanatory myth, used to explain why men submit, to the limitations on personal freedom entailed in submission to authority."

31. This should be considered with the *caveat* that both slavery of Africans and ethnic cleansing of indigenous Americans played a significant role in the development of the United States.

32. Ferdinand Tönnies, *Community and Association,* translated and supplemented by Charles P. Loomis (London, Routledge, 1955), xxv.

33. Ibid, xv.

34. Russell, 533.

35. Ibid, 670. Extract from Rousseau's social contract: "Each of us puts his person and all his power in common under the supreme direction of the common will."

36. Immanuel Kant, *Perpetual Peace: a philosophical sketch* (1795), accessed by David Hart"s library of E-texts on 10 July 2002. Kant maintained that: "... providence is justified in the history of the world, for the moral principle in man is never extinguished, while with advancing civilization reason grows pragmatically in its capacity to realize ideas of law."

37. General Wesley Clark typifies a certain nationalist sentiment when he says: "If there is nothing worth fighting and dying for, then there is nothing worth living for." Wesley K Clark, *Waging Modern War* (Oxford, Public Affairs, 2001), 420.

38. Benedict Anderson, *Imagined Communities* (London, Verso, 1983), 6. Anderson defines the nation as: "... an imagined political community – and imagined as both inherently limited and sovereign." He quotes Ernest Gellner: "Nationalism is not the awakening of nations to self-consciousness: it invents nations where they do not exist."

39. Samuel Huntington, The clash of civilizations and the remaking of world order (London, Simon & Schuster, 1997), 321.

40. Paul Hirst, War and Power in the 21st Century, (Cambridge, Polity, 2001), 147.

Cross-Track Approach: A Remedy to Post-Conflict Peace Building?

Agata Dziewulska

What inspired me to think about writing this article was a series of observations I made during my stay in Sarajevo in June 2002. I was doing a field trip to Bosnia in order to collect further materials for my Ph.D. thesis about the peace process there. During this visit to Sarajevo, I talked not only to the international organisations representatives but also to "ordinary people", for whom, after all, I thought, the whole effort with the construction of the peace should be made. One of my favourite places was a little restaurant in the Sarajevo market where I would have lunch everyday. Becoming a regular customer, one day I was invited by the owner himself to have a drink with him. He was sad about what had happened in Bosnia and could not comprehend it. He was sad about how things could never have come back to how they used to be. And then he started to tell me how things used to be and his perception of the reason for the war. I remember this particularly well as I collect these stories. His way of seeing the beginning of the war was that Yugoslavia had had a strong military industry:

- Were you producing Kalashnikovs? - I asked.
- Something similar only better and cheaper. Everything: and machine guns and especially anti-craft weapons. They were being sent to Iraq, Kuwait and to the developing countries of Africa. All around the world. And the competition was too big for the West. So they decided to arrange a war here and kill the competition. First they made war here now they are making peace.

Not really knowing how to relate to what he was telling me, I decided to change the topic.

- You have many internationals here - I was meaning his restaurant but he took it as if I were talking about Sarajevo as a whole. Apparently for him it was the same.
- Still less and less - he nodded.
- Why?
- They are going to make war somewhere else.

He was talking about the presence of the international forces as if these forces and the peace process had nothing to do with him and the reality of the ones like him - Sarajevans, Bosnians, "ordinary people". This particular impression I got for the second time a couple of days later when I was talking to a professor of the Sarajevo University.

- I left Sarajevo in 1993 in order never to come back – the professor said. – All that war was incomprehensible.

"Incomprehensible" was the word he was using most often to tell me how things were. He was lecturing in England and Korea and only recently decided to come back to Sarajevo.

- I can't understand what happened. – He went on – I was trying to write about the war but I soon gave up as the writing was equally incomprehensible.

Then he asked me about my research and what I had done in Sarajevo. I spoke to him for a long time and with real involvement as this research is really my passion.

- Yes... - he nodded – I don't have much interest in politics and peace processes. It is too incomprehensible. I'm interested only in my books, in literature.

When I remember these conversations once again, a striking similarity comes to my mind between the reactions of the people whom I spoke to in Bosnia and the Emir Kusturica film "Underground". There is one exceptional scene that just forces itself upon ones' notice here. It is when the main character Marko rescues his friend Blacky from the German confinement, leaves him in the cellar where a nice crowd of people is already well accommodated, and starts to chat up Natalija, an actress described on the video tape as of "easy virtue", that is desired by Marko and Blacky, and by yet another German officer. They are in his house, in a room which is all papered with pictures of her, articles praising her talent and of interviews she had given.

Natalija: "This room is dedicated to me! My room!"

Marko: "Right... Yes. This room and this house. And this country and the sky, stars, rain, sun, moon, and clouds even when the sky is bright..." – he goes on getting closer and closer to her.

Natalija: "It's all mine."

Marko: "Yes, all of it." – He whispers into her keen ear.

Suddenly, a bombardment starts. One can hear sounds of explosions nearing to the house.

Natalija (in panic): "Marko! Marko! Who's bombing us now?"

Marko (putting a record on, as if the explosions were not concerning him): "The Allies. When it's not the Germans, the Allies bomb us."

The room fills up with dust from the ceiling shaken by the blow of the explosion. With the irresistible charm of a sweet liar, Marko takes Natalija into his arms. They start dancing. The next shot is a notice that reads: "Easter, April 1944. The Allied bombs destroyed what the Nazis had left of Belgrade..."

This last counter of Marko, which sounds like the whole truth about the war – "when it's not Germans, the Allies bomb us" – represents the general feeling people, initially in Yugoslavia, and now in post-conflict Bosnia, seem to have. As if war was something that was not a disturbance to life but a way of living that comes and goes, that one would not choose if there was any choice to be made. But there isn't any choice. As if one could not help the war, and as if it would not matter very much who we are with and whom against, because whether enemies or allies, one could get bombarded by both and thus one should not rely on either of them too much. As the saying advises: if you can count, count on yourself. One does not have any control over a war.

I had a similar feeling when talking in Sarajevo to the Professor and the bar owner. These two meetings gave me a sensation of how the people who are the object of the peace-making process feel about it. They make only a small difference between the war and what happens after it is finished. As if neither the war nor the peace process was anything they could influence in any way: if the international forces decide to make war here, there will be war, if they decide to make peace, they will go for it. But the people whom the peace is supposed to be made for have nothing to say about the shape, direction, or timing of the peace process, and certainly not about the money that is directed at Bosnia from abroad. This is not in order to make a judgmental statement here and not in order to say that the people whom the peace is made for are the ones who should take all the actions into their hands. This is only in order to highlight the fact that looking at the behaviour and the attitude of the Bosnian societies one might be tempted to conclude, that they do not care whether they live in war or in peace.

Do people really not care whether they live in peace or in war? It is more than challenging to think of a situation in which one would not mind a life under bombardment, food and utilities shortages, and ever-present death and atrocities. This is hardly a challenge but would rather suggest that one should find another answer to this puzzle. It is not that they do not care about what happens – it is that they would like to change the circumstances but they have no influence over them. In fact, one can easily spot signs of their being preoccupied with the situation and their good will towards change, on an individual scale which is already implicit in the very fact of people meeting everyday "others" that were supposed to be the enemies during the war and not shooting at each other any more. The killing has stopped and although perhaps multi-ethnic Bosnia is still a long way away, people not only do not kill, but also cooperate with each other.

I was in Bosnia several times from 1997 on, and twice I saw something that then I classified as a positive phenomenon. One should mention here the Inter-Entity Boundary Line (IEBL) that divides Bosnia into two Entities: Federation of Bosnia and Herzegovina and Republika Srpska. This demarcation line was initially difficult to cross for citizens and the movement from one part of the country to another was rather dangerous.[1] Only recently the crossing of the IEBL became easy, although if one were a BiH citizen, one would not risk it without an explicit need.[2] But one occurrence was striking in this situation of mutual distrust and the making of each other's lives impossible: markets along the roads that cross the IEBL and national borders. I visited two of these markets: one near Stolac, in south-east Bosnia, where the Croat-dominated part of Federation meets Republika Srpska. This market was attended mostly by Croats and Serbs from the neighbourhood but also by Muslims from the nearby Mostar. What made a deep impression on me was not only the fact that all three groups would come there but also the look of the entire place. A narrow road goes along a valley, shut in by steep mountain slopes. Beside the road there was also a mountain river. Since the area was for several years a front line, all of the houses both in the little town of Stolac and in its surroundings were completely destroyed. The land was still heavily mined so that on my SFOR map the whole place was marked red, meaning that moving exclusively on the concrete roads was most advisable.[3] On the road, two cars could pass each other not without difficulty, and there was very little space between the road and the slope of the hills. Nevertheless, all along the road (for three hundred meters) there were wooden and iron stands, of a rather provisional look, on which marketers were presenting their goods. Luckily, I was there on a weekday, otherwise, in the weekends, the place is so popular and so overcrowded that it is impossible to travel on the road by car.

I saw another market in northern Bosnia, on the border between Republika Srpska and the Republic of Croatia. It was in the Serb town of Gradiška, where people from bordering areas of Croatia were coming to do their shopping. A new bridge was supposed to be opened for the traffic soon, the old one having been destroyed when the front line between Serbs and Croats stopped on the Sava river, which the town was situated on. This new bridge would finally be equipped with border control and customs checks.[4] However, the crossing of the river (and the border) was possible by means of a provisional bridge further up the river, on the outskirts of the town. This temporary bridge was built with the use of local resources and from the initiative of people living in the neighbourhood, precisely for the purpose of attending the market or visiting their previous places of living on the Croat side.[5] It was cheap and narrow and "just like" a military floating bridge, but served equally well to "ordinary people" who had "ordinary things" to do on the other side of the Sava river. These "ordinary people" made enough peace between themselves to build a bridge and to come to the market unthreatened.

This phenomenon of the markets was recognised as a sort of miracle by Charles G. Boyd in his article "Making Bosnia Work" where Boyd elaborates on the peculiarity of the Dayton provisions, saying at one point that the functioning of the Bosnian state "depends on cooperation by three parties (i.e. Serbs, Croats, Muslims) with little inclination to cooperate".[6] He also contrasts this hard-to-believe construction of a state with spontaneously set up markets, describing one of them: "[a]long SFOR's Route Arizona, on the inter-entity border between Doboj and Tuzla, a market has emerged spontaneously since the Dayton Accord went into effect.[7] Located just off the main road in a five-acre field, it consists of some semi-permanent wooden stands that are open daily".[8] The Arizona Route crosses the IEBL in Blaževac, where Muslim and Serb communities meet. As Boyd stresses, although both Serb and Muslim police routinely patrol the marketplace, no confrontation between these two forces, nor between the "ordinary people" ever happened there.

These three markets described here are really very similar and offer the same assortment of goods. One could get there everything imaginable, from CDs and jeans to building materials, cars (mainly German and from Germany), pharmaceutical supplies, sweets, toys and food (also often from Germany). What is not at hand there, one could order to be delivered in the next few days. Boyd goes further in the description of the market goods: "black market gasoline, cigarettes, prostitutes, and AK-47 are available, if that is what the buyer wants". He admits, however, that the core of the market are "building materials and home improvement items like sinks, heaters, roof tiles, tools, and hardware", since "most of the shoppers are in search of items to improve their families' lives".[9]

As to the absence of confrontation between the police forces as well as between the ethnic societies, the leading rule on the markets is not that of the ethnicity nor of the religion, but the guidelines of economy, where the historic differentiation on the basis of belonging plays only a secondary role. It would seem that Serbs, Croats, Muslims, and all the other ethnic minorities, are capable of cooperating and undertake this cooperation where it would benefit them.[10] One aspect of the existence of these markets which is especially worth paying closer attention to is the fact that only very shortly after the war came to a halt, "ordinary people" were able to cease shooting at each other and begin to run trade in peace.

This could be evidence that peace in Bosnia is possible, as is possible the cooperation between the ethnic groups. Boyd offers a hypothesis that perhaps "in the microcosm the Arizona market represents may lie a clue to building a functioning multiethnic society in Bosnia", as for the time being people feel secure only when surrounded by their own ethnic compatriots but the economic reasons that dictate cooperation make them get into contact with other groups so that after some time "the same people will gradually become confident that they can live again in a mixed society".[11] An alternative or perhaps expanding interpretation of the phenomenon of the markets could be that this will of the people to meet, trade, react with each other should be paid more attention to and more support should be given to their efforts as these markets are in fact almost the only actually functioning form of cooperation between groups, the rule being that the higher up in the structure of authorities one goes, the less cooperation one gets.

In this light, one would be entitled to be surprised at the little progress Bosnia has officially made on the road to reconciliation and stability. All reports on the progress of the implementation of the peace accords in Bosnia or of the progress in the implementation of reforms state that the changes that have been constituted from the time of the Dayton are hardly satisfactory.[12] The question of what it is that stops the progress springs to the fore. If people are capable of creating something that could be a good basis of peace, how does it happen that these foundations are not used? Such reasoning leads one to a closer look at how a peace process in itself is actually thought of.

Going back to the abstract level of thinking about peace building, one cannot but notice that the whole endeavour towards peace is dominated by giant international organisations. These organisations – UN, OSCE, EBRD, the World Bank, IMF, NATO, to name only the most powerful and those most engaged – have a very specific way of acting on the international arena. Being set up by governments, they are both subordinate to these governments as well as having the mission to extend the power of each single government so represented. One of the main features of these wide-ranging international organisations is that they most often interact with the governments themselves, whereas only sporadically and with crumbs of their resources connecting with other subjects in a state – for instance local governments or initiative groups.[13] Government is a structure they know how to deal with and consider this to be the proper level of authority with which a dialogue could be run.

At the same time, these big inter-governmental organisations are the main wheel in the machinery of peace-making in the world. They are the ones who decide about peace operations, together with economic and military interventions, aid delivery, deployment of forces, the conclusion of peace treaties and many other aspects of peace actions.

So in the case of Bosnia the main effort the international inter-governmental organisations make is towards the reconstruction of a state and state structures and thus they are interested in cooperation with the state government as well as the institutions of the Entities.[14] Exclusive attention is paid to the recovery of the state as if the state was the equivalent of its institutional framework. Later on these state structures are expected to take over the revitalisation of the particular sectors of a country: to initiate an upsurge in the economy, to rebuild the infrastructure, to start industry, to work towards the well-being of its citizens. The donor states hold this as the model idea of peace-building. Certainly, the poor results of the efforts aimed at the strengthening of Bosnia are the outcome of a whole volume of reasons, but it is also not untrue that the way international organisations and other third parties involved in the Bosnian peace process steer this process through the channel of state structures is one of them.

In a schematic way, one could describe the peace-making actions and the role of particular international and local bodies following the popular "track diplomacy" figure that distinguishes between Track I, Track II and Track III diplomacy. All of these "tracks" are the ways in which particular actors react to conflict in each of its stages: early, developed and when the fight comes to a stop. Track I diplomacy involves top-level international organisations that influence the top leaders of a state in question, by negotiating, arbitration, mediation, peace-making and peace-keeping operations, also with the threat of the use of force or with the use of force. Track II diplomacy happens between international NGOs, churches, academics, private negotiations of politicians and businessmen on the one hand and middle level leaders in the state on the other.[15] The measures used in Track II diplomacy would include good offices, conciliation, mediation, and problem-solving. Finally, there is Track III diplomacy which involves local forces such as local NGOs or other forms of groups and low-level leaders that interact between each other and possibly with the higher level of authority within the same state.

Table 1. Multi-track diplomacy

Track	"emitter"	"receiver"	means of interaction
Track I	Powerful inter-governmental organisations (e.g. UN, OSCE, NATO, EBRD, the World Bank), powerful governments	top-level leaders (e.g. government of the receiving country)	negotiation, peace-making, peace-keeping, peace-enforcement, economic measures (e.g. embargo), arbitration, mediation with muscle
Track II	NGOs, academics, businessmen, churches	middle-level leaders (e.g. local authorities, groups of initiative)	good offices, persuasion, pure mediation, problem-solving
Track III	local NGOs	Grassroots[16]	building social cohesion

Source: Self, on the basis of Hugh Miall, Oliver Ramsbotham, Tom Woodhouse, *Contemporary Conflict Resolution* (Cambridge: Polity Press, 1999).

Most of the time, "emitters" and "receivers" of one particular track interact only with each other, so that there is flow of information and assistance between those who take part in a particular track. One could call the way those involved work a layered one. That means that what is here called "emitters" of Track I diplomacy communicate with "receivers" of Track I diplomacy, mainly by the use of the means mentioned in the last column of Table 1. By analogy, Track II diplomacy is run within what could be read from Table 1 as Track II layer. As to Track III diplomacy, it is not very well described in literature and it very much depends on the ability of the local population to form into groups with a clear goal and the strength to go for it. Track III diplomacy, however, often receives support from "emitters" of Track II, and especially from international or foreign NGOs for which the evolution of local groups is one of the main objectives. In fact, when one looks at this table, Track II activities and actors seem to be most flexible of all in taking part in the interactions included in the table. They interact both with their "natural" Track II "receivers" and with Track III "emitters" (that is mostly local NGOs), as well as often with the Track III "receivers", that is giving a hand to "just people".[17] They are also active with the preparation of feasibility studies, reports on the situation and monitoring of various enterprises.

It is rather different with Track I, where the grand international organisations are interested in communication exclusively with top-level leaders. Only some of the donor financial resources that are to be spent on peace-building initiatives are directed at the post-conflict country through the foreign NGOs.[18] One must underline here that these Track I "emitters" are by far the most powerful actors involved in the entire peace process and therefore it is not without importance how they locate their resources. Diagram 1 below investigates the way multi-track diplomacy works:

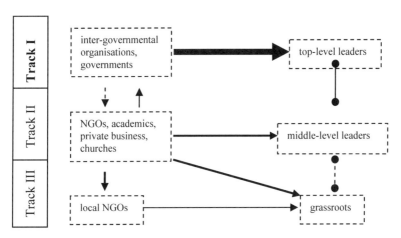

Diagram 1.   ***Multi-track diplomacy: directions of interaction.***

From this scheme one sees that the greatest wave of power and resources, that is available to governments and inter-governmental organisations, is directed almost exclusively along the Track I diplomacy layer, with some minor exceptions which occur when some of the finances are made available to the NGOs that operate in a country a particular government involved in the peace action would be interested in. As has been mentioned before, Track I diplomacy is run with the idea that the empowerment of the top level of authority of a country will stimulate it to lift the whole rest of the country in all the relevant areas. This current approach could be called "top-down": the main stream of assistance is directed at the central government that is supposed to be renovated in order to take over the reconstruction of the country.

Coming back to Bosnia, one can see that the top-down approach exercised there does bring rather poor results. The trap for top-down approach in Bosnia, like in many other post-conflict states, is that contemporary military conflicts are usually about the taking over of power in the state. So that the solidity of a state as well as its structure of authorities is challenged and frequently abandoned or simply crushed during the conflict or its aftermath. One of the characteristics of these military conflicts is that they are about the getting of control in a state, so that in effect a post-conflict area has rarely ever been governed by a unified centre of authority. Many centres claim that they represent the state while not possessing a network of institutions and a structure of channels with the help of which it will then govern this state. Certainly this description does not apply to the situations in which the regime from before a war comes back to power. In other different circumstances, however, it takes time to gain the compliance of all the power centres in a state, to create institutions such as government with all its ministries or a parliament, to create rules of communication and dependency between these institutions, to make a decision-making process effective and the implementation of law functional. One does not build a state structure from the beginning just in one day, even in the circumstances of advanced cooperation between particular groups of this state, not to mention a post-conflict country where this cooperation is more than unlikely to be obtained. Time and again, even what would appear to be a trivial problem can stop the state-building process interminably. For instance, the Bosnian state Parliament could not meet for several months after the first elections in September 1996 for two reasons: one was the reluctance of the Serb political establishment to do so (the ostensible reason being that the Muslims would not dismantle the old, war-time and Muslim-dominated government), the other one being the lack of a building that would accommodate all the MPs, as the old building of the Parliament was destroyed.[19] So that when the Serb agreement on the first session of the Parliament had finally been obtained (after more than three months), the legislators were meeting in a theatre.

One has to realise also that many of the states that emerge after a military conflict are new-born ones or such that had been independent only for a short time before the war. In the case of Bosnia, for instance, statehood had been obtained only a matter of hours before the violence started.[20] Before international recognition came, it had remained one of the Yugoslav republics, with a broad field for manoeuvre but still not an independent state, having spent most of the post-world war II era in a one-

(socialist)-party system, strongly tied to Belgrade, and acting at its command.[21] Although there had certainly been structures of power before the war – such as a parliament and the republic government – Bosnia had not been a state up until April 1992. Therefore, in 1995 when the reconstruction of Bosnia commenced, Bosnia required not a re-construction but the inventing of it from the beginning. One cannot any longer relate to any of the solutions of political engineering from before the conflict as these were not prepared to bear the burden of management of an independent and democratic state. Certainly, there were political connections and old dependencies but these are rather more destructive for the new Bosnian state now than supportive of it – favouritism and corruption dominate the behaviour of political elites, most of whom had already been involved in financial scandals.[22] In fact the use of the old relations makes illegal practices intertwine with politics.[23] In addition to that, the post-Dayton division of Bosnia and Herzegovina into Republika Srpska and the Federation was a complete novelty with no precedent. Even if there were old institutions and authorities networks, they were certainly not prepared to accommodate the solution adopted at Dayton.[24] In this situation, one cannot really talk about the reconstruction of a state in the area of its institutional composition but rather about the building of a state.

The international assistance programme as well as the entire way of peace-building, however, clearly show that their designers take the existence of state structures for granted. At least, they assume that the making of these institutions, the whole state management machinery, is a junior issue that would be solved just on the way to the initiation of this assistance programme. They formulate requirements to be addressed under these state institutions and they make funds available to them. Usually, the requirements and the availability of the money are tied to each other and made into what is called conditionality, a carrot and stick mechanism that is supposed to keep the new country on a track set up by the donors.[25] The rule is that compliance with the programme assigned by the donor parties is a condition for the delivery of the financial resources. As the entire international help is bunched and grants are often dependent on the obtaining of resources from another international organisation, there is practically no other way for this post-conflict country but to comply with the requirements. But this in itself is not all that harmful and perhaps in some cases even the only way to move some reforms forward. The startling occurrence is that the whole effort made by the third country governments and powerful international organisations is directed at structures that are either non-existent or not influential enough to comply with the international blueprint that is the precondition for this financial assistance. These structures, the institutional framework of a state, are often struggling within the state to keep this power and try to extend their ruling and strengthen its own spine, being at the same time expected by the donor parties to implement a programme of an in-depth reform that they are not strong enough to do.

The Dayton Peace Accords left Bosnia divided into two Entities that are constitutionally better equipped than the state they together create. In fact, the state for instance has no power to collect taxes and no defence competencies. In practice it means that the state level of government (i.e. not only the functioning of state structures but also the state budget!) fully depends on the finances from the Entities and the state has neither police nor military forces, which are the competence and the privilege of the Entities. Furthermore, the state institutions are regulated by the rules of composition and way of deciding, which are that each of the three major ethnic groups is guaranteed equal share in decision-making and government. All of this together deprives Bosnia of what is in most democratic countries the main stream of power interaction, that is the dispute between the lower and the higher levels of government over competencies. This dialogue is substituted in Bosnia by a conflict between two Entities that in the state structure are on the same, at a first glance lower than the state, level of government. What one could call here a vertical confrontation between the Entity level of government and a state level of government has been completely removed as the state, in the face of the lack of large constitutional competencies, is fully dependent on the good will of the leaders of the Entities.

Despite this relation of subordination, these are the state institutions that the international community has decided to have as partners, being faithful to the rule that an inter-governmental organisation would search out a state government (as it is supposed to be the top institution of the state) as its natural partner. This routine has a strong effect on the peace-building, in that it inevitably creates a trap: the peace process cannot progress faster than the construction of the state institutions that are to be partner to the inter-governmental organisations, and "ordinary people" that initially have a will to create peace get discouraged by the non-change. This lack of progress is what makes people feel resigned.[26] A Vukovar based Youth Peace Group Dunabe produces short films about how it is after a war. In one of them the ending speaker declares: "[n]egative things are not the worst that can happen to us. The worst thing which can happen is nothing".[27] The slow speed of change or simply the lack of it, so present in the feeling of the youth in post-war parts of Yugoslavia, makes them think that they have no future.

In these circumstances most of them think about emigration rather than building peace in their own country.

If one takes the Bosnian case, this internationally set up trap turns into the façade of peace-building as the state institutions are not constitutionally constructed and equipped to be strong (and the constitution was one of the Annexes to the Dayton Accords) and practically their every single action requires an agreement between Croat, Serb and Muslim politicians that are by "nature" not keen on agreeing with each other. As a result of this, today Bosnia is considered to be influenced if not run by organised crime groups, to have the lowest state income in Europe, and to have no great hope for a recovery.

Apart from the state 'representatives' and the Entities authorities, there are also canton governments in the Federation and local authorities in both Entities, interest groups, NGOs, business and finally "ordinary people", organised in different ways like for instance villages with their representatives. When one watches the political situation in Bosnia and when one talks to people, a dependence emerges between the will to live in peace and cooperate with other groups and the level of representation: generally speaking the higher the level of representation, the more difficult is this cooperation. The natural supporters of peace are "ordinary people" and the further away from them in authority structure one looks, the more tensions there are between the representatives of ethnic societies, up to the highest level on which there is almost structurally – that is "by definition" – no agreement. The official demands of the ethnic groups were not given recognition when constructing the Dayton Accords and a single Bosnian country was designed despite the fact that the entire war was fought in order to prevent this from happening, so that the parties at the high political level try to achieve their goals under new conditions, that is within state mechanisms and with international watchdogs.[28] The overriding policy of the representatives of all the groups is to gain the greatest influence possible and not to let the others have more. This indeed can hardly be called a policy of agreement and cooperation.

As the example discussed above of spontaneously built up markets in the places where the groups meet can show, a will to cooperate exists and is actualised on a much lower than the state or even political level. It exists in what is called in the table above Track III: all these parties that are between local NGOs and grassroots, meaning "ordinary people", their very close authorities, their forming into slightly bigger organisations – all that form of grouping that is difficult to notice from Track I. One could give examples of Track III units such as perhaps villages with their heads, towns with their mayors, lobbies with their activists, neighbour actions, small scale initiatives (in terms of the number of people involved not because of lesser importance for the peace process), all kinds of associations, as well as small and middle-size business. The main characteristic of this type of close to grassroots formations is the will to act combined with the lack of funding. They are the ones who would happily support peace actions if only they were given a chance. Unfortunately, because of the lack of recognition from Track I decision makers, limited financial resources and few possibilities are available to them so that their might remains unexplored.

In the light of these observations, one could be tempted to propose an alternative approach to peace operations. It would be useful to refer to already established track division of actors taking part in operations and their basic grading along "layers". I shall leave all the tracks composed as they were presented earlier. It is rather the scheme of interactions between them that calls for rethinking.

Coming to the conclusion that the present model of dealing with building a sustainable peace after a military conflict is not all that effective, I asked the question why, which was answered in the following way: because international, most powerful organisations and third party governments targeted the government of a post-conflict country as both the main receiver of the entire international aid, and as a body in charge of the reconstruction of this state in all respects. These post-conflict state institutions, however, are not prepared to bear the burden of the responsibilities the international donors require them to carry. The lack of preparation comes in the most part from the fact that whether within or outside state institutions, the parties that were previously the parties to a military conflict do not cooperate with each other. An alternative pillar of peace would be Track III units that, however weakly organised, are ready to commit themselves to development and also are vitally interested in changes towards peace. They, nevertheless, do not get important recognition from most powerful international donors, so that they do not receive efficient financial resources nor an easy green light for their actions. Track II is a very present and large, in terms of the number of organisations and fields of activity, buffer between Track I and Track III, keeping in touch with both, but with limited resources accessible and weakly coordinated as a unit, for the great number of organisations taking part in Track II diplomacy makes this coordination rather difficult.

Given this information I would suggest that the peace engineering could be more efficient if the attention of grand Track I organisations were diversified and fewer expectations addressed to state structures whereas more resources could be made available to Track II and III. The main objective of this "decentralisation" of scope would be to support the core of a good will to build peace, that is the grassroots. For practical reasons, this distribution of the aid to the Track III units would be better off perhaps passing through the Track II international or foreign NGOs. The advantage of using Track II NGOs as a kind of 'middleman' is that they already have contacts with Track III and are knowledgeable about the situation and needs at the grassroots level. Another advantage of the use of Track II organisations as a go between is the presence of well-trained and highly motivated personnel. The channel of Track II would call for reorganisation since, as has been mentioned before, there is only loose coordination between these NGOs. The combination of human resources which are the strong point of Track II "emitters" and the financial resources available to inter-governmental organisations which are the strength of Track I, all being directed at Track III would empower these Track III units and encourage them to work towards peace. Coming back to my observation from the beginning of this passage that people in Bosnia seem to make only a small difference between war and the peace process, as they do not feel that they have any influence over either of them, such re-direction of assistance as proposed here would change this attitude which would mean the beginning of real reconciliation and working towards well-being. One could call this new model one of "cross-track diplomacy" and present this re-direction of assistance as on the diagram below.

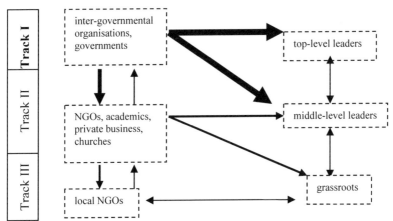

Diagram 2.   *Cross-track diplomacy: directions of interaction.*

What happens here is that the Track I "emitters", the most powerful in the whole puzzle, interact with the same strength in three directions, that is towards top-leaders, towards middle-level leaders, and towards Track II NGOs. The change compared to diagram 1 is that the energy of the international potentate is dispersed into three directions but not weakened. It allows the empowerment of more than one centre at a time (i.e. not only state institutions as on the previous diagram), as it goes both to the top-leaders and institutions, to the middle-level authorities, and – via foreign NGOs – to Track III. Another expected effect of this re-direction of assistance is the activation of communication between "receivers" of all three tracks, that is by the strengthening of the lower-level authorities one would make them better prepared for being partners for other levels of authority. The general idea is that instead of re-building the country with a top-down approach (as presented on diagram 1), the reconstruction of this country starts simultaneously at three levels. In fact, however, these three "layers" are classified in such a way that the governing bodies of all the levels of authorities and as many other kinds of groups as possible are somehow included into the scheme alike. In this way, one makes more than the one top level of government be in charge of the reform and reconstruction, so that the bigger share of both institutions and population is involved in the peace process. What seems to be equally relevant, is not only the numerical difference that is being pointed out here, but also the fact that these newly empowered forms of organisation are most often more highly motivated than the top leaders and in many cases more effective and cheaper than the top institutions.

On drawing to the end of this commentary, one would be tempted to point out another argument in favour of cross-track approach, which comes from a different order. The post-conflict reconstruction of a state means too often really in practice the creation of this state anew. That is where a question could be asked about how states were created and what a state in fact means. Not wanting to explore here this fundamental argument, I shall refer briefly only to one of the theories of state creation, that is to the contractual origin of a state, according to which a state is a result of an agreement between all its citizens to create this state. According to this concept, the state is set up in a bottom-up process, that is that the origins of the state are citizens who give their permission to the authorities to take over. When putting this blueprint onto the approach adopted for post-conflict areas, it does not fit, as the re-construction of this post-conflict state starts from the opposite end: from the top and goes to the bottom (if it gets there). This is not how the state was originally built. What we know today is that the bottom-up, contractual way of creating a state docs function but we lack any knowledge about democracies forced from the top. Why not use a model already well tested by history and provide support and finance for the putting into practice of such a bottom-up, contractual model?

Notes

1. Cousens elaborates on the situation after the Bosnian war, saying that the crossing of the IEBL just after the war, when the return of refugees was most important, was almost impossible for those who were entering the other Entity who were prosecuted by local police and paramilitaries at check points. Entities' authorities set taxes for the transporting of any kind of commodities, as well as introducing "visas" regime. Every ethnic community established separate symbol zones that were also put on the car licence plates. There were also three distinct currencies (although the German DM was a common currency in all three zones). See: Elizabeth M. Cousens, "Making Peace in Bosnia Work", *Cornell International Law Journal* 30 (1997): 789-818.

2. The easiness is largely due to the law imposed by the High Representative of the United Nations in Bosnia on car plates that are now identical in both Entities. After the unkept deadline for the introduction of unified license plates in January 1998, the High Representative issued a decision on new deadlines for the Uniform License Plates System in May 1998, deciding that no vehicle after 1 June 1998 will be allowed to cross a national border unless carrying new plates, and the deadline for the rest of the vehicles in Bosnia would be 31 August 1998. See: Office of the High Representative, *Decision on deadlines for the Implementation of the Uniform License Plate System*, 20 May 1998. Up until the implementation of this law, the signs on car plates differed – Croat plates had a white and red chess board, Muslim – blue and golden lily, and Serb – four "S" in old-Serbian on the framework of a cross. All three signs were the same as the ones previously used for the identification of forces during the war. The identification of the ethnicity of the travelling was, therefore, non-problematic and when on the "wrong" side of the IEBL, a BiH citizen would risk prosecution.

3. Penguin Hutchinson R*eference Suite* gives a data of approximately 3 million mines still deployed in Bosnia in 1997. See: Penguin Hutchinson *Reference Suite* (Oxford and London: Helicon Publishing Ltd and Penguin Books Ltd, 1998), s.v. "mine", CD-ROM. Sharp quotes the UN data on the share of the Bosnian territory still mined: at the end of 1997

approximately 300 square kilometres were still mined and the following 200 could have been at risk (the vagueness of the assessment is mainly due to the fact that many minefields were not marked on maps). The demining action is run only on a very small scale by the UN forces, the gross part of the job being done by amateurs, local forces and some NGOs. In mid-1997 the UN reported that about 1 % of the territory was mine-cleared. See: Jane O. Sharp, "Dayton Report Card", *International Security* 22/3 (1997/98): 101-137.

4. According to BBC News report of February 2001, there were 400 border crossing points in and out of Bosnia, only 4 of them being staffed and functioning along standards: with a border guard and customs officers. The rest of the crossings were unguarded. See: Andrew Bomford, "Sarajevo: Gateway to Europe", *BBC News*, 9 February 2001 <http://news.bbc.co.uk/1/hi/world/europe/1161989.stm> approached on 26 November 2002. The reason for such a poor performance is in the first place the lack of funds.

5. What is now the Croat bank of the river, was often before the war the seat of Serb households. When escaping the war from Croatia to Bosnia, people would leave their property in what appeared later on as Croatia, the wrong side of the river, where they would have a difficult come back. Driving along the Bosnian north border, yet on the Croatian side, one can see whole empty villages and abandoned fields, marked by the SFOR as mined. Everything is mined apart from the road so that one has to stick to the concrete surface. These places were previously belonging to Serb families. Still in 2000 no demining action was taking place there, although people are waiting to access their houses, thinking either about returning there or selling them.

6. Charles G. Boyd, "Making Bosnia Work", *Foreign Affairs* 77/1 (1998): 44.

7. The SFOR uses its internal nomenclature when talking about roads. It is only that in the lack of clear marking and naming of the roads, they introduce their own taxonomy, giving main roads names like Arizona, Python, New Jersey, Crow, Raven, Pelican, Tuna and others.

8. Boyd, 52.

9. Ibid.

10. Most often, one reads about only three ethnic groups in Bosnia, but in fact they are more ethnic groups represented there. According to the census of 1991, there were 44 % of Muslims in Bosnia, 31% of Serbs, 17% of Croats and 8% of "others". This data is quoted after: Susan L. Woodward, *Balkan Tragedy: Chaos and Dissolution after the Cold War* (Washington, D.C.: Brookings Institutions, 1995). All these 8% in the category of "others" seem to be forgotten by those who were constructing the Dayton provisions. See: Zoran Pajić, "The Dayton Constitutions of Bosnia and Herzegovina – a Critical Appraisal of its Human Rights Provisions" in *Constitutional Reform and International Law in Central and Eastern Europe*, eds Rein Müllerson, Malgosia Fritzmaurice, Mads Andenas (The Hague, London, Boston: Kluwer Law International, 1998).

11. Boyd, 52-53.

12. See for instance a series of International Crisis Group reports: International Crisis Group, *State Succession to the Immovable Assets of Former Yugoslavia* (Sarajevo: ICG Bosnia Report No. 20, 1997), International Crisis Group, *Dayton: Two Years On: A Review of Progress in Implementing the Dayton Peace Accords in Bosnia* (Sarajevo: ICG Bosnia Project – Report No. 27, 1997), International Crisis Group, *Is Dayton Failing? Bosnia Four Years After the Peace Agreement* (Sarajevo: ICG Balkans Report No. 80, 1999), International Crisis Group, *Bosnia: Reshaping the International Machinery* (Sarajevo, Brussels: ICG Balkans Report No. 121, 2001), International Crisis Group, *Implementing Quality: The "Constituent Peoples" Decision in Bosnia and Herzegovina* (Sarajevo, Brussels: ICG Balkans Report No. 128, 2002).

13. For instance the United Nations have the programme of UN Volunteers (UNVs) that are deployed in different post-conflict as well as disaster areas, who interact with local environments working together on projects aiming at the improvement of living conditions in these areas. UN Volunteers' way of working resembles very much the routine of NGOs. It is much rather NGO-type work than the UN itself: a standard UN mission would be based usually in main cities of a receiving country and dealing with high-level matters and state politics. For details consult: www.unv.org.

14. Previously, when trying to bring the fighting parties to negotiations, the international peace sponsoring parties were interested in a dialogue with the leaders of these fighting parties. These leaders, nevertheless, lost

much of their importance for peace sponsoring parties from the time they nodded to a single Bosnian state, so that at present the international dialogue involves most · often the state government. Apart from state institutions, there are other authorities: each of the Entities has a separate government and parliament, and a wide range of powers, so that in fact they are better equipped with competencies than the state itself.

15. Track II diplomacy started in the 1980s, when some diplomats and businessmen undertook private, quiet diplomacy and problem-solving as an activity that was complementary to the Track I efforts. For further reading about Track II diplomacy see: John W. McDonald and Diane B. Bendahmane, *Conflict Resolution: Track Two Diplomacy* (Washington D.C.: Foreign Service Institute, US Department of State, 1987), Louise Diamond and John W. McDonald, *Multi Track Diplomacy: A Systems Approach to Peace* (Washington, D.C.: Institute for Multi Track Diplomacy, 1993), or Joseph V. Monteville, *Track Two Diplomacy: The Development of Non-Governmental, Peace Promoting Relationships* (Mimeo: Foreign Service Institute, US Department of State, 1987).

16. I shall understand here by "grassroots" what I do when thinking about "ordinary people".

17. For instance Swiss Caritas was involved in the delivery of building materials for the restoration of villages in Kosovo. The aid was distributed directly to the local people on the basis of their declared needs. Some sort of a supervision mechanism was set up in order to prevent overuse of the aid and nepotism. This would engage a representative of a different village who was supposed to be outside the local networks.

18. For the description of how this communication between governments and NGOs often looks like see: Mary B. Anderson and Peter J. Woodrow, *Rising from the Ashes: Development Strategies in Times of Disaster* (Boulder, Paris: Westview Press and UNESCO, 1989). This book presents also a practical side of the work of an NGO dealing with areas of disaster and post-conflict states.

19. Parliamentary building is situated on what is now named Trg BiH 1, in Sarajevo, a place that was during the war a front line between the besieged and besieging. All the buildings on this line were heavily bombarded and almost completely destroyed.

20. Bosnia was first recognised by the European Union on 6 April 1992, and by the United States on the following day. Some authors suggest that

the recognition of Bosnia and Herzegovina was the last straw that pushed Serbs into war. See: Cousens.

21. The first multi-party elections were held in the Yugoslav Bosnia on 18 November 1990, giving power to nationalist parties.

22. See for instance: Office of the High Representative, *Decision of removing Edhem Bicakcic from his position as Director of Elektroprivreda for actions during his term as Prime Minister of the Federation of Bosnia and Herzegovina*, 23 February 2001.

23. One of the biggest problems both Bosnia as a state and the bordering European Union suffers from is not only corruption of politicians but also their involvement in different forms in organised crime practices: human trafficking, drugs, arm and cigarette trade. See a series of BBC and CNN articles: Andrew Bomford, "Sarajevo: Gateway to Europe", Paul Henley, "Sarajevo's refugee 'business'", *CNN News*, 24 April 2001 <http:// news.bbc.co.uk/1/hi/world/europe/1294011.stm> approached on 26 November 2002, Misha Glenny, "Criminal gangs running the Balkans", *BBC   News*,   28   April   2001   <http:// news.bbc.co.uk/2/hi/programmes/from_our_own_correspondent/1300684. stm> approached on 25 November 2002, Misha Glenny, "Balkans challenges for the West", *BBC News*, 1 July 2001 <http:// news.bbc.co.uk/2/hi/europe/1416145.stm> approached on 25 November 2002, Nick Hawton, "Balkans human trafficking 'set to rise'", *BBC News*, 26 November 2002 <http:// news.bbc.co.uk/2/hi/europe/2513703.stm> approached on 26 November 2002, "Europe targets Balkan crime lords", *CNNEurope*,25   November   2002 <http://europe.cnn.com/2002/WORLD/europe/11/25/balkans.crime/index. html> approached on 26 November 2002.

24. In order to illustrate the difficulties met in the aftermath of the peace conference decision on the division of Bosnia into two Entities, one could mention the networks of utilities, that were designed as units fitting Bosnia as a whole. After the separation of Republika from the Federation, these networks were cut across the IEBL leading to paradoxes. Networks such as these of energy, gas, telecommunications, banking system, radio signal broadcasting, postal services, road infrastructure, railways – they all became divided after the war, becoming the property of Entities. As a result of this incision, Bosnia was deprived for a long time of telephone connections between Entities, inter-Entity train services, a state-wide radio

and television signal is still lacking and postal services are done by three separate operators.

25. For more reading about conditionality see: Alvaro de Soto and Garciana del Castillo, "Obstacles to Peacebuilding", *Foreign Affairs* 94 (1994): 69-83. For the conditionality being applied in Bosnia see: Susan L. Woodward, "Bosnia After Dayton: Transforming a Compromise into a State", in *After the Peace: Resistance and Reconciliation*, ed. Robert L. Rothstein (Boulder, London: Lynne Rienner Publishers, 1999), 139-164.

26. The apathy of the population may well be measured by the elections' turnout. The results of the last general elections' attendance shows an immense decline in comparison to the previous elections. There were 65 % out of 2,35 thousand of the eligible voting in 2000 and only 55 % in the October 2002 elections. It is noticeable that young people were especially oblivious to the elections.

27. Adnan Popovic, *Idea* (Vukovar and Salzburg: TV Dunav, Studio West Salzburg, Video Factory Vukovar at Youth Peace Group Dunabe, 1999), videorecording.

28. For the interests and demands of the parties to the Bosnian conflict see: Paul Szasz, "The Dayton Accord: The Balkan Peace Agreement", *Cornell International Law Journal* 30 (1997), 759-768.

Bibliography

Anderson, Mary B. and Peter J. Woodrow. *Rising from the Ashes: Development Strategies in Times of Disaster*. Boulder, Paris: Westview Press and UNESCO, 1989.

Boyd, Charles G. "Making Bosnia Work". *Foreign Affairs* 77/1 (1998): 42-55.

Cousens, Elizabeth M. "Making Peace in Bosnia Work". *Cornell International Law Journal* 30 (1997): 789-818.

de Soto, Alvaro and Garciana del Castillo. "Obstacles to Peacebuilding". *Foreign Affairs* 94 (1994): 69-83.

Diamond, Louise and John W. Mcdonald. *Multi Track Diplomacy: A Systems Approach to Peace.* Washington, D.C.: Institute for Multi Track Diplomacy, 1993.
International Crisis Group, *Implementing Quality: The "Constituent Peoples" Decision in Bosnia and Herzegovina.* Sarajevo, Brussels: ICG Balkans Report No. 128, 2002.

International Crisis Group, *Bosnia: Reshaping the International Machinery.* Sarajevo, Brussels: ICG Balkans Report No. 121, 2001.

International Crisis Group. *Dayton: Two Years On: A Review of Progress in Implementing the Dayton Peace Accords in Bosnia.* Sarajevo: ICG Bosnia Project – Report No. 27, 1997.

International Crisis Group. *Is Dayton Failing? Bosnia Four Years After the Peace Agreement.* Sarajevo: ICG Balkans Report No. 80, 1999.

International Crisis Group. *State Succession to the Immovable Assets of Former Yugoslavia.* Sarajevo: ICG Bosnia Report No. 20, 1997.

Kusturica, Emir. *Underground.* Paris, Frankfurt and Budapest: CIBY 2000, Pandora Film, Novo Film, 1995. Videorecording.

McDonald, John W. and Diane B. Bendahmane. *Conflict Resolution: Track Two Diplomacy.* Washington D.C.: Foreign Service Institute, US Department of State, 1987.

Miall, Hugh, Oliver Ramsbotham and Tom Woodhouse. *Contemporary Conflict Resolution.* Cambridge: Polity Press, 1999.

Monteville, Joseph V. *Track Two Diplomacy: The Development of Non-Governmental, Peace Promoting Relationships.* Mimeo: Foreign Service Institute, US Department of State, 1987.

Pajić, Zoran. "The Dayton Constitutions of Bosnia and Herzegovina – a Critical Appraisal of its Human Rights Provisions". In *Constitutional Reform and International Law in Central and Eastern Europe*, edited by Rein Müllerson, Malgosia Fritzmaurice, Mads Andenas, 187-193. The Hague, London, Boston: Kluwer Law International, 1998.

Penguin Hutchinson. *Reference Suite*. Oxford and London: Helicon Publishing Ltd and Penguin Books Ltd, 1998. s.v. "mine", CD-ROM.

Popovic, Adnan. *Idea*. Vukovar and Salzburg: TV Dunav, Studio West Salzburg, Video Factory Vukovar at Youth Peace Group Dunabe, 1999. Videorecording.

Sharp, Jane O. "Dayton Report Card". *International Security* 22/3 (1997/98): 101-137.

Szasz, Paul. "The Dayton Accord: The Balkan Peace Agreement". *Cornell International Law Journal* 30 (1997), 759-768.

United Nations. Office of the High Representative in Bosnia and Herzegovina. *Decision of the High Representative of the UN in Bosnia and Herzegovina of 20 May 1998 on deadlines for the Implementation of the Uniform License Plate System*.

United Nations. Office of the High Representative in Bosnia and Herzegovina. *Decision of the High Representative of the UN in Bosnia and Herzegovina of 23 February 2001 removing Edhem Bicakcic from his position as Director of Elektroprivreda for actions during his term as Prime Minister of the Federation of Bosnia and Herzegovina*.

Woodward, Susan L. "Bosnia After Dayton: Transforming a Compromise into a State". In *After the Peace: Resistance and Reconciliation*, edited by Robert L. Rothstein, 139-164. Boulder, London: Lynne Rienner Publishers, 1999.

Woodward, Susan L. *Balkan Tragedy: Chaos and Dissolution after the Cold War*. Washington, D.C.: Brookings Institutions, 1995.

Notes on Contributors

Agatha Dziewulska is a PhD researcher at the European University Institute, Florence, Italy.

Asa Kasher is the Laura Schwarz-Kipp Chair, Professional Ethics and Philosophy of Practice at Tel-Aviv University and IDF College of National Security.

Bradd Hayes is a Professor at the Naval War College, Newport, Rhode Island, USA.

Christopher Macallister is a doctoral student in the Department of Politics & International Relations at the University of Kent at Canterbury.

Deborah Gómez is a Ph.D. Candidate, Department of History and Art History, George Mason University.

Edward Horgan is a retired officer of the Irish Defence Forces, has completed a BA, History, Politics and Social Studies, University of Limerick, M.Phil. (Peace Studies), Trinity College Dublin, and is currently a Government of Ireland Scholar, PhD. programme, Centre for Peace and Development Studies, University of Limerick, Ireland.

Jones Irwin is Lecturer in Philosophy at St. Patrick's College of Education and Liberal Arts, Dublin City University, Ireland.

Martin Bayer is studying War Studies at King's College London (2000–2003) with the main focus on European Defence, simulations, media, RMA, and civil-military relations. He previously worked in the computer games industry.

Maura Conway is a PhD candidate in the Department of Politics, Trinity College, Dublin, Ireland.

Michael Gross is a Lecturer in the Department of International Relations, University of Haifa, Israel.

Paul Gilbert is Professor of Politics at the University of Hull, UK.

Paul Rexton Kan is Assistant Professor of International Security and Military Studies at the Air Command and Staff College of the United States Air Force.

Susan G. Sample is Assistant Professor of Political Science in the School of International Studies and Department of Political Science at the University of the Pacific, Stockton, California, USA.